TOTEMS TO TURQUOISE

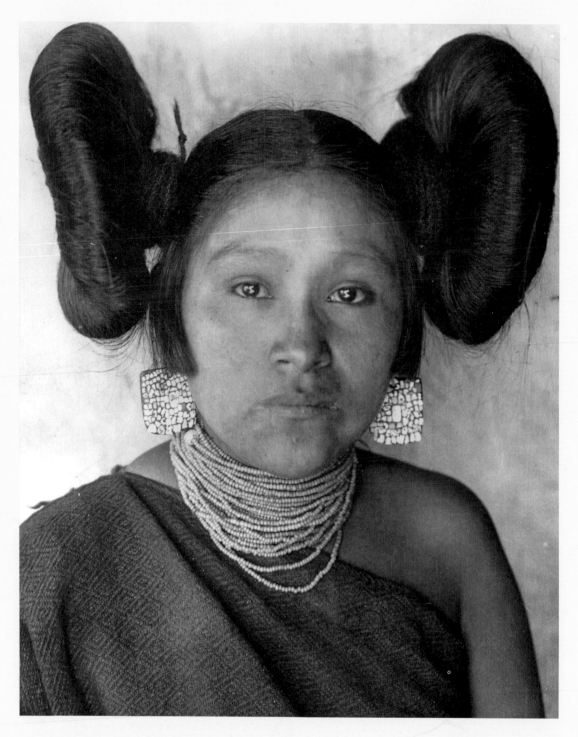

A Hopi girl wears the "butterfly whorl" hairstyle indicative of her marriageable age. She is adorned with earrings of turquoise-mosaic and glass beads reminiscent of ancient shell beads. 1901. Courtesy of the Southwest Museum, Los Angeles

TOTEMS TO TURQUOISE

native north american jewelry arts of the northwest and southwest

kari chalker, general editor

lois s. dubin and peter m. whiteley, contributing editors

with essays by

kari chalker, lois s. dubin, peter m. whiteley, martine reid, martha albrecht, and jim hart

principal photography by kiyoshi togashi

Lois S. Dubin

harry n. abrams, inc.

in association with the american museum of natural history

CONTENTS

THE SOUTHWEST

FOREWORD

Ellen V. Futter, President, American Museum of Natural History

Bears, whales, eagles, ravens, butterflies, land-scapes, and the night sky—for centuries, Native artists of the marine Northwest and desert South-west of North America have turned to these images both to describe the world around them and to communicate deeply held spiritual beliefs. Though distinct in many ways, these two regions have rich and unique jewelry traditions that marry personal adornment with cultural expression.

Over time, technological innovations, trading opportunities, access to new materials, and fashions have changed some of the practices and products of Native jewelry artists, but in these regions, a strong thread of tradition can be traced from the archaeological record, throughout recorded history, to the master jewelry artists working today. In a context of commercial, cultural, and technological complexity, today's leading Native artists are ushering in a renaissance in the jewelry arts, extending traditional crafts into full-fledged modes of artistic expression while continuing to communicate a wide range of cultural ideas and spiritual beliefs.

Displaying a dazzling array of classic and contemporary jewelry, this book and the special exhibition it accompanies honor the remarkable depth, continuity, and growth of Native North American artistic traditions. In addition, by presenting the finest Native jewelry arts in cultural, historical, and environmental contexts, they train a light on the vitality of Native North American cultures while promoting the cultivation and revitalization of Native cultural identities.

Such efforts are in perfect alignment with the work of the American Museum of Natural History, which has, since it was founded in 1869, studied the cultures of North America. The Museum has expertise in interpreting and displaying cultural artifacts, holds extensive collections of Native North American artifacts, and has a continuing dialogue with Native American peoples.

This exhibition and book were truly team efforts, and it is my privilege to acknowledge the exhibition's outstanding curatorial team: curators Peter Whiteley and Lois Dubin, and advising artists Jim Hart and Jesse Monongya. I thank as well the many people on the staff of the Museum and of institutions throughout North America whose contributions made the exhibition and book possible. I am grateful to the book's editor Kari Chalker and photographer Togashi who worked in tandem with the curatorial team to reflect the exhibition themes and images in this beautiful volume.

Finally, I would like to salute the artists them-selves, whose words and works are represented here and in the exhibition. Their craftsmanship is dazzling, their creativity astonishing. But perhaps most significantly, they succeed brilliantly in bridging the often thorny divide between personal artistic vision and cultural expression, giving us works that are not only examples of beautiful jewelry but also moving and timeless cultural objects.

Ancestral Pueblo (Anasazi)
turquoise-mosaic pendants
from Canyon de Chelly, ca.
AD 1100–1200. Width, 3⅛".
Collection American Museum
of Natural History, 29.1/879,
29.1/880

ACKNOWLEDGMENTS

Conceived as a companion to the *Totems to Turquoise* exhibition originating at the American Museum of Natural History in New York, this book was brought about through the efforts of many people, and we are grateful to them all.

To the private collectors who contributed their knowledge and their treasured belongings goes our sincere appreciation. Their willingness to share is remarkable. Thanks go to Mary Ann Abrams, Dan and Martha Albrecht, Michael Bernstein, Erly Crazy Horse, Victor Dukowski, Jean MacKay-Fahrni, Susan Garland, Eleanor Tulman Hancock, Jim and Lauris Phillips, Colleen Reeks, Jim and Val Reeks, Edna Rober and family, Gregory and Angie Schaaf, Dolores Schapiro, Joe and Cindy Tanner, Arch Thiessen, Daune and Austin Turner, Gene and Ann Waddell, Edwin Wade, Rita Yokoi (founding director of the Museum of Native American Jewelry), and others who prefer to remain anonymous. In many cases they allowed their valued belongings to leave their hands to be photographed in locations across the city, across the state, or across the country, often at their own expense. Special acknowledgment goes to Jim Phillips and Arch Thiessen for producing their own beautiful photography, and to Martha Albrecht for her essay.

Several institutions have provided photographs. These include the Arizona State Museum at the University of Arizona, the Heard Museum, the University of British Columbia Museum of Anthropology, the Royal British Columbia Museum, the Peabody Museum at Harvard University, the University of Pennsylvania Museum, the Haida Gwaii Museum of Qay'llnagaay, and the National Museum of Canada, Canadian Museum of Civilization.

Bill McLennan, curator and designer at the University of British Columbia Museum of Anthropology, helped in many ways, including facilitating a photography session at the museum, contributing substantial knowledge and edits, and taking his own excellent photographs.

Jim Hart, advising artist for the exhibition, has helped shape this project from the beginning. Besides taking on the monumental task of coordinating the logistics for the Vancouver photo and interview session, he also contributed an essay and made painstaking edits to the Northwest Coast introductory chapter.

Jesse Monongya, advising artist for the exhibition, shared with us not only his knowledge of and thoughts about his culture, but also his intelligence, humor, and generosity of spirit.

Appreciation also goes to Martine Reid for contributing an outstanding essay and much knowledge. And a thank you goes to Tanja Dorsey for all her help and introductions.

Many thanks to American Museum of Natural History staff members Karen Miller, Sonia Dingilian, Susan Parrs, and Audrey Farolino for their consistently cheerful and professional help and support, and for pulling the pieces together. Thanks go as well to the Museum's executive producer of exhibition media, Geralyn Abinader, for her close collaboration over the course of the two photo and interview sessions. We are also grateful to Gary Zarr, the Museum's senior vice president for communications and business development, for encouraging the project.

To the book's primary photographer, Kiyoshi Togashi, goes much appreciation for his consistent attention to detail and excellence, even under difficult circumstances and challenging shoot schedules.

Thanks to Karen Hayes for her incisive editing talents and for her moral support.

Finally, we express our deepest thanks to the artists for their talent, enthusiasm, intelligence, and willingness to participate, and especially for sharing insights into their lives and work with such openness.

"*Tsawatenok* Girl." A Kwakwaka'wakw girl wears abalone shell earrings and a cedar bark cloak. Ca. 1914. According to author Ruth Kirk, these abalone shell squares may have at one time adorned a button blanket. Royal British Columbia Museum, PN 7377

EDITOR'S PREFACE

Kari Chalker

For Native Americans, indeed for all people through time, jewelry and other forms of adornment such as clothing, blankets, and headdresses express personal and cultural ideas of beauty and convey beliefs about relationships to other people and to the natural world. Adornment connects people to each other and distinguishes people from one another, and it helps express a sense of place in the world and the cosmos.

The exhibition and the book, *Totems to Turquoise*, explore the many facets of jewelry and adornment in two remarkable cultural regions of North America, the Northwest Coast and the desert Southwest. The book was intended to be a companion rather than a direct catalog of the exhibition, and indeed, over the months of its creation, the text took on a life of its own—the result of many voices, talents, and life experiences. Artists from both regions share their thoughts about the role of jewelry in their lives, in their cultures, and in their individual and collective histories. Although each artist has his or her own beliefs, strengths, and motivations, taken as a whole this assemblage of perspectives and images becomes a collective statement, verbal and visual, of the history and richness of the jewelry of these two regions.

It was Togashi, the book's photographer, who suggested that we feature portraits of contemporary artists. Photography sessions were scheduled in two locations—in Vancouver, British Columbia and in Albuquerque, New Mexico. *Totems to Turquoise* exhibition curators Peter Whiteley and Lois Dubin,

and advising artists Jim Hart and Jesse Monongya, compiled lists of artists who represent accomplishment and connections to their cultural roots. Once a gathering of artists was underway, it was then decided that a video crew from the American Museum of Natural History should participate as well to gather video portraits of the artists. Geralyn Abinader, the museum's executive producer of exhibition media, and I collaborated on the interview questions, knowing that the brief time we would have with each artist had to satisfy the needs of both book and video.

We interviewed fifteen artists in Vancouver and nineteen in Albuquerque. I conducted interviews by phone with an additional five artists. It is important to note that the artists included in the book represent remarkable ability and commitment, and yet they are not the only ones of their caliber. Many excellent artists from both regions could not participate for various reasons including conflicts of schedule, community obligations, and busy careers and lives. A number of pieces included in the exhibition are not presented in this publication and some pieces featured here are not part of the exhibition.

The artists' portrayals of themselves and their art bring to life the themes of the exhibition. Throughout the interviews, it was striking that many artists expressed similar values, ideas, and thoughts. Jim Hart and Jesse Monongya each describe the impact that the original exchange program between the Haida and Southwestern jewelers has had on their lives and work (see

Curators' Introduction). Recurring themes include a desire to give back to one's community, hopes that children will carry on the traditions, and a firm belief that, to be most effective, artists need to be rooted in their culture. At the same time it is generally acknowledged that tradition, especially in artistic styles, is ever-changing, and there must be room for innovation and growth. Several artists express a feeling of spiritual connection to the natural and supernatural worlds. For others, that spiritual connection is not openly discussed but deeply felt nonetheless. It was notable that many artists brought their hands to their hearts as they spoke, emphasizing how personally central these topics are.

The focus of this book is on contemporary artists, their work, and their thoughts on individual roles and responsibilities in supporting their cultures and communities. The book also briefly traces the development of the jewelry traditions and the histories of the various groups to place them in context. Introductory chapters discuss each region and their landscapes, cultures, and histories. An essay by Martine Reid, an anthropologist and the widow of Haida artist Bill Reid, explores aspects of Haida beauty and the transfer of Haida tattooing principles into jewelry. Exhibition curator Peter Whiteley discusses an emphasis on the painterly aesthetic in the Southwest and its relationship to people and culture. An essay by collector Martha Albrecht provides insight into the world of art collecting and the feeling of connection to the cultures that this has brought her and her

husband. The relationship between artist and collector often becomes one of valued friendship and mutual appreciation. Without thriving art markets, many artists would not be able to turn their creativity into sustaining careers.

When the artists were asked to comment on the meaning and importance of jewelry, again and again they responded that jewelry is " . . . a reflection of who you are." If this book adequately and accurately reflects who the artists are and opens a window to their outstanding talent and commitment, it is because of the sincerity they brought to the project that, in turn, inspired me to try to live up to their integrity.

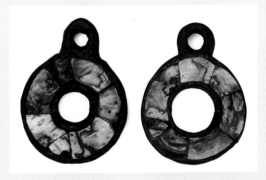

Men's horn and abalone earrings. Tlingit. Prior to 1915. Length, 1¼". Collection American Museum of Natural History, 16.1/1557

A NOTE ABOUT TRIBAL NAMES

Many of the popular names used to refer to Native American tribes (known as First Nations in Canada) have little or nothing to do with what the people call themselves. Over the years, incorrect names—often the results of improper pronunciations and misunderstandings on the part of the early explorers and other outsiders—became embedded in the anthropological and popular literature. However, in the last few decades, many Native groups have been bringing these misnomers and misunderstandings to the public's attention and today prefer to be called by the name they use for themselves. Often this name is the word from their language for "the people." In some cases, groups have chosen new names for themselves that reflect a shared characteristic. While this has sometimes created confusion, it is a matter of respect to call someone by the name they prefer. Therefore, throughout this text, Native-preferred names will be used. For clarification, the new, preferred names and the old names, some with notes about their origins, are listed here.

Northwest Coast

The Haida, Tlingit, Tsimshian, Nisga'a, Gitxsan, and Haisla are popularly known by the names they call themselves.

Kwakwaka'wakw—Kwakiutl

Kwakwaka'wakw is the collective name for speakers of the language Kwakwala. The anthropologist Franz Boas applied the word Kwakiutl to all the peoples on the central coast whose language root was Wakashan (of which Kwakwala is one example). The Kwakiutl (*Kwagu'l*) are actually one group of Kwakwala speakers who live at Fort Rupert (Bill McLennan: personal communication, 2004).

Nuu-chah-nulth—Nootka

Nuu-chah-nulth roughly translates as "all along the mountains" and is a name this west coast group has chosen to collectively refer to themselves. The former term Nootka was a misunderstanding of a word that Nuu-chah-nulth ancestors called out to Captain James Cook as he sailed into their waters in 1778.

Heiltsuk—Bella Bella
Nuxalk—Bella Coola

Both Bella Bella and Bella Coola are misnomers.

Southwest

Navajo–Diné

Both terms are still in popular use, although Diné is becoming more accepted. The word Navajo was a Tewa place name adopted by the Spanish to refer to these people, originally, "Apaches de Navajo."

Pueblos

The Hopi, Zuni, Acoma, Zia, Nambé, Pojoaque, and some other Pueblos have retained their original names, or approximations of their names. For those Pueblos who have taken the name of their patron saint, such as San Juan or Santo Domingo, the people do have names for themselves in their own languages, but the Spanish names are still generally accepted and used.

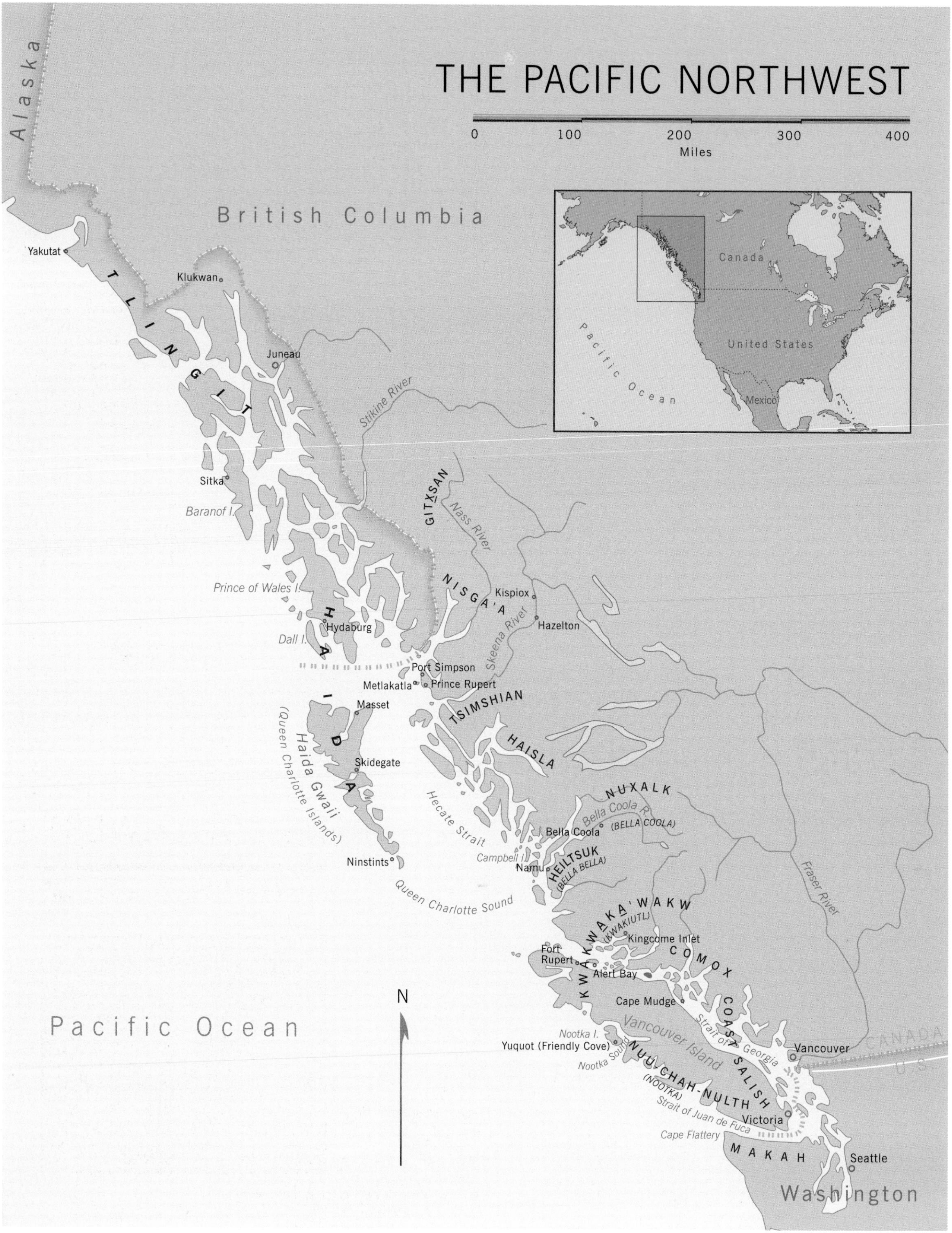

THE PACIFIC NORTHWEST

0 100 200 300 400
Miles

Alaska

British Columbia

Canada

United States

Pacific Ocean

Mexico

Yakutat

Klukwan

T L I N G I T

Juneau

Stikine River

Sitka

Baranof I.

GITXSAN

Nass River

Prince of Wales I.

NISGA'A

Kispiox

H A I D A

Hydaburg

Skeena River

Hazelton

Dall I.

Port Simpson

Metlakatla   Prince Rupert

Masset

TSIMSHIAN

Haida Gwaii
(Queen Charlotte Islands)

HAISLA

Skidegate

NUXALK

Hecate Strait

Bella Coola R.

(BELLA COOLA)

Ninstints

Bella Coola

Campbell I.

HEILTSUK
(BELLA BELLA)

Namu

Queen Charlotte Sound

KWAKWAKA'WAKW
(KWAKIUTL)

Kingcome Inlet

Fraser River

Fort
Rupert

C O M O X

Alert Bay

COAST SALISH

Cape Mudge

K W A K W A K A ' W A K W

Vancouver

Pacific Ocean

N

Nootka I.

Vancouver Island

Strait of Georgia

Yuquot (Friendly Cove)

Nootka Sound

NUU-CHAH-NULTH
(NOOTKA)

Victoria

CANADA
U.S.

Strait of Juan de Fuca

Cape Flattery

M A K A H

Seattle

Washington

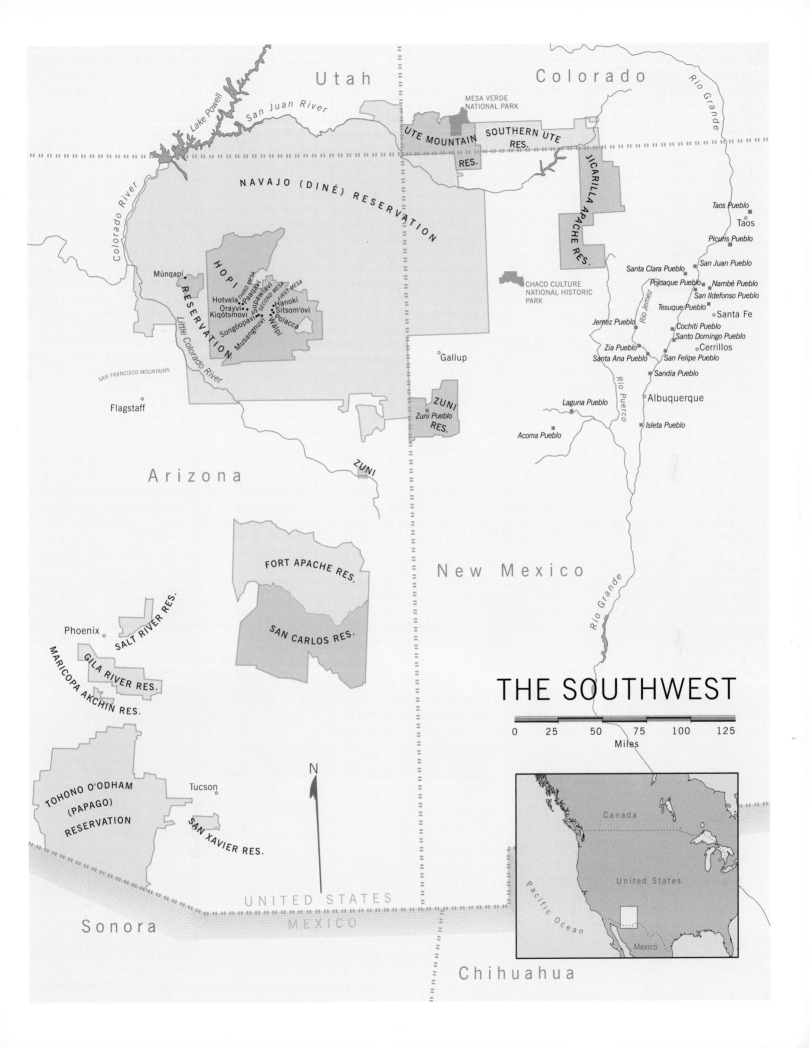

THE SOUTHWEST

Utah

Colorado

Lake Powell

San Juan River

MESA VERDE NATIONAL PARK

UTE MOUNTAIN RES.

SOUTHERN UTE RES.

Rio Grande

NAVAJO (DINÉ) RESERVATION

JICARILLA APACHE RES.

Colorado River

Taos Pueblo

Taos

Picuris Pueblo

Mùnqapi

HOPI RESERVATION

THIRD MESA
Hotvela Paaqavi
Orayvi Supawlavi
Kiqötsmovi SECOND MESA
Songoopavi FIRST MESA
Musangnuvi
Hanoki
Sitsom'ovi
Polacca
Walpi

CHACO CULTURE NATIONAL HISTORIC PARK

Santa Clara Pueblo
San Juan Pueblo
Pojoaque Pueblo
Nambé Pueblo
San Ildefonso Pueblo
Tesuque Pueblo
Santa Fe
Jemez Pueblo
Cochiti Pueblo
Santo Domingo Pueblo
Cerrillos
Zia Pueblo
Santa Ana Pueblo
San Felipe Pueblo
Sandia Pueblo

Little Colorado River

San Francisco Mountains

Gallup

ZUNI RES.
Zuni Pueblo

Albuquerque

Rio Jemez

Rio Puerco

Laguna Pueblo

Isleta Pueblo

Acoma Pueblo

Flagstaff

Arizona

ZUNI

New Mexico

Rio Grande

FORT APACHE RES.

SAN CARLOS RES.

Phoenix

SALT RIVER RES.

GILA RIVER RES.

MARICOPA AKCHIN RES.

N

TOHONO O'ODHAM (PAPAGO) RESERVATION

Tucson

SAN XAVIER RES.

Sonora

UNITED STATES
MEXICO

Chihuahua

0   25   50   75   100   125
Miles

Canada

United States

Pacific Ocean

Mexico

CURATORS' INTRODUCTION: JEWELRY AS A VISUAL LANGUAGE

Lois S. Dubin and Peter M. Whiteley

"For our people, what we wear is who we are. Our jewelry and our clothing represent where we come from. We wear our history."
—Jim Hart, Haida Chief and Carver

Within two artistically sophisticated but vastly different regions—the Northwest Coast and the Southwest—jewelry and adornment comprise a visual language that communicates on many levels. Native American jewelry frequently embodies larger cultural themes in miniature, making cosmic theories accessible and understandable at a human scale. In the Northwest Coast, identical imagery of supernatural creatures is displayed on totem poles, Chilkat blankets, tattoos, and bracelets. Masks are scaled down to pendants. The vast Southwestern sky is encapsulated on a Navajo inlaid bracelet, while a bolo tie from Zuni Pueblo embodies a *katsina*, or spirit being.

Exploring commonalities of world view and unique artistry within strikingly contrastive Northwest Coast and Southwest cultures is the central theme of *Totems to Turquoise: Native North American Jewelry Arts of the Northwest and Southwest.* The extraordinary quality and beauty of contemporary artistic production in each region flows from a shared strength of cultural persistence. That cultural persistence partly owes to similar histories in some respects: while suffering much hardship as a result of non-Native contact and colonization, none of the tribes involved was radically displaced from their traditional homeland. Despite their differences, the tribes share parallels in their social lives and in their adaptations to the environment.

The Origin of the Exhibition

Totems to Turquoise originated from a cultural exchange program in 2000 that brought five Haida artists to Arizona and New Mexico and then took ten Southwest Native artists to British Columbia. Although the Southwest and Northwest Coast contemporary Native art markets are two of the strongest in North America, the artists tend to

Monument Valley bolo tie. Jesse Monongya (Navajo-Hopi). For a benefit auction, Monongya created this scene of a Monument Valley rock formation with a dramatic night sky lit by an opal moon. Bear paw bolo tips represent the hands of Preston Monongye (Jesse's father) and Charles Loloma, two of Jesse's mentors. Lapis lazuli, coral, opal, sugilite, shell, dolomite, turquoise. 2001. Bolo length, 2¾". Private collection

Opposite page:
Woman in the Moon pendant. Jim Hart (Haida). Hart explains, "I've wanted to do a series of moon faces. Woman in the Moon is a crest for *Yakulanaas*, or Raven, clan at home, a clan that people from my Eagle clan have always intermarried with. I've been working on this idea for years, and I'm really happy with this design. A Haida woman from the community of Old Masset acquired the piece as a gift from her husband, and she wears it quite happily." 22-karat gold inlaid with abalone. 2003. Diameter, 2". Private collection

have limited knowledge of work outside their own region. The exchange program introduced talented Haida, Navajo, and Pueblo jewelers to each other while building bridges between differing Native groups and creating a dialogue through the arts.

The program was a great success. The artists shared information and experienced each other's lifestyles. All felt, however, that the most potent aspect of the trips was their unexpected and deep bonding with one another. The artists discovered that, regardless of distinctions in expressions of their culture and art, they shared many values. These commonalities derive from similar ways of seeing the world or "world views." Haida chief and carver Jim Hart, a trip participant, describes that common sensibility: "We have feelings that come from the same place. Our connections to each other come out in different ways, not just jewelry and art. We share a way of life in a sense." Jesse Monongya, a Navajo master jeweler and also a trip participant, adds: "We share a lot . . . sometimes we Indian people don't appreciate what surrounds us, until we're outside and then we appreciate what our traditions mean."

Out of this exchange, a conversation developed between Lois Dubin, who organized the exchange program, Dr. Craig Morris, Dean of Science at the American Museum of Natural History, and Dr. Peter Whiteley, curator of North American Ethnology at the Museum. *Totems to Turquoise* is the result of that conversation.

Co-curators Whiteley and Dubin worked with advising artists Jim Hart and Jesse Monongya to select items and artists for the exhibition. Hart and Monongya strongly recommended that any contemporary artist whose work was included must be connected to their culture. Contemporary jewelry comprises approximately seventy percent of the exhibition; ancient and historic contextual material accounts for thirty percent. The items have been assembled from the American Museum of Natural History's collection and many contributing institutions and private collectors.

Universal Connections

When Jim Hart discussed the feelings shared by the exchange program participants, he described, in a broad sense, a core set of common values. These values operate within similar perspectives, shared across Native America, on the natural world and the cosmos. In essence these commonalities are: the significance accorded to tradition; an emphasis on reciprocity, harmony, and balance; a sense that circuits of knowledge and communication animate relations among human beings, the natural world, and the supernatural realm; and, not least, the profound importance placed on quality and creative dynamism in producing, to use Haida master-artist Bill Reid's terms, "the well-made object" (Shadbolt 1986:83). As for Jim Hart's sense that the feelings "come from the same place," it is hard to imagine two more dissimilar physical environments than the desert Southwest and the marine Northwest Coast. What Jim refers to is a philosophical place—both metaphysical and ethical—that surpasses differences in the surface forms of the landscape.

The dialogue between humanity and nature is a primary focus in both areas. The universe is conceived as a web of interconnections between the celestial and the terrestrial, between natural phenomena and the human condition. In many Native North American views, the cosmos is divided into three primordial layers: the heavens, the earth, and the underworld, each with its own pantheon of opposing spirit forces. Duality (paired opposites) is implicit to the fundamental Native belief in harmony. Humanity's role is to identify and mediate between opposing forces, to maintain the harmony and balance of life, an idea expressed in stories, ritual, daily life, and the arts.

In this world view, people think of themselves within a universe that is an organic whole. Individual creatures, plants, and terrestrial and celestial phenomena—bears, killer whales, eagles, ravens, butterflies, cedar, turquoise, maize, mountains, springs, sun, moon, wind—provide a

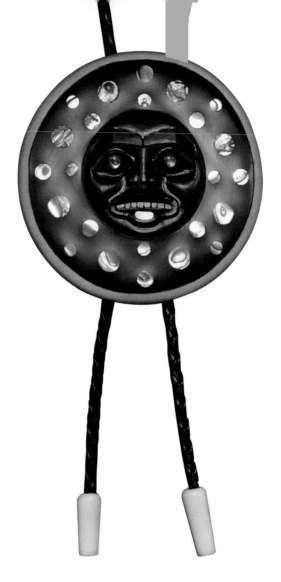

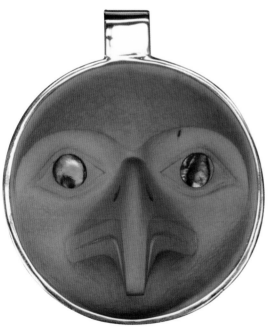

Top:
Man in the Moon bolo tie.
Donnie Edenshaw (Haida).
Edenshaw was a participant
in a workshop held by Jesse
Monongya on Haida Gwaii
(Queen Charlotte Islands)
in a 2002 extension of the
original 2000 cultural
exchange program. This bolo
tie inlaid with disks of abalone
is a direct result of Jesse's
teaching and an example of
the mutual influence inspired
by cultural exchange. Wood,
argillite, abalone. Diameter, 3".
Collection American Museum
of Natural History, 16.1/2646

Left:
Eagle face pendant. William
Kuhnley (Nuu-chah-nulth).
Wood, abalone, 18-karat
gold. 2003. Diameter, 2½".
Collection American Museum
of Natural History, 16.1/2644

Blue corn bolo tie. Victor
Coochwytewa (Hopi).
Turquoise, silver. 2003.
Height, 3⅝". Collection
Schaaf

fund of literal and metaphorical images. People express important values and meanings through such images as clan names for the Hopi and Zuni (Bear, Badger, Spider, Dogwood), or social divisions for the Rio Grande Pueblos (Turquoise and Squash people, Winter and Summer people), or the Eagle and Raven moieties of the Haida and the Wolf clan among the Tlingit and Tsimshian.

Southwestern cosmologies, such as those of the Navajo, relate sacred landscape features (mountains and lakes), food (maize), and jewels (shell, turquoise, jet) to the origins of the first people. On the Northwest Coast, Raven discovered Haida humankind emerging from a clamshell. Salmon were thought to dwell as Salmon People in their own big houses under the sea, where they removed their scaly robes and carried on an existence remarkably similar to that of humans. Humans, animals, and other earthly beings are thus of the same stuff, sharing in each other's being and substance.

Traditions in both regions emphasize transformation: from self to spirit, nature to humanity, geography to morality. The concept of simultaneity within different aspects—coexistent realities, only one of which is typically revealed at any given time—is pervasive. Kwakwaka'wakw composite masks (page 51), for example, include multiple beings "...with little indication of where one ended and another began." (Furst and Furst, 144)

The idea of circularity and cyclical process informs much Native American thought and art. All of life participates in a continual cycle of birth and rebirth. Phases of the moon coincide with agricultural cycles in the Southwest and with ocean tides in the Northwest. Time revolves around seasons and patterns of ritual. The cosmic circle, symbolized by the sacred sun and motifs related to the four cardinal directions, is a recurring theme in Native iconography. Therefore, wearing a brooch with the sun and four-direction motifs miniaturizes the universal within the personal and the cosmos within the intimate.

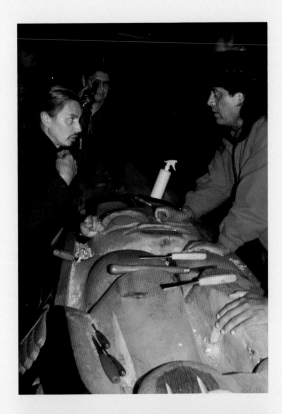

Top:
Jim Hart and Jesse Monongya discuss carving techniques and tools over an unfinished totem pole during the exchange program between Haida and Southwestern jewelers, 2000.

Bottom:
Salmon pin. Lyle Wilson (Haisla). 18-karat gold. 1993. Length, 2¾". Collection University of British Columbia Museum of Anthropology, Nb3.1471

Through storytelling and ritual drama, Native elders teach cultural and moral values to the younger generation. Tricksters, like the Southwest's Coyote and the Northwest Coast's Raven, and sacred clowns make social rules explicit by acting out challenges to society's taboos. Hero and jokester, creator and destroyer, the trickster's and the clown's actions serve to remind of realities beneath idealized surface appearances. Artisans have always added an important dimension to oral tradition, recording the beliefs of their people in a visual language of motifs and symbols. Stories continue to inform Northwest and Southwest tribal jewelry.

Ceremonies—often described as "dances" or "doings"—provide opportunities to wear one's finest garments and jewelry. Ceremonial regalia, the major form of visual artistic expression on the body, unite clothing, ornaments and body decoration to enhance the individual's self-presentation.

Northwest Coast ceremonies emphasize reciprocity through public displays of gift-giving. Social status and power accrue to those who give. Acquiring prestige, more important than the accumulation of wealth, requires generosity. Dispersing a cache of silver and copper bracelets at a nineteenth-century potlatch (a ceremonial giveaway) brought prestige to the giver (page 43). Gifting at a potlatch remains important today. Similarly, gift-giving pervades ceremonial practice in the Southwest: giveaways, as in the women's society Basket Dances of the Hopi, reinforce the basis of community life in sharing and mutuality.

Historical Connections

The exhibition goes back into the archaeological past to reveal aspects of cultural history, and ancestral forms of adornment, such as tattooing in the Northwest and body-painting in the Southwest, to show their connections with contemporary jewelry. In the Southwest, there are shell beads and turquoise mosaic work a thousand years old nearly identical to works created today. Artifacts adorned with classic Northwest Coast formline art have been found at archaeological sites hundreds of years old.

The exhibition also explores intertribal trade networks through which materials and ideas were circulated. Some of the more intriguing connections are between the Southwest and Northwest regions themselves. A marvelous nineteenth-century Tlingit shaman's necklace astonishingly includes an ancient Southwest Hohokam shell pendant (page 55). Plumed serpent iconography extends from Mexico through the Southwest to British Columbia, hinting at unexplained but fascinating linkages.

Tribal Traditions and the Individual

In addition to showcasing commonalities and tradition, it is equally important to show change. As noted, Northwest and Southwest cultures have always traded and borrowed. Traditions come alive and remain alive by innovations and new introductions.

At certain historical moments, major technical and other innovations occurred in both regions: the introduction of iron adzes on the Northwest Coast dramatically enhanced artistic production; silversmithing in the Southwest altered a pre-existing emphasis on stone and shell. Within the last century and a half, traders and the commercial market have produced further dramatic changes. Contemporary jewelers owe much to historic cultural icons such as Charles Edenshaw (Haida), Leekya Deyuse (Zuni), and Fred Peshlakai (Navajo). Since the 1960s, individual artists like Bill Reid (Haida) and Charles Loloma (Hopi) have helped transform artistry into full-blown "art," paving the way for today's masters like Jim Hart and Jesse Monongya.

At present, the emergence of uniquely individual artists within distinct tribal traditions has reached a higher plateau. At its core, this exhibition illuminates contemporary individual styles as they develop within tribal genres.

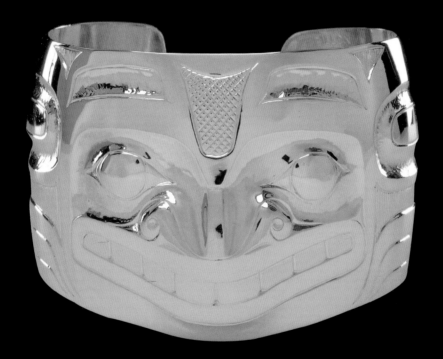

Bear bracelet. Jesse Brillon
(Haida). 22-karat gold. 1½"
high. 2003. Private collection

Parrot motif necklace. Lambert
Homer, Sr. (Zuni Pueblo).
Silver, turquoise, mother-of-
pearl, spiny oyster shell, black
marble. Ca. 1950. Diameter
of pendant, 3⅛". Challis L.
Thiessen Collection

Opposite page:
Turquoise necklace. Joe and
Terry Reano (Santo Domingo
Pueblo). The Reanos are
among the very few artists
who still create turquoise and
shell beads in the old way—
cut, drilled, and polished by
hand. Bisbee turquoise, gold.
1980. Length, 15". Collection
Tanner

Art or Craft?

Whether Native arts are "art" or "craft" is often discussed in art circles. Does appreciation of a fine carving or bracelet require familiarity with cultural context? To a certain degree objects stand on their own merits—when something is intrinsically beautiful, it is a pleasure just to look at it, even if one knows nothing about its meaning. Perhaps the most important message of *Totems to Turquoise*, however, lies in how much one's appreciation can be deepened by an awareness of cultural symbols, meanings, and values. Knowing an object's cultural context immeasurably enriches an enjoyment and understanding of its artistry.

The Continuum

Native North American jewelry provides a window into culture while explaining Native art through the lens of culture. The continuum of designs from past to present illustrates that iconography is deeply rooted in a series of cultural traditions. Above all, this continuum acknowledges a vibrant cultural persistence. Culture is not some vaguely remembered notion, but guides Native peoples' lives in the present. Contemporary pieces, even when transformed through market influences and new materials and techniques, illustrate the continuation of deeply held beliefs. Authenticity relies on the ability of an artist to retrieve the sources of tradition to speak in the language of symbolic value.

"With this exhibition we hope to show who we are as a people and how we think about art," says Jim Hart. "It's a well-thought-out thing. In the outside world art is, more or less, a separate thing. But in our art it's our job to bring forward the supernatural depths. Today we are becoming more contemporary, and we're pushing the old styles, but they still have meaning. That's really important to all of us. That's the bottom line: where it comes from."

Above all, attention to the highest standards of craftsmanship—"the well-made object"—continues to generate an extraordinarily evocative body of work among the jewelers of the Southwest and Northwest Coast. We trust that *Totems to Turquoise* will promote greater understanding of Native American artistic traditions and will illuminate the remarkable continuity and vitality of Native cultures.

Human and eagle bracelet.
Russell Smith (Kwakwaka'
wakw). Silver and abalone.
1981. Height, 1". Collection
University of British Columbia
Museum of Anthropology,
Nb3.1459

COLLECTING IS AN INCURABLE DISEASE

Martha L. Albrecht

Collecting is an incurable disease that afflicts many. The first symptom is curiosity; from there it progresses to love, passion, and even obsession. Involvement may become total, including time, energy, and finances. Some may even require psychological assistance to "get over" this disease.

Collecting means amassing a group of things that bear a resemblance to each other (such as a group of stamps), that are related to each other (like a group of furniture from a certain period of time and place), or that come from a particular area (such as the art of the Southwest) and learning about these items. The collection may vary from stuff that is found in refuse piles to items of great cost and significance. But the symptoms are the same from person to person. Only the degree of the illness varies, along with the nature of the collected items.

My husband and I were both collecting before we met. Dan had had a number of these attractions, selling one so that he might move on to another, while I had built only one modest collection of Southwestern Native art. Dan had built a significant collection and was considered a notable collector in the field of Southwestern Indian art when he suddenly sold it all. About that same time I made my first significant acquisition by purchasing a black feather-design plate by Maria Martinez of San Ildefonso. When I met Dan a few years later I learned that this plate had been in his collection!

For us, collecting from the Southwest has also meant the opportunity to meet artists, since we live in the Southwest. We are both on boards of "living museums" where the artists are as integral and important as are their various arts. New friendships have become an important aspect of our collecting. In return, these friendships have increased our understanding and appreciation of the people, their arts, and their ways.

We have only recently begun collecting arts from the Northwest. And this began with meeting some of the artists as they appeared at large Native American functions here in the Southwest. The work is appealing and very visual. The Northwest and the Southwest are quite different: the Northwest uses bold design and vibrant color while the Southwest designs are smaller and the colors more subtle and subdued; both are related to the intrinsic nature of their environments. Nature in the Northwest has been generous in supporting its people while in the Southwest it has been more reserved, even sparing. The designs used by these two peoples reflect their respective spiritualities as well as their native artistic abilities, their appreciation of the beauty of their surroundings, and their joy in making everyday things pleasing to the eye.

There is great joy in living with art . . . we buy only what we love. We have recorded stories of how we acquired many of these items and keep careful notes of description, provenance, cost, and details of where, when, and how each item was collected. For us, that's the fun of collecting.

Bolo tie. Edison Cummings
(Navajo). Ironwood, turquoise,
gold, silver. Bolo height,
2¼". Collection Dr. and Mrs.
E. Daniel Albrecht

THE NORTHWEST COAST

"The soul of our art form goes back to a time when there was a great flood. Once I asked one of my elders how the old artists invented the designs. He said, 'They didn't invent them, they were a gift from the Creator after the flood.' When the floodwaters receded, the people found the designs carved in the sand. All the beautiful formlines, the swirls and twirls, the intensities and the splits and everything, it was all carved in the sand for them, a gift from the Creator. And now, as the modern artists apply those same techniques, it's continuing from that very day when the gift was given in the flood. Ever since, artists have been trying it this way, trying it that way, changing it a little bit this way and that way. It all fits together, it all works." —Beau Dick

ABUNDANT WORLD OF WATER AND WOOD: THE NORTHWEST COAST

Kari Chalker

Along the Northwest Coast, mountains covered in lush, dense forests meet the ocean along a narrow border of rocky shoreline. Island groups veiled in mists protect interior waterways, and inlets, coves, and river deltas offer shelter from winter storms. Waves crash along sand and pebble beaches as killer whales hunt and eagles soar overhead. Salmon move in seasonal rhythms between the ocean and the rivers.

People have made this rich edge between land and sea their home for thousands of years, living in ways that, until European contact, changed slowly over time, but, in general, relied on similar resources and lifeways. They fished, hunted, and gathered. They stripped bark from red and yellow cedar trees to pound into soft fiber for clothing and padded baby cradles. They traveled over ocean and rivers by canoe, trading for necessary goods and exotic items. Large cedar-plank houses, known as big houses, offered communal protection, warmth, and comfort.

The Northwest Coast people lived as actively in the supernatural world as they did in the natural environment, enacting tales of mythic ancestry with carved masks and lavishly adorned regalia. Their social and ceremonial lives were as rich as the lush region in which they lived.

Kwakwaka'wakw artist Beau Dick describes the scene that first greeted European explorers: "When the invaders came to the coast, they saw a sophisticated people with a high standard of living. They lived in beautiful cedar houses with great, carved monuments. Their jewelry and even their tools were decorated with ornate designs. It was all an expression of wealth. Not only was their society powerful and sophisticated, their art form was magnificent. They put so much love and care into the things that they made."

The People

The ancient ancestors of those sophisticated people had lived similar lives that grew more complex over time. Although fluctuating sea levels, weather, and decomposition have almost obliterated the earliest archaeological record along the Northwest Coast, enough evidence remains to show that people have lived in this area for at least 12,000 years. Between 5,500 and 1,500 years ago, people lived in complex cooperative communities and caught large quantities of salmon, preserving their catch for later needs. Recovered items include lip plugs known as labrets—evidence that the early people expressed their beliefs through art and adornment and placed value and meaning on their appearance. Stone-tool kits indicate that woodworking assumed major importance, and stains of post-hole locations suggest that people built large houses covered with cedar planks along the rivers and coasts 2,000 years before those of today's descendants. Dentalium shell from the west coast of Vancouver Island was traded widely, and carved pendants in the shapes of humans, birds, animals, and supernatural creatures may represent shamanic charms or the beginnings of Northwest Coast crest art.

Today's descendants—the Tlingit, Haida, Tsimshian, Nisga'a, Gitxsan, Haisla, Heiltsuk, Nuxalk,

The Northwest Coast land-
scape is characterized by rocky
shoreline, sand or pebble
beaches, and vast forests
reaching to the ocean's edge.

Oweekeno, Kwakwaka'wakw, Nuu-chah-nulth, Ditidaht, Makah, and Coast Salish—share many traits, but they express those traits in distinct ways.

The Haida occupy primarily Haida Gwaii (the Queen Charlotte Islands) with another group living in what is now southeast Alaska. Recognized as great carvers, warriors, and traders, the Haida covered enormous distances in sea-going canoes. So great was their reputation as canoe-builders that they traded their canoes up and down the adjacent mainland coast and up into Alaska. They traded with all groups for goods not found on their islands—most importantly "grease," the valuable eulachon oil derived from the eulachon or candle-fish, a small fish that many groups netted, boiled down, and aged to produce a much-valued food source. They acquired mountain goat wool for Raven's Tail and Chilkat blankets, mountain goat and mountain sheep horns for finely carved spoons, ladles, and bowls, and maple wood for carving frontlets (a carved masquette that fronts a chief's headdress).

The Tlingit live along the archipelago of south-eastern Alaska and also were known as great traders, bartering copper and blankets made of mountain-goat wool for exotic shell jewelry and slaves. As the European, market-driven fur trade increased, the Tlingit expanded their trade connec-tions to receive goods from tribes farther inland, including the Tahltan, and controlled the flow of those inland goods, such as furs and hides, to the coast.

The Tsimshian occupy islands and mainland along the mouth of the Skeena River. The Gitxsan live farther upstream along the Skeena, and throughout their history, they have lacked direct access to a coastline, relying instead on river and mountain resources, including the hunting of land mammals. The Nisga'a today occupy four villages along the Nass River.

The central coast, including Vancouver Island, is home to many different groups. The Kwakwaka'wakw live along northern Vancouver Island and the adjacent mainland, and the Nuu-chah-nulth occupy the outer, Pacific, coast of Vancouver Island. With Washington State's Makah group, and the Ditidaht, from the southern tip of Vancouver Island, the Nuu-chah-nulth were ocean-going whale hunters. On the mainland are the villages of the Heiltsuk, the Nuxalk, and the Haisla, who live farthest north, having frequent contact with and influence from the Tsimshian.

Carving along the central coast, especially Kwakwaka'wakw carving, included attachments like wings, beaks, and arms that gave house poles animation. As non-Native paints became available, bright reds, greens, blues, and whites were added. In addition, these groups took the exuberance and drama of Northwest Coast culture to great elaboration, developing winter ceremonials into lively theatrical events.

Shared Traits

Despite distinctly different languages, origin stories, and art styles, many characteristics are shared throughout the Northwest Coast cultural region. With varying degrees of emphasis, all the groups made their living from the sea and rivers. Salmon were vital for several reasons: They were abun-dant, predictable, and the flesh could be preserved for storage, creating " . . . a year-round staple rather than only a seasonal delicacy, allowing develop-ment of dense populations, complex social organi-zation and elaborate material culture" (McMillan, 1995, 196–197). Societies of this complexity do not normally develop without an agricultural base.

Countless foods from the ocean included shellfish, crabs, and seaweeds. Sea mammals— seals, sea lions, and whales—were hunted. Forest resources such as salmonberries, huckleberries, fern roots, and edible bulbs and tubers were also gathered.

The cedar tree was one of the most important resources and vital as an artistic medium. Cedar bark and spruce roots provided warp and weft for woven blankets, hats, baskets, and mats, some

Top:
A chief displays a button blanket adorned with his crest. Fort Rupert, 1894. American Museum of Natural History, 335772

Bottom:
Kwakw̱aka'wakw houses line the beach at Hope Island, 1881. American Museum of Natural History, 42298

Opposite page:
Bill Reid Respect Pole. The University of British Columbia Museum of Anthropology commissioned Jim Hart to replace a pole that Bill Reid and Doug Cranmer had carved in 1962 and which was deteriorating. Instead of replicating the existing pole, Hart designed a new pole in honor of Bill Reid. Over the course of eight months, he and his team of three apprentices, Oliver Bell, Paul White, and Nika Brown, granddaughter of Bill Reid, carved the pole, and Hart's new design took shape. The bottom figure, considered to be the most important because it holds the others up, is the wolf, representing Bill Reid's crest. Above that are Raven and Eagle to represent the two clans of the Haida. Three Haida watchmen figures, on guard for danger in the natural and supernatural worlds, top the pole. As Hart explains, "The pole represents Bill holding up the Haida people." The pole was raised in October, 2000.

This page, top:
Bentwood box carved with bear motif. Tlingit. Bentwood boxes were constructed of one plank that was partially cut through at three spots, then steam-softened and bent to form corners. Boxes were ubiquitous containers, some so well constructed that they were used for cooking by adding hot rocks to boil liquids. Wood, opercula, abalone, metal, pigment. Ca. 1894. Length, 33½". Collection American Museum of Natural History, E/2295

This page, left
Silver "bentwood" box and lid. Earl Muldoe (Tsimshian). 1973. Height including lid, 4⁷⁄₁₆". Collection Royal British Columbia Museum, 14082a,b

woven to waterproof tightness. The vast forests provided an ample supply of trees to choose from for creating canoes, crest (totem) poles, bent-wood boxes, and for big house materials including planks, beams, and posts. There is no evidence that any group on the Northwest Coast except the Haida and southern Tlingit carved exterior crest (totem) poles before European contact. All groups, however, carved house posts to display their crests (Bill McLennan: personal communication, 2004). House planks were valuable possessions. During moves to seasonal locations, some groups would remove planks from structures to take them along. Haisla artist Lyle Wilson describes connections between woodworking and other aspects of the natural world: "The wild beaver is a symbol of industriousness. . . . Precontact carvers used a chisel with a beaver-tooth blade, so the beaver has played an important part in our wood-carving traditions" (Wyatt, 86).

Copper, used by Native groups before European contact, was soft and workable without forging, and it became associated with wealth, high rank, and power. It was hammered flat and shaped into highly valued, particular figures of varying sizes called Coppers. Each Copper had its own name and value that could increase according to presentation. Adds Jim Hart, "A Copper was a living thing among the people and was part of our banking system." Copper was hammered and twisted into bracelets, anklets, rings, and earrings—all valued representations of the wearer's power and status.

Also incorporated into adornment and other objects of power were cut pieces of abalone shells inlaid into masks as shining eyes and tied to blankets as reflective ornaments. Dentalium shells, gathered by the Nuu-chah-nulth in deep water off the west coast of Vancouver Island, were traded great distances along the coast and inland trade trails and were made into earrings, headpieces, and necklaces, and used to outline crest designs on aprons, tunics, leggings, and blankets. Long sea lion whiskers formed part of the structure of chiefs'

headdresses, supporting the carved frontlet and creating a framework to hold eagle down. These headdresses were danced during special occasions and as the dancer moved, eagle down was gently released to bring peace, goodwill, and blessings.

Mythic Histories and the Supernatural

The Northwest Coast's abundant resources were gathered within a framework of respect for the natural world's connection with the supernatural world. "In mythic times humans and animals were essentially the same, and animals were believed to retain the ability to transform from one realm to another. The Salmon People, Killer Whale People, Wolf People and others were viewed as having their own houses, where they took off their animal cloaks and lived parallel lives to humans. . . . Because the Salmon People voluntarily left their underwater villages to offer [themselves] to humans, it was essential that they be respected" (McMillan, 199). The cedar tree, too, was thanked any time a strip of its bark was taken to create clothing and other woven objects.

Mythic stories are told in the "visual language" referred to by exhibition curators Dubin and Whiteley in their introduction. Northwest Coast artists depict their own mythic history and connections to the natural and supernatural worlds on their houses, poles, canoes, bowls, masks, tools, clothing, and jewelry. Thunderbird, a supernatural being whose image is found on many items, ". . . darkens the sky with its great shape; the clapping of its wings causes thunder, and the blinking of its wild eyes causes lightning. . . . Thunderbird can swoop down to grasp its favourite food, a Killerwhale, in its talons" (Wyatt, 11). This change in relative size and scale is in keeping with the blending of supernatural and natural worlds in Northwest Coast cosmology and with the artists' abilities to adapt the scale of a motif to a totem pole or a pendant.

Jewelry represents connections with the natural and supernatural and indicates people's relation-

Pendant incorporating *sisiutl* (serpent) and Copper designs. Lloyd Wadhams (Kwakwa̱ka̱'wakw). Silver. Ca. 1968–1971. Length, 3½". Collection University of British Columbia Museum of Anthropology, Nb3.1465

Opposite page:
Mountain goat horn bracelets.
Tlingit or Coast Salish. Horn,
shell, pigment. Ca. 1800.
Height of bottom bracelet, 4¾".
Collection Peabody Museum,
Harvard University, photo
T1659

This page, right:
Tlingit potlatch guests at
Yakutat. American Museum
of Natural History, 328740

This page, below:
A Kwakwaka'wakw chief at
Fort Rupert gives away a
Copper, a shield-shaped
object highly valued among
Northwest Coast groups,
in honor of his son. 1894.
American Museum of Natural
History, 106707

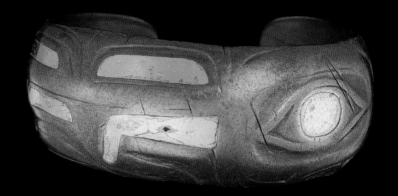

Opposite page:
Copper bracelet with gold
inlay. Northwest Coast artists
who have examined this
bracelet believe it was
originally inlaid with abalone
(Bill McLennan: personal
communication, 2004).
Tlingit. Ca. 1850. Height,
1³⁄₁₆". Collection University of
British Columbia Museum
of Anthropology, Nb22.97

At the Kwakwa̱ka'wakw village
of 'Yalis (Alert Bay) men pose
with potlatch gifts to be distributed including blankets and
silver bracelets stacked on
cedar stakes. Ca. 1910. Royal
British Columbia Museum,
PN1098

Copper and abalone bracelet.
Tlingit. Prior to 1896. Length,
3⅛". Collection American
Museum of Natural History,
E/2612

44

Top:
A Haida woman wearing a
labret weaves a hat at the
village of Yan, Haida Gwaii.
1881. American Museum
of Natural History, 42290

Bottom:
Francine Hunt, wife of George
Hunt, the Kwakwa̲ka'wakw
man who assisted Franz Boas
and others in documenting
and collecting objects from
the Kwakwa̲ka'wakw. 1914.
Courtesy University of British
Columbia Museum of Anthropology

Raven bracelet. Phil Janze
(Gitxsan). Gold. Width, 1⅝".
Collection University of British
Columbia Museum of Anthro-
pology, 2594/2

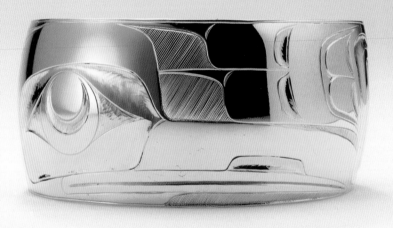

ships to their history and to others. In 1803, an English sailor named John Jewitt was taken captive and enslaved by Maquinna, a Nuu-chah-nulth chief. Jewitt later described the people of Maquinna's household: "Their ornaments consist chiefly of ear-rings, necklaces, bracelets, rings for the fingers and ankles, and small nose jewels (the latter are wholly confined to the wives of the king or chiefs). These are principally made out of copper or brass, highly polished and of various forms and sizes; the nose jewel is usually a small white shell or bead suspended [from] a thread. The wives of the common people frequently wear for bracelets and ankle rings, strips of the country cloth [woven cedar bark] or skin of the [elk] painted in figures . . ." (Stewart, 83). Although the common people had no access to valuable goods like metal, they still placed a value on adorning themselves.

The strict social ranking of nobles and commoners was inherited. One's social status was determined at birth, although commoners and slaves could change status. Chiefs and nobles held important names, rights, and access to resources. Commoners did not hold titles or privileges, but shared in the general identity of the group and, along with slaves, were the labor force. Slaves, captured from other Native groups, may have been high-ranking people in their own groups, but became considered part of the wealth owned by a chief. Membership in a kin group was inherited through the group's descent from supernatural ancestors who, in mythic history, had been transformed into human beings. Along with kin membership came the rights to portray images of the ancestors, as well as rights to fishing territories and other resources.

Crest (totem) poles distinctly varied in style from region to region. Most poles grandly exhibited the particular ancestry or crests of the chief or noble whose house it graced. Respected artists were commissioned to carve these poles and also to depict the family crests on many objects including masks, rattles, and large feast dishes.

Today's artists feel it is their responsibility to maintain Northwest Coast mythic histories. Explains Beau Dick: "When my ancestor, the wolf, came down the mountain in ancient times, he found a nice place to build his house. He summoned four spirits to be the support pillars. These four spirits represented four different person-alities: the spirit that welcomes and feeds you; the one who dances, sings, and entertains you; the one who takes care of business and keeps things in order; and the one who gives you gifts and wishes you well on your way. Wolf then summoned two double-headed serpents to drape themselves across the heads of these four spirits so he could build the roof. If one of those characters is missing, the house won't stand up. We need each other for the different roles we play in society—to hold each other up, to hold our house up. For our people, that's what the artist's role is—knowing the old stories. It's the artist's responsibility to be a historian, to incorporate the teachings of the mythology into his artwork, to carve the masks that are used in ceremonies. So the artist has to learn the meanings of the items he carves. What does it represent? Where does it originate? Who owns it? It's the artist who finds credible answers to these questions."

Northwest Coast peoples have many ways of interacting with the supernatural world. Shamans were integral to Northwest Coast life and could enter the supernatural world, changing form to interpret its mysterious workings. With the use of charms (see page 55), drums, rattles, songs, and the knowledge of healing, shamans could retrieve missing souls and cure ailing individuals. They had great powers and were respected by the people.

Although shamanism was an important aspect of Northwest Coast beliefs, other, more public, interactions with the supernatural world occurred in ceremonials held in the big houses. Through elaborate masks, costumes, and choreography, tales of supernatural ancestry are told by flickering

Silver bracelet. Art Thompson
(Nuu-chah-nulth). 1979.
Width, 1 7/16". Collection Royal
British Columbia Museum,
16665

firelight as in the *hamatsa* ceremony of the Kwakw<u>a</u>ka'wakw people, which tells of Cannibal-at-the-North-End-of-the-World. His village is guarded by three large cannibal birds: the *Huxwhukw*, the Cannibal Raven, and the Crooked Beak. The *hamatsa* dancer is believed to have lived there, apart from civilization, as a wild cannibal. When he returns, he must be tamed and pacified, while the monster cannibal birds dance in attendance, clacking moveable beaks in elaborate wooden masks.

Most important of all Northwest Coast ceremonies is the potlatch, which continues today despite having been banned from 1884 to 1951. The potlatch is a public feast in which gifts are given to invited guests to validate or make official certain important events or life transitions. By listening to a recitation of the host's virtues, history, and hereditary rights, and by accepting gifts, guests become witnesses to the transition. Historically, valuables such as bracelets, blankets, and Coppers were commissioned from respected artists, and eulachon oil and other goods were purchased to be part of the potlatch giveaways. Today, jewelry remains an important potlatch gift. It may take a family many years to accumulate enough goods for a potlatch. Gifts are given according to rank, the most valuable going to the highest-ranking visitors. Potlatches were sometimes competitive, when rival chiefs strove to outdo each other with their generosity. With the acquisition of European trade goods, chiefs became even wealthier, and the scale of giving and demonstrations of scorn for material wealth increased. Vats of eulachon oil were burned. Coppers were cut to pieces and the pieces distributed to rivals, setting a challenge for a rival to buy back all the pieces, reassemble the Copper, and best the disgraced owner (Bill McLennan: personal communication, 2004). Today, the potlatch remains a vital part of Northwest Coast cultures.

Style Conventions

Northwest Coast art follows style conventions that vary from group to group but in general, make use of formlines to create design units known as ovoids and U-forms. Described by scholar and artist Bill Holm in his landmark book, *Northwest Coast Indian Art: An Analysis of Form*, formline art dates back centuries and is followed assiduously by today's culturally sensitive artists. As described by Holm, "formlines swell and diminish, rarely retaining the same width for any distance. Generally they swell in the center of a given design unit and diminish at the ends." The ovoid is called by Holm "the most characteristic design unit in the art . . ." and is used to depict eyes and joints and to fill space. The top of the ovoid is always convex, giving it a downward cast. U-forms are also ubiquitous and " . . . result when both ends of a formline turn in the same direction and each tapers to a point at their inevitable juncture with another formline."

Today's artists have great respect for the rules of formline art and find room within it to develop their own personal styles. Remarks Tsimshian artist Corey Moraes, "It's amazing what has been created with basic elements—the ovoid, the U-form, and tertiary spaces have been the basis for countless creatures, poles, and masks. Every day I come up with new ideas, and it all stems from these same basic elements." Because of this flexibility and creativity within a style structure, Northwest Coast art continues to grow and evolve, while still respecting the old conventions. Adds Tahltan-Tlingit artist Dempsey Bob, "The old pieces were valid in their time and they're still valid, but today we have to make it real for ourselves here and now, and that's the challenge for an artist."

Contact and Change

European explorers were first represented by the Spanish and the Russians in the early 1770s; both groups explored the area with competing hopes of controlling the vast and rich territory. Major contact

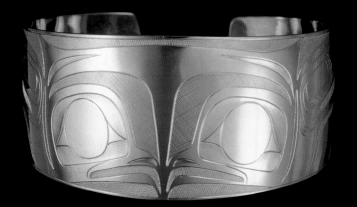

This page, left:
Raven of the Sea transformation mask in closed and open positions. Kwakwaka'wakw. Prior to 1901. Wood, pigment, hide, iron, fiber, cord. Length, 32⅜". Collection American Museum of Natural History, 16/8529

This page, below:
Killer whale feast dish. Kwakwaka'wakw. Prior to 1901. Wood. Length, 30¾". Collection American Museum of Natural History, 16/8528a,b

51

Opposite page, top:
Silver bowl. Tony Hunt (Kwakwaka'wakw). 1980. Length, 7". Collection Royal British Columbia Museum, 16788

Opposite page, bottom:
Owl bracelet. Francis Williams (Haida). Silver. Height, 1¼". Collection University of British Columbia Museum of Anthropology, Nb1.729

and trade did not begin, however, until Captain James Cook sailed into Nootka Sound in 1778. By the 1780s, a lively fur trade between the Native peoples and American, English, Spanish, and French companies was in place. Ships' holds were emptied of non-Native trade goods such as vermillion, iron axes, glass beads, guns, and cloth, and were in turn filled with sea otter pelts destined for China.

Foreign diseases, for which the Native people had no resistance, killed tens of thousands of people up and down the coast. The survivors gathered to maintain a foothold in their ancestral villages as fur trading outposts and other interests took over previously held territories. In the early 1850s, treaties were enacted with some groups, especially in the south, that made already-settled lands the property of European colonists, but beginning in 1858 reserves were established for the groups based on traditional use. Christian missionaries arrived not far behind the traders, intent on bringing the light of a new and "better" life with God. Many people adopted the new beliefs either completely or in combination with their Native practices. But the old beliefs remained, especially the outlawed potlatch. Families often continued to potlatch in secret, with the result that by the 1920s numerous Kwakwaka'wakw were prosecuted and jailed. A major victory for

traditional beliefs was won in the 1970s with the return to the Kwakwaka'wakw of many masks and ceremonial items that had been seized in the 1920s. The U'mista Cultural Centre, a museum in the Kwakwaka'wakw village of Alert Bay built in the style of a big house, now holds these invaluable pieces.

Today's Revitalization

In the face of significant cultural devastation and near annihilation, artists have played an important role in the survival of tradition. As the artists interviewed in this book reveal, Northwest Coast culture is experiencing a period of revitalization and renewal. An intense pride in one's heritage pervades today's Northwest Coast cultures, jewelry, and art. Master artists like Haida carver Charles Edenshaw and a few others maintained these arts through the most difficult years, providing a vitally important link to the old ways. Artists and scholars like Bill Reid and Bill Holm came together to examine and discuss the old masterpieces. Bill Reid played a pivotal role in today's revitalization by turning the world's attention to Northwest Coast art and by passing on his talent, skills, and enthusiasm to younger artists who now further the process in their own ways, with their own talents. Although some of today's artists have moved away from their home villages to cities like Vancouver, Victoria, and Seattle, many still take active roles in the ceremonial lives of their communities, creating jewelry, masks, and regalia for their own people as well as for a burgeoning art market. Museums and cultural institutions are supporting artists in their studies of the old masterpieces, and they loan objects to communities for use in ceremonies. Young artists study under masters, perpetuating not just the styles and techniques, but the teachings and the connections to the traditions. As Dempsey Bob puts it: "Art lifts people's pride. Art makes you see who you are. It reflects the culture, and culture is what you do, where you live, what you believe."

Chilkat blanket. Tlingit. Mountain goat wool, cedar bark, goat wool, fur trim, leather straps. Ca. 1911. Width, 74". Collection American Museum of Natural History, 336105

Opposite page:
Tom Price and John Robson, descended from Haida nobility, wear Chilkat blankets and frontlets, small panels or forehead masks that front a chiefly headdress. American Museum of Natural History, 45608

THE BODY TRANSFORMED: BODY ART AND ADORNMENT AMONG PREHISTORIC AND HISTORIC NORTHWEST COAST PEOPLE

Martine Reid

The underlying assumptions of this essay are, first, that aesthetics, the perception of the beautiful in nature and art, "does not exist in itself as an independent category of thought.... Aesthetic judgments are predicated on a system of values ... manipulated by rules which are ... culturally specific and historically determined" (Shelton 1992:209–210; Wittgenstein 1970). One cannot separate Northwest Coast aesthetic expressions from Northwest Coast cultural and historic experience. To understand and appreciate them one must describe the context in which they occurred, their meanings, explicit and implicit, formal and semantic, their symbolic associations to other categories, and their relationship to the world itself. "Art is an experience of certain objects, not just the objects themselves." (MacGaffey 2003:258–59)

Secondly, the desire to alter, or mark, or "adorn" the surface and the structure of the body, temporarily or irreversibly, is one of man- and womankind's most universal characteristics. Early Northwest Coast people have used several means to this end: body piercing, painting, tattooing,[1] head deformation, and dental modification, as well as clothing and jewelry, all of which are evidenced in various forms in the archaeological record.

With these assumptions in mind, and through analysis of early forms of body art and adornment in terms of their substance, forms, and contextual use, we hope to provide an insight into the aesthetics of Northwest Coast people.

Northwest Coast Aesthetic Expressions in Archaeological Time

Northwest Coast people have a long and dynamic history spanning at least 12,000 years. Knowledge of the cultures of the Pacific Northwest of the Early Period (12,000 to 5,500 years ago) is rather thin. A belief system is evidenced by ritualistic use of red ocher,[2] which suggests body painting,[3] and a few animal teeth pendants, which may well have been charms associated with spirit power beliefs. (Carlson 1983:21) Favorable environmental and material conditions gave rise by the end of the Middle Period (5,500 to 1,500 years ago) to the antecedents of the general cultural and intellectual tradition that existed when the first Europeans arrived. (Borden 1975:98–116; Carlson 1983:13–32; Fladmark 1986: chap. 9; Mitchell 1990:352) At the end of the Middle Period a sophisticated artistic tradition which, in itself, "suggests full-time artisans and commissioned art," was present. (Carlson op. cit. 28) This tradition was maintained by the politically and spiritually successful, and manifested, although with some degree of regional variations, in the symbolism of their cultural and aesthetic expressions. Wealth, in the durable forms of small disc beads laboriously ground from stone or shell, as well as dentalia,[4] beads of amber and jet, and copper ornaments, was found in the major burial centers of the coast, providing evidence of trade over wide areas.

Trade and the desire for exotic goods burgeoned with the coming of the Europeans, who brought

Shaman's necklace. Tlingit. Ca. 1820–1880. Exotic and powerful amulets strung on twined string include a carved shell believed to be from the prehistoric Hohokam culture of the southwestern United States, an iron bird possibly from Siberia, and carved and incised ivory likely traded in from the Eskimo. Length of carved antler, 4⅝". The University of Pennsylvania Museum, negative number 138191

brass, silver, and iron. Exoticism was not the exclusive prerogative of the secular world. Shamans were equally attracted to foreign materials or ideas as evidenced by a nineteenth-century Tlingit shaman's necklace made up of several pendants including an ivory bird of Eskimo origin, the shell figure of a frog from the Aboriginal Southwest, and a metal bird from Siberia. The inclusion of objects of such exotic and mysterious provenance added to the power of the object. During the ethnographic period, i.e., the time following contact with Europeans during which ethnographers observed Northwest Coast cultures, Russian crosses and trade beads, Chinese coins, and Athapaskan bracelets found their way into the shaman's kit, while Chinese mother-of-pearl shell buttons added their magic qualities to the aristocrats' ceremonial attire.

Early explorers commented on the surprisingly rich and sophisticated cultures of the Northwest Coast. Charles Pierre Claret de Fleurieu, a member of the expedition led by Etienne Marchand (1790–1792), himself an admirer of art and architecture, while in the Queen Charlotte Islands wrote: "What must astonish most . . . is to see painting everywhere, everywhere sculpture, among a nation of hunters." (Fleurieu 1801:281) It is not surprising then that these people would treat their bodies with the same artistic fervor with which they decorated their houses and possessions.

Body Ornaments

We should emphasize the very close association between forms of adornments and social category on the Northwest Coast. Ornaments were an important indication of social classification, differentiating, classifying, and ordering in the same way as titles of nobility do. Hence, they formed a "second skin" through which the individual manifested her or his identity.

Personal body adornment was a means for a cultural specialist—be it a shaman, a chief, or an aristocrat—of assimilating, accruing, and storing supernatural power. Powerful thoughts were

contained—consciously or subconsciously—in artfully made potent devices or objects of adornment. Adornment and spiritual empowerment were synonymous.

Copper Ornaments

Native copper ornaments were found in burial sites by 500 BCE in the northern area, inhabited by the Tlingit, Tshimshian, and Haida, including bracelets, earrings, nose rings, and neck rings. (MacDonald (1983:105–106) The effectiveness of copper objects depended much less on copper's inherent qualities[5] than upon its symbolic associations, which had been established within the cultures that used it. These had to do with its red color, the color of life and salmon. Its smell was further associated with that of salmon: Kwakwaka'wakw mythology often refers to the metallic scent of copper linking it to that of salmon. (Widerspach-Thor 1981:159) Native copper's symbolic properties of curing disease when used by shamans, its association with sunlight (Boas-Hunt 1905:3520), its rarity and mysterious provenance, established its dominance as the most significant metallic substance in the symbolic system of Northwest Coast peoples. Copper was their gold. These properties coalesced in the historic period in the Copper plates (made of imported sheets of smelted copper), which embodied wealth and were valued in terms of mountain goat furs (or wool blankets) or slaves. (Widerspach-Thor, op. cit.:157–174)

Horn Ornaments

Engraved Salish mountain-goat horn bracelets—some with shell inlay—were collected by early explorers.[6] Mountain goat was a rare commodity hunted by men. Associated with the supernatural world of the high mountains, mountain goat horn and wool connote the spiritual world; objects created with these substances were used during cleansing rituals. Women transformed the soft, white fur into woven blankets, which in turn became symbols of wealth and a ritual currency.[7]

Eagle bracelet. Raymond
Stevens (Haida). Silver. 1980.
Diameter, 2¼". Collection
University of British Columbia
Museum of Anthropology,
Nb1.751

Abalone Shell (Haliotis) Ornaments

The long-standing symbolic association between the iridescent, white and blue-green abalone shell, traded up from the Californian coast, and light or the brightness of the sun[8] has established this substance of aquatic origin as a much-favored element for decoration. Many sculpted objects— containers, masks and headdresses, and even faces—were enlivened with haliotis pieces. Haida people, who painted crest designs on their faces for festive occasions, glued to their cheeks small pieces of abalone shells to symbolize sunlight. (Boas 1898: in Jonaitis 1995:111) In addition to light, haliotis connotes good fortune, everlasting-ness and well-being. (Grubb 1977:110)

Items used for self-decoration such as copper, mountain-goat horn and wool, and haliotis were also valuables that circulated in ritual exchanges at marriage and potlatch ceremonies.

Stone and Bone Ornaments

Most shamans' charms used in healing ceremonies were carved out of durable material such as stone, bone or ivory, antler, and the teeth of various animals. Small, prehistoric, three-dimensionally carved and incised stone "worms" found in the Middle Period, and other carved stone pendants[9] may have been part of shamanistic paraphernalia (Carlson 1983:27).

Stone connotes invulnerability or eternity as Northwest Coast mythology attests. Mythic ances-tors were sometimes turned into stone[10] to live "everlastingly as reminders of the circumstances that caused their transformation, and of their lasting implications for men." (Duff 1975:18)

A shaman's attire included, among other things, carved bone pins to keep his untidy hair in place and a bone worn through his septum (Swanton 1905:40). Several curved bone bracelets worn by Tlingit shamans in the north reveal two-dimensional, incised "geometric" designs that have been interpreted as "stylized vertebral columns, eyes, teeth and scales." (MacDonald 1983:106–107)

Northern-style shamans' charms of the historic period were deeply carved with narrative scenes often exhibiting skeletal features that could have suggested the wearer's death and his return to life, the ultimate transformation.[11] Shamans' bone ornaments were ritually potent and their protective powers stemmed as much from their substance as their form. Because bones are the longest-lasting parts of the body—they outlive death—it is believed that they are the source of, or the catalyst for, life. Amulets were literally and metaphorically deeply carved,[12] in the sense that "the design carried the charge that invested the images with their life form and hence their meaning, empow-ering them, in short, to be carved deeply into the consciousness of the people who used them." (Shadbolt, 1986:86)

Body Piercing

The wearing of ornaments such as earrings, nose rings, or labrets was the prerogative of the elite and made various grades of status visible, according to gender. Slaves were not permitted to alter their physical appearance in any way. (Emmons 1991; Niblack 1970)

The human body is more than a biological entity. It is a cultural artifact, the boundaries of which are unclear.[13] (Wilson 1985:2) Particular features of the face, such as earlobes,[14] nose septa,[15] and lips, were pierced for appending ornaments. Large steatite ear-spools[16] and nose rings made of copper, shell, or bone have been interpreted by some as devices to prevent illness, the cause of which was believed to be the loss of soul. Potent ornaments would prevent the soul from exiting the body from those orifices, as it was believed that the soul, which resides in bones, could seep out slowly through the orifices and joints.[17] The use of arm- and neckbands, finger rings, and necklaces during the Middle and Late Periods could be seen as stemming from the same preoccupation to avoid seepage of the soul from the joints. "Joint mark" features, typical of

Chief Xana and men in
ceremonial clothing including
two masked shamans. Masset,
Queen Charlotte Islands. 1881.
On the far right stands Chief
Xana, whose arms and chest
are tattooed with charcoal,
depicting his hereditary crests.
American Museum of Natural
History, 337197

Northwest Coast iconography, could be interpreted accordingly.[18] (Shuster 1951; Carpenter 1988)

Labrets, or lip plugs, were worn by both sexes in the north and in the south in prehistoric times.[19] They caused much discussion and gruesome description by all early travelers.[20] During the ethnographic period labret wearing became specifically a female attribute. Interestingly, people in the southern area, the Wakashan and Salishan, who practiced head deformation, historically did not wear labrets, which was the practice of the Haida, Tsimshian, and Tlingit.

Labrets were made of various materials[21] and were worn through perforations in the lower lip. Most commonly interpreted as indicators of high rank,[22] they came in different shapes and sizes. Acquired during childhood, the labret indicated a girl's eligibility for marriage;[23] its size increased according to the rank of the wearer and to the number of children she had borne. Symbolic of the emphasis the society placed upon female fecundity,[24] its size seems to have increased toward the beginning of the Common Era as evidenced by a few extremely large examples. (MacDonald 1983:104;[25] Gunther 1966:61– 62; Boas 1916:299–300)

Labrets continued to fascinate the newcomers, and Haida artists exploited that attraction to their advantage. They carved numerous masks of labret-wearing women for the tourist trade, while actual lip and nose piercing fell into disuse rather rapidly after contact. (Swan 1876:4)

Haida Tattooing

Tattooing was a widespread custom on the coast. In the north and the central coast some women wore geometric designs on their arms and legs and, in a few areas, on their chins. The Tsimshian tattooed their wrists and ankles, while the Nuu-chah-nulth reserved tattoos for the arms and breast. Farther in the south, among the Kalapuyans, tattooed designs were often to be seen on the arms and legs of both men and women. Wealthy men

gauged the value of bead and dentalium-shell string lengths with reference to tattooed horizontal lines on their upper arms. (Zenk, in Suttles 1990:548)

The Haida were, as far as is known in historical times, the only ones to have tattooed their whole bodies—hands, fingers, knuckles, wrists, arms, breast, back, legs, ankles, feet, and toes[26]— with conventional Haida designs. These designs, we assume, were linked with other Haida art forms, painting and carving styles, and techniques, and suggest broader associations with other aspects of Haida traditional culture and society. We hope an exploration of context, function, iconography and meaning of tattoo designs will shed more light on Haida aesthetics.

To date, archaeological contexts have not provided clues as to the antiquity of Haida tattooing. However, considering the high level of sophistication deployed by this art form, the convention of which extends back at least 4,500 years (Fladmark 1986), we can safely surmise that it has had as long an existence as that of other forms of Haida art.[27]

Tattooing among the Haida was achieved by two methods: sewing and pricking. Ethnographers did not witness the earlier practice; their informants, however, offered information about it. According to Mrs. Stingess of Masset:

Formerly the Indians got the wool of the mountain sheep and spun it into thread and soaked it in black pigment and then with needles sewed in under the skin, the thread then being drawn through left the black mark. The needles were made of copper until the white man. Then the system of tattooing with needlepoint was introduced. (James Swan Diary, May–Sept. 26, 1883)

Swan (1876) provided the only firsthand account of the second tattooing technique and reproduced a good number of Haida tattoo designs. Male specialists performed tattooing by puncturing and rubbing soot into the wounds. According to Reverend Freeman (c. 1904–1910), tattoo designs were pricked into the skin in red and black. Both

Swan and Boas were struck by the fact that "tattoo patterns were exactly analogous to the paintings and carvings of those people." (Boas 1889: 115–116)

Tattoos as Art Forms

Haida art displays two fundamental means of artistic expression. Sculpture tended to be realistic, while two-dimensional art forms were more symbolic and abstract. Art created by males—sculpture and two-dimensional art—had a representational intention; art created by females—weaving and plaiting—was non-representational, "decorative" or, in Boas's view, "without meaning."[28] In fact, female art was also representational, but of a different intention. As Carpenter pointed out, "The horizon of 'decorative' or 'non-representational' art in tribal societies recedes steadily as our knowledge increases, and we may soon reach the point where we can say with confidence that all tribal art, is, or once was, representational." (Carpenter 1988:2:3:669)

Haida people saw themselves as a part, not the center, of a vast cosmic system. They believed that animals and humans were linked in the intimacy of having been a single being in the beginning. At one time their ancestors had been able, with the easy donning or removing of a skin, to slip into another creature's identity. Humans were animals who had shed their skins, a view that was reiterated in rituals and ceremonies and was enfolded deeply into the art.

From Swan's description we can infer that tattooing was essentially a two-dimensional painting technique. The skin—the "threshold" of the body—is a potent zone, charged with potential powers of transformation, and becomes the privileged design field or the canvas on which to make visible forever that oneness with the ancestors.

Regardless of the designs (simulated stitching or engravings) being tattooed on skin or woven in wool, tree-bark, or root, earlier and later tattoo designs were representational of the wearer's personal and/or social identity. In that regard, tattoo images resemble an underlying principle of the two- and three-dimensional northern art forms: They contain and wrap the body. Skin robes (which undoubtedly preceded woven robes), tattoo designs, and decorated garments are therefore one: the skin (and bones) of the ancestors.

Tattoos as Markers of Personal and Tribal Identity and Rank

Tattoo designs are ancestral crest figures of the person on whom they were tattooed; they have to be examined in relation to Haida social structure.

Traditional Haida society was stratified and organized around two matrilineal moieties: Eagle and Raven, as well as clans or lineages or "houses." Much of Haida art was heraldic. Crests were carved on heraldic columns, engraved or painted on household utensils, boxes, and feast dishes, painted or appliquéd on ceremonial garments, painted on the face, and tattooed on the body.[29] All objects on which crests were applied were forms of containers,[30] literally, symbolically, or both. Tattoo designs expressed rank,[31] and tattooing was a major factor in advancing one's rank in Haida society. Leaders used tattoo art to validate ranking in a competitive system.[32] (Swanton 1905:170) The potlatch coinciding with the building of a house was a means of conferring rank on the donor's own children who were initiated and tattooed at that time (Murdock 1936:19).

According to Boas, tattoo "'Decoration' differs according to the rank and wealth of the wearer. The full and rather realistic representations of animals are considered of greater value, and as indicating higher rank, than conventional representations which consisted of symbols of the animals" (Boas 1898, in Jonaitis 1995:108).

The first tattoo designs to be received by youths at puberty were the most general crests of their lineage. As a youth reached higher social rank by repeated distributions of property among the

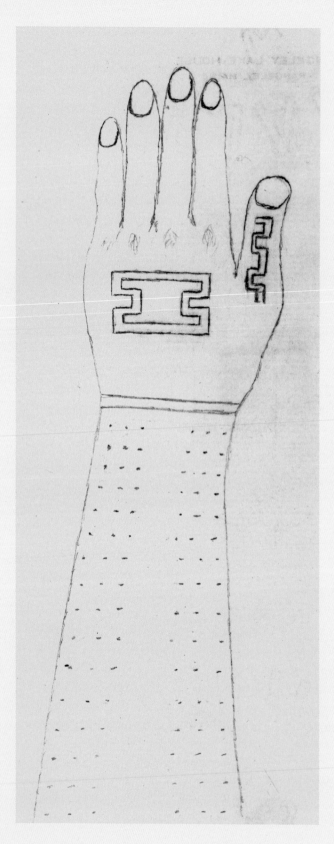

This sketch made by ethnologist G.T. Emmons in 1889 shows tattoos on the hand and forearm of a very old Tlingit woman. The lines at her wrist represent a bracelet. Along the Northwest Coast, the location of tattoos frequently became the place jewelry was later worn. American Museum of Natural History

members of the opposite moiety, he/she became entitled to the wearing of other crests. However, only a chief could use all the crests belonging to one particular lineage. (Boas, op. cit. 109) Florence Davidson, daughter of renowned Haida carver and chief, Charles Edenshaw, recalled that her "Dad was tattooed at his parents' potlatches. He had no clean skin he was so tattooed. Even his back, his arms, his legs, his chest, his hands were tattooed." (Blackman 1981:70) Tattooing not only conferred humanity, identity, and a name; it also brought the force of art closest to the individual person by linking him/her with his/her cultural heritage and identity. That oneness or complete-ness was achieved when the natural and the cultural personae merged. Without tattoos human beings were not complete persons.

Haida women were also known to have mythic figures tattooed on lower phalanges. According to Niblack (1970 [1890]:257), "The designs on their forearms invariably extend down over the back of the hands and knuckles, and this alone serves to distinguish the Haida women from those of other tribes on the coast. Frequently the tattooing on the hands represents finger-rings and bracelets." According to Florence Davidson,

My mother was tattooed at the doing my grandfather held; she had a long dogfish[33] on one leg, a grizzly bear on the other, and a quarter moon and lady on each arm. The tattoos were done in red and blue. They tried to put a tattoo on her chest but she didn't want it and wouldn't let them do it. She was ashamed of the tattoos on her hands. She used to wear gloves to hide them whenever she went out. (Blackman, op. cit. 68) (*See Swanton 1909: Pl. XXI for Isabella's tattoos.*)

Tattooed images on each joint of the hand would reinforce the view expressed earlier that tattoos prevented soul leakage from the hands, and "could be viewed as guardian figures that kept the soul from leaving the body causing death."[34] Niblack's observation would corroborate this view. "A Haida woman, who had on her person a figure of a halibut laid open, with the face of the chief

of her tribe shown on the tail, told Poole [Francis Poole] that it would protect her and her kin from drowning at sea." (1970 [1890]:257)

Women, Men, Chilkat Blankets and Tattoos
Ethnographers have shown that, in Haida society, men and women filled complementary roles in ceremonialism. Both sexes hosted potlatches. Males usually sponsored the house building and mortuary potlatches, while females were in charge of the puberty potlatches. "Both men and women were recipients of potlatch wealth and, as children at their father's potlatches, received equal attention in the form of tattoos and honorific names." (Blackman 1981:36–37)

However, a woman, and particularly a father's sister (or, more generally, a female of father's lineage) played the most important ceremonial role that was not matched by any comparable male ritual role. She cut her brother's children's umbilical cords and tended to her brother's daughters during their puberty seclusion. More importantly, she was the *ritualistic but not the actual* tattooist of the children, as she should have been. As we have said earlier, Haida aesthetics reflected male/female dualities in which two- and three-dimensional representational art, including tattooing which was crest art, belonged to the male domain,[35] while female art was non-representational and geometric. The division of labor as applied to aesthetics served to rationalize why women, who were assigned the ritual task of tattooing a brother's child, delegated the task to a male. (Blackman, op. cit. 38; Murdock 1936:8; Curtis 1916:125)

On the other hand, division of labor was reversed when men asked women to weave repre-sentational designs on the well-known Chilkat robes.[36] Women were not the originators of the designs, only the executors; they followed "pattern boards" that men had painted to that effect.

Consider the Raven's Tail robes. Collected by eighteenth-century explorers,[37] they were the ancestors of later, well-documented, nineteenth-century Chilkat blankets. Raven's Tail robes show a plain white field with repeated black motifs of concentric rectangular designs, vertical tassels, and borders. What was the meaning of these geometric representations? Were they symbols of heraldry as the more realistically decorated later Chilkat designs attest? More importantly, was the Raven's Tail robe entirely a purely feminine conceptual product, that is, one that had been thought out, created and executed without male's intervention? What triggered such profound dramatic changes between the two types of blankets in a relatively short period of time?

Emmons provides valuable information while considering the designs on the Raven's Tail robes. (Emmons 1903:273)

The tattoo pattern, literally "old person-hand-back-of-tattooed" (kaa jikool kajoolans) is possibly the most interesting, as it is one of the most ornamented and widely used characters on basketry.... It does not seem to have had any totemic significance.... The design was tattooed on the back of the hand... on the metacarpals of the fingers... [or] on the metacarpal of the thumb.... The origins of these figures is wholly forgotten by the present generation who know them only as basket designs.

These geometric designs seem to have belonged to the female realm, so we wonder if, in ancient times, women could have been the actual tattoo sewers? Or, did women delegate the task of sewing female tattoo designs to male tattoo artists? Or, was there, then, a division of labor applied to this practice at all?

Based on the fact that in "Several parts of the world, especially in Asia, motifs tattooed on fingers represented ancestors, genealogy being reckoned on the fingers," Carpenter speculated on the view that finger tattoos could be seen as genealogical charts (1988:2:3:687). Could Raven's Tail robes be interpreted accordingly? One question remains, however: How do we distinguish genealogical patterns (descent) from heraldic figures on the Northwest Coast?

We are faced with two possible scenarios: 1) In a remote past, geometric tattoo designs were perhaps sewed (or stitched) by women, and were perhaps related to genealogy. These designs are also found on women's works such as blankets and basketry weavings. 2) In a not so distant past, representational tattoo designs were pricked (or carved) by men, and were heraldic symbols that were also found on every decorated two- and three-dimensional work done by men. They were (and still are) crest figures representing mythic ancestors.

Who were the male tattoo artists? To which moiety or lineage did they belong with regard to the women who hired them? An in-depth research and analysis of mythic-related material pertaining to the origins of processes and techniques of tattooing, paralleled with a study of women's geometric art-forms of older antiquity, would be required to further elucidate uncertainties around tattooing, a research we intend to continue in the future.

Conclusion

Body art and adornment were more than emblems of nobility and symbols of rank in the social hierarchy. They were expressive means for each individual to exhibit his or her participation as part of a social unit, a moiety, a lineage, or a group of names. They also went beyond words or names: they were icons through which the identity could be physically explained, changed, and transformed during social transactions (Crocker 1977; Reid 1986b). A Haida individual, for example, who might say, "I am a Five-Finned Killer Whale from the Eagle moiety," would be entitled to wear ornaments with Five-Finned Killer Whales and Eagle representations. Not only did these attributes offer visual proof of who their owners were by affirming and confirming their identities; they also reinforced their owners' ideas of who they *thought* they were. The attributes translated their owners' dreams into matter and mediated between supernatural and human worlds.

Perhaps it is not coincidental that with the demise of permanent traditional body markers under the multiple influences of contact the tradition of making jewelry carved with crest designs blossomed. Even in the face of authoritative disapproval, heraldry prevailed. Bracelets, necklaces, and rings adorned bodies that would previously have been tattooed. It is of amusing interest that today's youths are choosing to have themselves tattooed—permanently or temporarily—with various exotic designs. In the not-too-distant future we may see the revival of traditional tattoo designs among the Haida and other Northwest Coast peoples.[38]

NOTES

I gratefully acknowledge the critical reading given the preliminary draft of this essay by Dr. George MacDonald. I am also grateful to Nika Collison of the Haida Gwaii Museum, Skidegate, for information surrounding Haida tattooing practices and to Dr. R. Allan Badger for his intellectual input.

1. Archaeological sites in Alaska have found prehistoric burials with evidence of tattooing (Van Stone 1974).

2. Red ocher (hematite), which was traded, was found on sculptured stone carvings, rock carvings and petroglyphs at intertidal areas.

3. Painting the face with red ocher was widely practiced on the Northwest Coast. Native peoples said, at a later date, that the paint prevented the face from getting painfully sunburned by the glare on the water while fishing, but the addition of blue and white to red was undoubtedly for other, perhaps aesthetic, reasons. (Gunther 1972:32) For ceremonial occasions Native peoples threw sparkling sand on their faces, which adhered to the paint (Haswell 1884, p. 61). According to Hill-Tout, one of the favorite decorations of the Salish was that "effected by sprinkling particles of mica over their faces and bodies upon a groundwork of grease" (probably mountain-goat tallow). "This gave their bodies a glistening appearance." (Hill-Tout in Maud 1978:46)

4. Mainly found on the south coast and western shores of Vancouver Island, dentalia shells were highly valued during the historic period and approached the status of a true currency. (Fladmark 1986:76)

5. Strength, malleability, and durability.

6. For descriptions of several horn bracelets collected by eighteenth-century explorers, see Gunther 1972: 227–228.

7. Like Coppers, they formed part of a noble woman's dowry. During a woman's puberty ritual, which celebrated the onset of her awesome power to bring forth renewed human life, young Wakashan and Salishan females wore bands made of mountain-goat fur (or wool) on their heads, wrists, and ankles. This would ensure that they would have good temper and beautiful legs, and that they would be "heavy" (Boas 1921:963; Goldman 1975:184; Reid 1986a:77; 2004). At the closing of her puberty ritual, the young lady wore a mountain goat wool blanket covered with abalone and dentalia shells, a shell-decorated hat, and large abalone shells hanging from her ears. The walls of her room were adorned with shells, and a Copper plate would be standing next to her. This ritual would contribute in putting "weight" on her. (Reid 2004)

8. A Kwakwaka'wakw myth portrays a man who "dreamed of [himself as] a well-dressed man with large abalone shells hanging all over his blanket, and abalone shells hanging from his ears, and abalone shells hanging from his nose." (Boas-Hunt 1921:1271) "A man like the brightness of the sun." (Boas-Hunt: op. cit. 1268)

9. Such a stone pendant, shaped like a hand with six fingers and an eye in its center, was found at Gitlakdamiks, Nass River.

10. Stone-Body is a character from Kwakwaka'wakw mythology. He is a warrior who makes war around the world to acquire great wealth for his tribe. His guardian spirit is the invincible Sisiutl (Double-Headed-Snake), who turns his enemies into stone. (Boas and Hunt 1905:165–247) In another narrative, a powerful man named Wawalis turns his wife into stone so as to keep her forever. (Reid 2004)

11. Shamans' aprons, dating from the historic period and displaying so-called "x-ray imagery," in which both the inner and outer parts of the body—the organs and the skeletons—are shown, suggest the same theme.

12. In the Haida language the aesthetic judgment expressed as "well made" is synonymous with "deeply carved." (Shadbolt 1986:84)

13. Does "the body" end with the skin or should it include hair, nails? The ambiguous boundaries of the body between outside/inside are what marginal beings such as shamans are concerned with; they never cut their hair or their fingernails.

14. According to Holmberg (1985: 13–14), a fulfilled Tlingit individual had his ears pierced eight times.

15. Haida shamans are reported to always have worn a bone through their septum. (Swanton 1905:40)

16. Ear-spools of various soft stones were found in the south, where some prehistoric sculptures depict figures wearing pulley-shaped ear ornaments. (Fladmark 1986:74) These sculpted objects may have been used in secret rituals involving Guardian Spirit beliefs.

17. George MacDonald: personal communication, 2003. Eyelike grooves carved at the knuckle of a wooden Tlingit charm, which were explained as "spirits emerging from the knuckles," would support that view. (Carpenter 1988:873)

18. Northern two- and three-dimensional art forms often display a human face (or an eye) at the articulation points of a human figure. Tlingit sculptured spirit figures (yakes), which guarded shamans' graves, had their knee-joints carved with faces. (Carpenter 1988:1:3, p. 893; Emmons 1930: 282–292)

19. Tooth-wear resulting from labret use is found in burials 4,500–5,000 years old, in the north on the Queen Charlotte Islands and in the south on Pender Island. (Fladmark 1986:61)

20. Gunther (1972:11); Johnson (1911:59); La Pérouse (1798:165); Cook (1784); Crespi (N.d.)

21. Labrets were made from plain dark stone or slate (black or dull red), steatite, lignite, serpentine, marble,

bone, whale-tooth ivory and wood, sometimes with shell inlay.

22. Among the Tsimshian the labret represented "the weight of status." (Miller 1997:83)

23. Bernard Magee, the first officer of the Jefferson, was among the Haida in 1794 where he witnessed a potlatch during which incisions on the lips and noses of two grown and two small girls were performed.

24. Jonaitis 1988:191–205.

25. 500–1000 CE: Three zoomorphic labrets with bird head decorations were found at Prince Rupert Harbour. (MacDonald 1983:104)

26. Haida seemed to have very seldom tattooed their faces. Only a few facial tattoos, primarily on the cheeks, were reported in ethnographic times. (Swan Sept. 1883; Freeman op. cit.) However, faces were painted temporarily for festive occasions with a profusion of abstract crest designs. (Boas 1898, vol. 2, pp. 13–24)

27. According to MacDonald (1983: 215–216, and 108) all the main stylistic elements and object types of the historic period were already in place by about 100 CE. Several prehistoric bone combs show the "joint marks" at major articulation points, and a combination of several elements conformed to the stylistic features of the classic northern style.

28. In his pioneering Primitive Art (1927), which was virtually restricted to formal analysis, Boas distinguished "art" from "decoration" by the presence of meaning. An artwork had meaning that could be interpreted as representing some object or idea, realistically or symbolically. (See also MacGaffey 2003:253)

29. Swanton (1905:113–115) listed seventy distinct crest figures, while Newcombe (1906) claims to have recorded more than twice that number. (In Blackman 1981:249) Most of them are zoomorphic, though, rainbow, rockslide, evening sky, cirrus, stratus, and cumulus clouds occur.

30. The concept of containment is deeply woven into the fabric of Northwest Coast culture beyond the field of art, a fact attested by Sturtevant (1974). He points out that in Tlingit language, for example, a single word conveys the meaning of "box, coffin, bivalve, shell, womb, opposite moiety" —in short, a container—which identifies a key central concept around which Tlingit life and thought can be seen to have been organized.

31. Crests identified lineages in symbolic forms and, in cases where an individual claimed exclusive right to a crest, they were indicative of individual rank within the lineage.

32. Usurping someone else's crest was a serious offense that could nearly lead to war. (Swanton 1905:142)

33. Haida artist Bill Reid reproduced as a gold brooch the original dogfish tattoo design drawn by Charles Edenshaw.

34. George MacDonald; personal communication: 2003.

35. This division of aesthetic labor has persisted well into the twentieth century.

36. Tlingit "Chilkat" robes are said to have originated among the Tsimshian.

37. See Cheryl Samuel's (1982) The Chilkat Dancing Blanket, and (1987) The Raven's Tail.

38. Native Northwest temporary tattoos have been available for quite some time.

WORKS CITED

Blackman, Margaret
1981 *During My Time: Florence Edenshaw Davidson, A Haida Woman.* Seattle: University of Washington Press.

Boas, Franz
1889 "Tattooing of the Haida." *Transactions, New York Academy of Science, 1889.* Pp. 115–16.

1898 "Facial Paintings of the Indians of Northern British Columbia." *American Museum of Natural History Memoirs* 2:13–24. New York.

1916 "Tsimshian Mythology. Based on Texts Recorded by Henry W. Tate." Pp. 29–1037 in the *31st Annual Report of the Bureau of American Ethnology for the Years 1909–1910.* Washington, D.C.

1921 "Ethnology of the Kwakiutl (Based on Data Collected by George Hunt)." 2 pts. Pp. 43–1481 in the *35th Annual Report of the Bureau of American Ethnology for the Years 1913–1914.* Washington, D.C.

1927 *Primitive Art.* Cambridge: Harvard University Press. (Reprinted: Dover Publications, New York, 1955.)

Boas, Franz and George Hunt
1905 "Kwakiutl Texts." Pp. 165–247 in the *Publications of the Jesup North Pacific Expedition* 3(1–3); *Memoirs of the American Museum of Natural History* 5(1–3). New York. (Reprinted AMS Press, New York, 1975.)

Borden, Charles E.
1975 "Origins and Development of Early Northwest Coast Culture to About 3000 B.C." *National Museum of Man Mercury Series, Archeological Survey of Canada Paper* No. 45: 66–76. Ottawa.

Carlson, Roy L.
1983 "Prehistoric Art of the Central Coast of British Columbia." Pp. 121–129 in *Indian Art Traditions of the Northwest Coast.* Roy L. Carson, ed. Burnaby, B.C.: Archaeology Press, Simon Fraser University.

Carpenter, Edmund
1988 *Materials for the Study of Social Symbolism in Ancient and Tribal Art: A Record of Tradition and Continuity. Based on the Researches and Writings of Carl Schuster* 2:3:669. New York: Rock Foundation.

Cook, James
1784 *A Voyage to the Pacific Ocean Undertaken by the Command of His Majesty, for Making Discoveries in the Northern Hemisphere.* 3 vols. [Vol. 3 by James King], London: Printed by W. and A. Strahan for G. Nicol and T. Cadell.

Crespi, Juan
N.d. *Diario de su viage con Pérez en la "Santiago" con el objeto a explorar las costas de las Californias hasta los 60 grados.* Original: Archivo General de las Indias, Seville, Spain. Translated by George B. Griffen.

Crocker, Christopher
1977 "Les réflexions du soi (The Mirrored Self)." Pp. 157–179 in *L'identité.* Séminaire dirigé par Claude Lévi-Strauss. Paris: Grasset.

Curtis, Edward
1916 *The Haida: The North American Indian* 11:115–175, 186–193. Norwood, Illinois: Plimpton Press.

Duff, Wilson
1975 *Images: Stone: B.C.: Thirty Centuries of Northwest Coast Indian Sculpture.* Seattle: University of Washington Press.

Emmons, George T.
1903 "The Basketry of the Tlingit." *Memoirs of the American Museum of Natural History* 3(2): 229–277. New York.

1930 "The Art of the Northwest Coast Indians: How Ancestral Records Were Preserved in Carvings and Paintings of Mythical and Fabulous Animal Figures." *Natural History* 30(3): 282–292. New York.

1991 *The Tlingit Indians.* Ed. by F. de Laguna. Seattle: University of Washington Press.

Fladmark, Knut
1986 *British Columbia Prehistory.* Ottawa: Archaeological Survey of Canada, National Museums of Canada.

Fleurieu, Charles Pierre Claret de
1801 *A Voyage Round the World Performed During the Years 1790, 1791, and 1792 by Etienne Marchand.* 2 vols. London: T.N. Longmans and O. Rees. (Reprinted: Da Capo Press. New York, 1970.)

Freeman, B. C., Reverend
N.d. *The Methodist Young People's Forward Movement for Missions,* Series No.5, circa 1904/1910. Wilson Duff manuscript records at the UBC, Museum of Anthropology Archives, folder 6–21:"Photostats & Reprints." Vancouver.

Goldman, Irving
1975 *The Mouth of Heaven: An Introduction to Kwakiutl Religious Thought*. New York: John Wiley & Sons.

Grubb, David McC.
1977 *A Practical Writing System and Short Dictionary of Kwakw'ala (Kwakiutl)*. Canadian Ethnology Service paper no. 34. Ottawa: National Museums of Canada.

Gunther, Erna
1966 *Art in the Life of Northwest Coast Indians. With a Catalog of the Rasmussen Collection of Northwest Indian Art at the Portland Art Museum*. Portland, Oregon: Portland Art Museum.

1972 *Indian Life on the Northwest Coast of North America As Seen by the Early Explorers and Fur Traders during the Last Decades of the Eighteenth Century*. Chicago and London: The University of Chicago Press.

1984 "Vancouver and the Indians of Puget Sound". *Pacific Northwest Quarterly*, vol. 51, no.1.

Haswell, Robert
1884 "A voyage round the world on board the ship 'Columbia Rediviva' and the sloop 'Washington' 1787–1789." In A. L. Bancroft, ed. *History of the Northwest Coast,* vol. 1. San Francisco.

Hill-Tout, Charles
1978 See Maud, Ralph, ed.

Holmberg, H.J.
1985 *Holmberg's Ethnographic Sketches*. Ed. by M. W. Falk and translated by F. Jaensch. Fairbanks: The University of Alaska Press.

Johnson, Margaret Olive
1911 *Spanish Exploration of the Pacific Coast*. M.A. thesis, University of California at Berkeley.

Jonaitis, Aldona
1988 "Women, Marriage, Mouths, and Feasting: the Symbolism of Tlingit Labrets." Pp. 191–205 in Arnold Rubin, ed. *Marks of Civilization*. Los Angeles: Museum of Cultural History, University of California.

Jonaitis, Aldona, ed.
1995 *A Wealth of Thought: Franz Boas on Native American Art*. Seattle: University of Washington Press; Vancouver and Toronto: Douglas & McIntyre.

La Pérouse, Jean-François Galup Comte de
1798 *La Pérouse's voyage round the world performed in the years 1785–1788*. Translated from the French in 2 vols. London: G.G. and J. Robinson.

MacDonald, George
1983 "Prehistoric Art of the Northwest Coast." Pp. 99–120 in Roy L. Carlson, ed. *Indian Art Traditions of the Northwest Coast*. Burnaby, B.C.: Archaeology Press, Simon Fraser University.

MacGaffey, Wyatt
2003 "Structural Impediments to Translation in Art." Pp. 269–283 in Paula G. Rubel and Abraham Rosman, eds. *Translating Cultures: Perspectives on Translation and Anthropology*. New York and Oxford: Berg.

Magee, Bernard
1794 *Log of the "Jefferson."* Unpublished manuscript. Massachusetts Historical Society.

Maud, Ralph, ed.
1978 *The Salish People: The Local Contribution of Charles Hill-Tout. Vol. II: The Squamish and the Lillooet*. 4 vols. Vancouver: Talonbooks.

Miller, Jay
1997 *Tsimshian Culture: A Light Through the Ages*. Lincoln: The University of Nebraska Press.

Mitchell, Donald H.
1990 "Prehistory of the Coasts of Southern British Columbia and Northern Washington." Pp. 340–358 in Wayne Suttles, ed. *Handbook of North American Indians*. Vol. 7: *Northwest Coast*. Washington, D.C.: Smithsonian Institution.

Murdock, George Peter
1936 "Rank and Potlatch Among the Haida." *Yale University Publications in Anthropology* 13:1–20. New Haven, Conn.

Newcombe, Charles F.
1906 *Letter to George Dorsey, Dated Nov. 5, 1906*. On file at the Field Museum of Natural History, Chicago.

Niblack, A. P.
1970 [1890] *The Coast Indians of Southern Alaska and Northern British Columbia*. Washington, D.C.: U.S. National Museum Annual Report for 1888. New York: Johnson Reprint.

Reid, Martine
1986a "The Significance of Colour among the Kwagiutl." In D. Jensen and P. Sargent eds. *Robes of Power. Totem Poles on Cloth*, UBC Museum of Anthropology. Note 17: 76–77. Vancouver: University of British Columbia Press.

1986b "Silent Speakers: The Arts of the Northwest Coast." Pp. 201–236 in Julia Harrisson, ed. *The Spirit Sings: Artistic Traditions of Canada's First Peoples*. Toronto: McClelland & Stewart; Calgary: Glenbow Museum.

Reid, Martine, ed.
2004 *Paddling To Where I Stand: Agnes Alfred, a Qwiqwasut'inuxw Noble Woman*. Translated by Daisy Sewid-Smith. Vancouver: UBC Press.

Samuel, Cheryl
1982 *The Chilkat Dancing Blanket*. Seattle: Pacific Search Press.

1987 *The Raven's Tail*. Vancouver: University of British Columbia Press.

Schuster, Carl
1951 "Joint Marks," Koninklijk Instituut voor de Tropen, Mededeling no. xciv, *Afdeling Culturele en Physische Anthropologie* 39. Amsterdam.

Shadbolt, Doris
1986 *Bill Reid*. Vancouver and Toronto: Douglas & McIntyre.

Shelton, Anthony
1992 "Predicates of Aesthetic Judgement: Ontology and Value in Huichol Material Representations." Pp. 209–244 in Jeremy Coote and Anthony Shelton, eds. *Anthropology, Art, and Aesthetics*. Oxford: Clarendon Press.

Suttles, Wayne
1990 "Central Coast Salish." Pp. 463–475 in Wayne Suttles, ed. *Handbook of North American Indians*. Vol. 7: *Northwest Coast*. Washington, D.C.: Smithsonian Institution.

Sturtevant, William
1974 *Boxes and Bowls: Decorated Containers by Nineteenth Century Haida, Bella Bella, and Tsimshian Indian Artists*. Washington, D.C.: Smithsonian Institution.

Swan, James J.
1876 "The Haidah Indians of Queen Charlotte Islands, British Columbia. With a Brief Description of Their Carvings, Tattoo Designs, etc." *Smithsonian Contributions to Knowledge* 21 (4):1–18. Washington: Smithsonian Institution.

1883 *Diary,* May–Sept. 26, 1883. Archives, Box 3, Notebook 32. Suzzalo Library, University of Washington, Seattle.

Swanton, John R.
1905 "Contributions to the Ethnology of the Haida." *Publications of the Jesup North Pacific Expedition* 5: *Memoirs of the American Museum of Natural History*. 8(1): 1–300. New York.

1909 "Tlingit Myths and Texts." *Bureau of American Ethnology Bulletin* 39. Washington.

Van Stone, James W.
1974 "An Early Archeological Example of Tattooing from Northwestern Alaska." *Fieldiana: Anthropology* 6:1. Chicago: Field Museum.

Widerspach-Thor, Martine de (aka Martine Reid)
1981 "The Equation of Copper." Pp. 157–174 in Donald N. Abbott, ed. *The World is as Sharp as a Knife: An Anthology in Honour of Wilson Duff*. Vancouver: British Columbia Provincial Museum.

Wilson, Elizabeth
1985 *Adorned in Dreams. Fashion and Modernity*. Berkeley and Los Angeles: University of California Press.

Wittgenstein, Ludwig
1970 *Lectures and Conversations on Aesthetics, Psychology and Religious Belief*. Cyril Barrett, ed. Oxford: Blackwell.

Zenk, Henry B.
1990 "Kalapuyans." Pp. 547–553 in Wayne Suttles, ed. *Handbook of North American Indians*. Vol. 7: *Northwest Coast*. Washington, D.C.: Smithsonian Institution.

NORTHWEST COAST MASTERS

CHARLES EDENSHAW

Chief *7idansuu*
Haida

The supernaturals were here first. Then—Raven came. Raven the trickster, Raven the creator. Creating the sun, moon, and stars. Giving us water and fish. Raven discovers the first people, and creates man and woman so that they would not be bored. On and on. . . .

Haida—"the people"—and Haida art flourish; a deep culture, a wonderful art form. Haida are a people tempered by their surroundings: the forest, the ocean, the weather. Bountiful seafoods allow time for their ceremonies and their arts.

Then the European world discovers Haida lands—Haida Gwaii, now known as the Queen Charlotte Islands. These new-comers are a people interested in "riches." Sea otter furs, bountiful around Haida lands, become goods sought after by the new explorers. A vigorous trade starts. Now Haidas have iron, cloth, beads, and guns.

In 1839, not long after first European contact, a boy was born in Skidegate, a village in the south of Haida Gwaii. He was born into clan privileges, born into nobility, born into the powerful *Saangga.ahl Stastas* Eagle lineage, and born with the rights to carve. His name was *Tahayghen*. His father and his uncle, his hereditary chief, Chief *7idansuu* [pronounced Ee-dan-su], were good carvers, and Tahayghen began carving Haida crest figures and story images in argillite. In the Haida way, carving was, and still is, one of the most respected things a person could do. The carved pieces show who you are, your privileges, your stories, your crests, and your histories.

Tahayghen's mother, Chief 7idansuu's sister, wished for him to move to the north end of Haida Gwaii to marry. Tahayghen was heir to the chieftainship, and Chief 7idansuu also wanted Tahayghen to come north so that Tahayghen could stay with him and learn from him to be a bigger part of the social structure. And Tahayghen further honed his carving skills by working with Chief 7idansuu on totem poles and many other carvings.

Through an arranged marriage, Tahayghen married a young woman named *K'woiyong* in a traditional Haida ceremony. Twelve

years later they decided to be Christianized. To be baptized, they had to choose Anglo names, a first and last name. They chose "Charles" and "Isabella," names affiliated with European royalty. Because Europeans could not easily say 7idansuu, they chose Edenshaw (an approximation of the Haida pronunciation). Chief 7idansuu also took a royal name, Albert Edward Edenshaw.

Charles and Isabella Edenshaw raised a family and became well known up and down the Northwest Coast, for Charles traveled extensively to the different trading centers to carve and receive commissions and to sell his works and Isabella's spruce-root weavings. Isabella wore tattoos to display her crests and lineage. But the Europeans made the Haida women feel self-conscious about their tattoos and labrets, so Haida women began to wear their crests as wonderfully carved metal bracelets and anklets—something new. It has been said that Charles started the silver and gold jewelry-carving among the Haida, and he excelled at it. Melting down coins and then pouring the metal into bands, he would shape them by hammering. He tied the shaped band of metal onto a round "donut" of wood that had a hole in the middle for his thumb. That way he could hold the piece to carve, using engravers that he made out of old files. He developed a method of carving by pulling the engraver toward himself, rather than the European method of pushing it away.

Charles was one of the survivors of the European-introduced smallpox epidemics. Not many did survive; many loved ones died. The remaining Haida on the north end of Haida Gwaii—just over 300 souls—gathered at the village of Masset. On the south part of Haida Gwaii there were little more than 200 souls left, and they drew together to live at Skidegate. And up in Alaska, the surviving Haida gathered at Hydaburg.

Not only was Charles a survivor, he was a surviving *carver*; one of the very few. These surviving carvers, who had witnessed so much death and near annihilation, decided to record Haida history and carved, carved, carved—for the

Haida and their future. It is important to understand that Charles came directly from Haida ruling class and Haida hierarchy, with all of the old social standing and the rights. This gave him the power to carry on with great integrity. He was ensuring our existence on Haida Gwaii; ensuring our existence with the supernaturals. Natives and Europeans up and down the coast had, and still have, a lot of respect for who he was and what he could do. He had high standards for creating Haida art.

Charles constantly kept in touch with his clan people. He used to make long canoe voyages with his uncle and chief, Albert Edward, to check on fellow clan members, making sure they were safe and reinforcing their clan ties. Albert Edward Edenshaw died in 1894. Charles was next in line for the position of chief, and he potlatched and took on the name 7idansuu, becoming the chief of the Saangga.ahl Stastas Eagle clan.

Charles survived many changes, socially and physically, and yet he raised his family the Haida way, giving many potlatches. Over the course of his life, there were ten potlatches given for Charles Edenshaw. At each potlatch he received another Haida name and more crest tattoos. He had tattoos over his hands, arms, chest, back, and legs.

Charles carved late into his life and died in 1920. His works are in many museums and private collections throughout the world. His influence on the Haida, and on all Northwest Coast artists, is great. One wish Charles had was that he could pass on his hands to his people. And he has. His many descendants, male and female, on both sides of the family, Raven and Eagle, show his great talent. We are carrying on. Charles Edenshaw—Chief 7idansuu—my great, great grandfather and the great carver, lives on. JIM HART

Deep Sea Frog bracelet.
Charles Edenshaw (Haida).
Silver. Late 19th century.
Width, 1⅝". Collection
University of British Columbia
Museum of Anthropology,
Nb1.736

Opposite page:
Charles Edenshaw seated
next to examples of his
argillite carving

BILL REID

Haida

Bill Reid (1920–1998), born to a Haida mother and American-German-Scots father, was raised outside the Native culture. It was not until he was in his early twenties that he journeyed to Haida Gwaii (the Queen Charlotte Islands) to visit his maternal grandfather, argillite carver Charles Gladstone, who had lived with Charles Edenshaw as a youth. Through his grandfather, Reid met Haida elders who retained both memories of the old traditions and pride in their ancestry and themselves. Drawing strength from the island's people and landscape, Reid thereafter returned as frequently as possible.

An early broadcasting career preceded any thoughts of art. In 1948, however, Reid began to study and master the techniques of European jewelry and was drawn to Scandinavian industrial design. At the same time, he carefully analyzed old Haida collections stored in museums up and down the coast and in Toronto and New York. With a growing understanding of Haida traditions, Reid explored his own style. He started working on a larger scale in the late 1950s, when he briefly helped Mungo Martin, Kwakwa̲ka'wakw carver, re-create a totem pole. Reid appreciated equally Martin's abilities as a teacher of the old ways and as a storyteller who sometimes sang when he worked. Shortly thereafter, Reid assisted in the rescue of Haida poles from abandoned villages in Haida Gwaii and worked with others to build a permanent home for the rescued poles, which resulted in the Museum of Anthropology at the University of British Columbia. Together with Bill Holm and Wilson Duff, Reid also decoded the ancient Northwest Coast vocabulary of formlines, helping transform classical Haida forms and their essence into new mediums: boxwood, silkscreen prints, cast gold, and bronze.

Reid's artist career originated with jewelry. "His monument sculptures," wrote Robert Bringhurst, have "grown out of objects that you could hold in the palm of your hand." Although Reid's jewelry was initially influenced by nineteenth-century Haida metalwork—particularly that of Charles Edenshaw—his introduction of overlay, repoussé, and casting resulted in the creation of wearable sculpture rather than simply two-dimensional etched designs. While pivotal in rekindling the rich Haida artistic traditions, Reid had an intensely individual vision. As a master of both European techniques and Native art traditions, he was a "mediator not only between two art traditions but also between two worlds," wrote Doris Shadbolt in her book, *Bill Reid*. She added that Reid delighted "in making connections" and wanted the Haida to apprehend that "only three generations ago, they lived richer, fuller, more satisfying lives" and "came from *marvelous* men." Above all, Bill Reid was a committed maker of things with quality, in love with and sensitive to materials with which he had a special affinity, be it cedar, argillite, bronze, or gold. "The well-made object was a moral imperative that guided his life," said Shadbolt.

Reid drew upon the richness of Haida oral literature, where physical and aesthetic sustenance came primarily from animal sources. Innovations in Reid's work included freeing his animals from the restrictions of the crest and totem poles, allowing them to be seen on their own as three-dimensional sculptures and carved bracelets. Although diagnosed in 1973 with Parkinson's disease, he continued to conceive and create art of monumental power, such as the inspired *Spirit of Haida Gwaii*, a twenty-foot-long bronze canoe

sculpture steered by Raven and brimming with potent Haida mythical beings.

"I consider myself one of the most fortunate of men, to have lived at a time when some of the old Haidas and their peers among the Northwest Coast peoples were still alive, and to have had the privilege of knowing them," Reid stated in the introduction to *The Raven Steals the Light*, the book of Haida tales he illustrated and wrote with Robert Bringhurst. During a profoundly moving, seven-hour memorial service held for Reid on March 24, 1998, at the University of British Columbia Museum of Anthropology, more than sixty speakers, dancers, and singers, including First Nations elders and youth, returned the tribute. Seated among the totems he had rescued from Haida Gwaii in the museum building that houses them today, one was clearly reminded—through a myriad of Native and non-Native perspectives—of Reid's seminal role as a thinker and doer, storyteller and shaman, spokesperson and artist.

"We are indebted to Bill Reid, that incomparable artist," wrote Claude Lévi-Strauss, "for having tended and revived a flame that was so close to dying. That is not all; for Bill Reid by his own example and by his teachings has given rise to a prodigious flowering, the results of which the Indian designers, sculptors, and goldsmiths of British Columbia offer today to our wondering eyes." LOIS S. DUBIN

Excerpted with permission from "North American Indian Jewelry and Adornment: From Prehistory to the Present" by Lois S. Dubin.

Sea Bear or *Snag* bracelet. Bill Reid (Haida). The owner of this bracelet asked Reid to make a totem pole she could wear. Gold, fossilized ivory. 1964. Height, 2⅛". Collection Jean MacKay-Fahrni

Opposite page:
Bill Reid with his two favorite female figures, Dogfish Woman and Bear Mother. 1989

Whale Box. Bill Reid (Haida). Gold. 1971. Length, 4". Collection Royal British Columbia Museum, 13902a,b

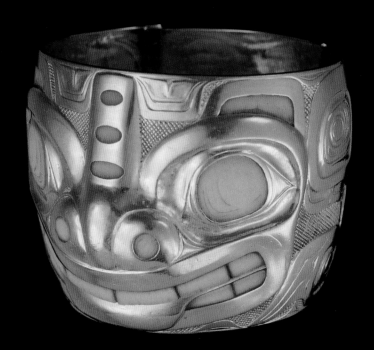

NORTHWEST COAST CONTEMPORARY ARTISTS

JIM HART

7idansuu
Haida
Saangga.ahl Stastas Eagle Clan
Old Masset, Haida Gwaii (Queen Charlotte Islands),
British Columbia

My uncle passed on the traditional name, 7idansuu, to me, and when he did that, it meant that I became chief and head of our clan. To make it official, I potlatched it in 1999 at a memorial inauguration potlatch with the help of friends and the *Yakulanaas* and Saangga.ahl Stastas Eagle clans. At home, taking on a chief's name means taking on a position and a lot of responsibility. It's something you have to set your mind on; it's not a game. It's not for fun. When you talk, you have to keep in mind that you're representing your history. And when you wear your regalia at potlatches, you're wearing the crests that represent who you are. The regalia, including the jewelry, is not just adornment, it's old, old history. So, it's a lot more than just standing there looking good. You're standing there as a pinnacle of all that's behind you. It's a continuation of your clans and your history. The regalia can be passed on, generation to generation, and what you wear also depends on what stage of life you're at. Now, I have the right to wear a Chilkat blanket with full honor.

It was in late high school that I realized we, Haida, have a great art form—something worthy. In 1979 I made the decision that carving was what I wanted to do for the rest of my life. When I was a kid, my great-aunts would tell me how valuable our art was. But I took it all for granted. It was only as I got older that I began to realize that we, as a people, have an art style and a culture that are truly great.

In 1982 I went to Italy. I'd heard there were some Haida pieces in museums there, and I wanted to see them. I like to go to museums to visit our pieces—it's like visiting your ancestors. In the midst of all these wonderful paintings and sculptures from different countries, different people, different artists through time, I saw Haida work, and I realized that it's just as creative and powerful as any art form out there. I was walking around proud as heck after that. Once I realized for myself the depth of our own art form, I was totally focused, and I started in very seriously.

I get so excited to see the old pieces. It just makes me want to carve, carve, carve. The art these old-timers created was amazing. The Haida art form has a strict set of rules—rules to be bent, mind you—and, knowing that it also contains the old history, I realized it was our written language. It was written by feelings. And once you start learning how to read something by feelings, it's a whole different way, but it's still reading. The carvers are telling you the stories right there, but you have to understand that that's what's going on.

I love making art for my home communities—that's where it comes from. That's where *we* come from. Our being is there. And we grew to be the people we are today because of the feelings we get from our environment. We're a strong, hardy people honed by our winds and weather. The oceans were our sidewalks and highways. Canoes were our mode of getting around, food gathering, visiting, fishing, hunting, warring. Our ancestors were dealing with waves and weather, and you had to be pretty hardy because it was all manpower and woman-power.

For the Haida, being an artist, a good carver, is one of the highest things we can do. It is highly respected. We make representations of who we are, our stories, our crests, our history. The supernatural world is all around. My experience is that if you think about these things, believe in them, they're real. They become part of your everyday existence. We come from that world, and we bring that world to life; we make it physical, so you can see supernatural creatures in three-dimensional view.

And when you realize that, you realize we're still connected to nature, and nature hasn't forgotten we're connected to it. As I go along in my life, it's so good to see that connection, and to feel it, to be part of it. I have witnessed special events between our people and nature, and it reminds you that nature is still connected to us and the connection runs deep. Nature hasn't forgotten even if we have, here and there. Because of this we won't forget. The respect is still there.

It's *all* connected—the ceremonies, the regalia, the masks, the songs, the dances. And through those things, we're part of a very old history. We've had a disruption in that line with the arrival of Europeans and all the new stuff that came along with contact; and we've had to deal with it. Our people are going to school and learning how to become lawyers and doctors. Of course we need all of that, because we're in that world, too. So we're doing both, we're keeping the traditions while incorporating the new. We're struggling to make it work for ourselves in our own way.

With European contact came the selling of our art, and the design rules started to change. Carvers began to play around with images that didn't belong to their own families, and it allowed them to capitalize on what was happening. That was the beginning of using our traditional figures for something other than ceremony. It was still being done out of a base of who we were, but it became more commercial and for different reasons.

Today, our traditions are becoming stronger. We're working with other people on the coast, and we're strengthening each other and moving forward in a direction that's positive.

And now we're working with the Southwest artists. When we traveled down to Arizona and New Mexico, we visited Jesse Monongya in Scottsdale, and then we headed—I'd say up the coast, but it's not—up north to meet more people. It was fabulous, and so different for us. It's desert country . . . sandy and dry. You can see where rivers could be—gullies with bridges over them—but there's no water. We learned that for these people, most of their prayers and ceremonies are directed for water, for the rain to come. It's not like that for us; for us, everything is water. We have it all around us, it's not a problem.

When we met these people, we didn't know anything about who they are or their art. But as we went along, we knew right away they're great people. So now we've made new friends, and we talk and exchange thoughts about our ways and our workmanship. It's getting pretty exciting, and it's just the beginning. For the Northwest Coast people, our art form is engraved in our systems; it's who we are as a people. To see what they're doing in the Southwest and where they've taken their traditions is exciting. The possibility

of incorporating their techniques and their use of the different stones is really exciting. It feels like our relationship with them is going to bring our art forms to another level; we can add their techniques to our art, and it can add to our art form and not take away.

When I first started getting serious about Haida art, I wanted to carve totem poles, because to me, a totem pole is always out there, and I thought it was really important to show people that we're not gone; we're still here and still alive. I still make totem poles, but I don't feel quite like that anymore. Because we *are* here. And what we're doing with the exhibition at the American Museum of Natural History, being part of this group of artists, continues to prove that. Up and down the coast, we know of each other—our different tribes, our different people. We keep an eye on each other, and we carry on. It helps with our direction for the future. Because we're realizing that this is a responsibility, not as a single person, but as a unit. We're thinking of the future of our cultures, and not just of making a living as individuals. As an artist, you're an ambassador for your people, because this art represents all our people. So the art is healing, because we believe in it so much.

Bear mother and cubs bracelet. Jim Hart (Haida). 22-karat gold. 2000. Height, 1¾". Collection American Museum of Natural History, 16.1/2639

Opposite page:
Jim Hart wears a button blanket while eagle down, a bearer of blessings for Northwest Coast people, floats around him.

80

NORMAN TAIT

Nisga'a
Eagle Clan: Beaver Crest
Vancouver, British Columbia

My native name is *Gawaak'*, which means "beaver swimming with a side paddle." It was given to me by my grandfather. When I raised the totem pole in Chicago, he decided that it was time for me to take his name, so he gave it to me at that pole raising, and I will pass it on to my nephew before I go.

I got into carving by accident. I was trained as a mechanic and moved to Vancouver. I applied for a job in a sawmill, and they told me I would be on-call and to sit by the phone and wait. As it happened, there was a construction site behind my motel, so I went back there to see if they might have a job for me while I was waiting. They didn't, but on my way back to the motel, I picked up a piece of wood, and I sat down and whittled. And the rest is history.

I didn't know I could carve until then. And I realized that I didn't know that much about my culture, my history, my people. So I carved and sold my carvings, and then I bought a plane ticket to Ottawa to look at Nisga'a art in the museum there. I ran out of money, so I came home and carved again. And then I went to Chicago and studied the Nisga'a art pieces there; they have a marvelous collection. Then, when I ran out of money I went home again and carved some more before going to New York. I jumped back and forth to study the art, including to London, Paris, and Madrid. I kept going back to UBC [the University of British Columbia Museum of Anthropology] and asking where else there would be Nisga'a art that I could look at. And they just kept giving me a list. Wherever they sent me, they sent an introductory letter asking if the new museum could help me. Every time I arrived at a foreign museum, they'd assign a secretary to help me study.

Nisga'a art is quite similar to Haida and Tlingit art. So, I'm caught just about halfway between. I learned quite a bit from Bill Reid and Bill Holm. They were both accomplished artists; they could switch to any style and achieve it. Once, I asked Bill Holm to explain Nisga'a art to me. I was quite honored when he turned to me and said, "You're Nisga'a art."

I try not to copy pieces in the museums; I try to do my own style. My inspiration is usually a story that belongs to my family, and there are quite a few. Sometimes, I do a sculpture called the "Wind Mask." My uncle told me the story of the Wind Mask because we had a family of ten, and since money was scarce back then, I would go hunting to get meat on the table. The wind is a ghost that travels throughout the mountains. When you go out hunting you have to keep your mind on what you're doing. You can't think of a warm bed, you can't think of your girlfriend, you can't think of your mother. You have to pay attention to what you're doing. If you start to wander off that track, the wind will sneak up behind you, blow in your face and pull your mouth aside. A lot of hunters get lost that way; they suddenly find themselves in the control of the wind. They wander off into the mountains; and they're never seen again. So, the moral is, you have to keep your mind on what you're doing. At that time it was hunting. And then, later on, carving.

I'm an acting shaman. When I was first born, my aunt looked into my crib, and she called out an old woman's name . . . a shaman who had been dead a hundred years. But my aunt said "That's her in the crib. Although it's a boy, that's her in the crib." My aunt told me many stories that sounded familiar. My uncle said to me, "Those stories have to go on. That's how come you were born. So take those stories and remember them." And it just so happens I started carving. So, my art is very connected to the stories of my family.

When I first started carving, I had so much fun that I started carving images of fun characters. One time there was a lady photographer who was writing a book on a totem pole that I was doing. She was there just about every day taking lots of pictures. When the totem pole was finished we had a ceremony. I had carved a mask of a human face with a camera stuck in the front of it, and so at the ceremony we did a "camera-woman dance." People started saying to me, "You're a mischievous man." So, later I carved the "Mischievous Man" as I saw him. That's how legends begin, I guess, and that's the fun part of carving.

But there's a serious side of carving. I have to carve to make a living, but when my family is planning a feast, I'm notified right away. Naturally they expect me to carve some bracelets. Jewelry is the most valued thing among the Native people now. I'm in the process of carving bracelets for my four sisters. I thought I'd better do it now, or they're not going to have any to pass on to their nephews and daughters. I've got one done, and I'm going to leave it up to my mother to hand it out. That's how important jewelry is.

Those things are a little bit more precious than what I sell. Although, sometimes, they get sold; especially if there's a death in the family. I lost my son about five years ago. I carved a memorial bracelet in his honor, and I wore it in a feast, up north. And eventually that got sold. Because my mother said to me, "It's time to let go; he's gone now. Don't delay him for his journey to the grandfathers. If you don't let go he's going to feel sorry for you and he'll hang around and he'll never see his grandfathers. Doesn't mean we'll forget him. Just time to let go." You're given a year to mourn, and then you turn back to life itself, and you throw a feast and you have fun at that feast. So, that's the ups and downs of carving.

The art is carrying on our tradition. Just like my name, I'll pass the Nisga'a art on to my nephews. Both the name and the art are inheritances that have to be kept up. It's the same for the Kwakwa̱ka̱'wakw, and the Haida, and the Tlingit; they'll all pass it on to their children.

The songs, the dances, regalia —they're all intertwined, and they all mean something. The button blanket that I wear has an eagle design on the back. When I stand up at a feast, it tells everybody I'm of the Eagle clan, and they recognize my grandfather, my mother, and my uncles.

—Norman Tait

Killer whale bracelet. Norman Tait (Nisga'a). Silver. 1977. Height, 2⅛". Collection University of British Columbia Museum of Anthropology, Nb7.339

LYLE WILSON

Haisla-Kitamaat
Eagle Clan: Eagle, Halibut, and Frog Crests
Vancouver, British Columbia

I wasn't trained as a traditional artist of the Pacific Northwest Coast. I took regular art classes in high school. At the University of British Columbia I studied in the Native Indian Teacher Education Program. I then graduated from the Emily Carr Institute of Art and Design. These institutions honed my interests and skills, and helped shape my outlook in life, art, and learning.

I had a grounding in my people's own history because my grandmother used to tell traditional tales of the Haisla people to us children—my brother, sisters, and cousins. My uncle, Sam Robinson, I credit for sparking my interest in art simply because he was there and carving at a time when it wasn't popular.

I have a deep reverence for wood. I used to hunt with my grandfather and my uncles. Hunting and trapping meant the company of the trees, and some of those trees were giants! Our house was heated by a wood stove; while growing up, I'd help collect logs from the ocean to cut for firewood. And I used to watch my uncle carve. Once, our extended family was having dinner downstairs and he was upstairs carving. Everything was dark, except for one light shining overhead. The shavings seemed to flow off the wood in crispy curls before disappearing into the dark. To my impressionable eyes, it was a magical scene that I've never forgotten.

The link between the mediums of wood and metal lies in my carving technique. I became very comfortable carving and shaping metal into jewelry. My goal in jewelry is to create layers, forms, and textures that highlight the creative process. The finished work is not so much jewelry but a miniature carving. I also prefer a surface that is not highly polished and reflects the light in a diffused manner—this allows the carving rather than the metal to "shine."

One thing people have to understand is that Northwest Coast art style is animistic in its subject. When I was growing up, Kitamaat Village was only accessible by boat or air; it had no road. You'd see wildlife everyday. Killer whales still come right past the village beach chasing the salmon. When the eulachon [fish] spawn there are predatory clouds of sea gulls and herds of sea lions and seals. While hunting you might spot bears, deer, moose, mountain goats, foxes, and wolves. To outsiders, this profusion of life was incredible, yet to us it was natural in its entirety. So it is easy to see why animals figure so prominently in our art style.

A lot of the artists I know have a great combination of talents; they're chiefs, *and* they're singers, *and* they're dancers, *and* they carve. Because so much of our artwork is gone from the villages, as an artist, it's quite natural to feel empathy for these communities. To replace what's gone is a daunting task that everyone can contribute to. Many artists do so by carving or painting regalia for their people. This attitude of giving seems like the one strand of original culture that survived the onslaught of time, people, and plagues. It's an ideal that I've long admired. I've adjusted to contemporary times by focusing on the local Haisla elementary school so that children can derive some benefit from my artistic journey.

The market for Pacific Northwest Coast art causes conflicting emotions in me. If you look at it from the point of view of art history, it's positive because more people will be exposed to our culture. On the other hand, as an individual artist, you devote so much time and energy to making and selling your art that it is impossible to nurture your home community as befits its traditional importance. I think most artists would gladly give their work to their communities to rebuild, maintain, or build upon their traditional culture. Like me, most artists do what is realistically possible for their people.

Beaver-Eagle bracelet. Lyle Wilson (Haisla). "I was born into Beaver Clan and was later adopted into my father's Eagle Clan. These two crests [are] portrayed on this bracelet. . . ." Using hatched and cross-hatched lines to create positive and negative effects, the bodies of the beaver and eagle occupy complementary spaces. The eagle's head (not shown) faces the back and is deeply carved. The beaver's head was carved in wax and then cast in gold. Silver, 18-karat gold. 1993–1995. Width, 1⅞". Collection University of British Columbia Museum of Anthropology, Nb3.1475a-b

BEAU DICK

Kwakwa̱ka'wakw
British Columbia

When I was five, my mother decided that home wasn't the place that could offer me the best education for these modern times, and decided she'd rather bring me to the city where I'd have a better education. I guess it might have worked.

I was fourteen or fifteen years old when I returned home to Alert Bay and began to do the artwork with my father and my grandfather who were traditional carvers. I was searching for my identity, I suppose. I was involved with art already, doing my own style of paintings and drawings with pastels. I took a great interest in surrealism and Renaissance art, Greek, ancient Mesopotamian, Egyptian . . . all these different cultures of the world just fascinated my mind. Of course, even as a young boy I realized that although it was wonderful, it was somebody else's culture. It wasn't my own.

When I first returned home, I lived with my grandfather. I helped him with things like gouging masks out, sanding, drawing the designs, and painting. I was allowed to use my grandfather's tools only when I was working on his work. He'd go away from time to time and lock his tools up with a padlock in his great tool chest. He'd be gone for days at a time and I wouldn't have much to do except draw and paint. But I really wanted to carve my own pieces. So I figured out that I could unscrew the hinges on the back of his tool chest. I only did it a couple of times, but the second time, he came home early. I had just come home from down the road and was making myself a sandwich. I heard someone coming up the stairs and I thought, "No, it can't be Gramps, he won't be back for a few days." Got back to my sandwich. Then I could feel him walking towards me, and I thought, "Uh-oh, that's my grandpa." And then boom! I got a kick in the butt. It really hurt. I cried because it hurt physically . . . the pain of the boot hitting the butt. But even more than that was the anger and the emotional trauma I suffered from getting a boot in the ass from my grandfather. But he never locked the tools on me again. And I think even though my grandfather was annoyed, he was proud too because I took it on myself to fulfill that hunger I had.

Our histories are told in the artwork. My younger daughters are Nisga'a, and in their origin history, their ancestors were bad children who learned a lesson when they tortured and killed two beautiful little frogs. The mountain spirit was so upset that her frog-children had been mistreated, that she erupted into a volcano, spewing lava all over, and destroyed the people's village, killing everybody except the two children. The Raven was sent to tell them, "Now, you must take on the frog crest as a reminder that this will never happen again." My other daughter is a Haida, and her origin is different. Her ancestors were found by Raven in a mussel shell. My mother's ancestor came from a wolf that transformed himself into a human. That's what totem art is about, that's what the totem pole or the painted house front represents, the lineage of the people who lived in that house. The designs and motifs on the poles and jewelry, bowls and ladles— everything—represented the people's history, their identity, and their very essence. It's all told in the artwork.

In the potlatches, they give away jewelry. The potlatch is about distributing wealth. To receive a bracelet at a potlatch is important. You can show it off and say, "Look what I got at the potlatch, isn't that beautiful?" And people say, "Gee, those people had a great potlatch. They gave away wonderful stuff. They have a lot of class."

We had begun to lose our culture, begun to lose our language; our lifestyles had changed. Rock and roll was coming in, and there was a big world out there, and for a couple of generations this old Indian stuff didn't seem that important anymore. But then, all of a sudden, we started desperately clinging to it and trying to restore it, so we have what we have today. The artist's role in the community— whether they be a weaver, a jeweler who makes bracelets, a carver of masks, a singer, or a dancer—is that they provide the identity for the people. Without these sacred things that we reflect on as our identity, we have nothing. Although our old lifestyle is gone, the art form and the ceremonial side of us are still real and still alive. And it's often the artists who, in addition to their art form, also take an interest in learning the songs and the dances. All of these things are intertwined.

Today we also bring our work to the marketplace, and it ends up in Milwaukee, Chicago, New York, Germany, Tokyo. But it's still our identity; it represents who we are. Just as I was interested in other cultures' art forms as a child, this is a way for people of other cultures to appreciate the greatness of Northwest Coast art. Native people have something to share with the other cultures of the world, a beautiful gift.

Burned chief mask. Beau Dick (Kwakwa̱ka'wakw). "With the potlatches, they would try to outdo each other. And sometimes, the lengths that people would go to weren't healthy. To demonstrate their contempt for wealth, they would do things like throw eulachon oil on the fire as if to say 'I'm so wealthy and powerful I can just throw eulachon oil away, the most valuable commodity we have; I can just burn it.' This mask shows what happens when you go too far." Wood, paint, cedar bark. Collection Dukowski

EVELYN VANDERHOOP

Haida
Eagle Clan: Beaver, Frog, and Wood Spirit Crests
Old Masset, Haida Gwaii (Queen Charlotte Islands),
British Columbia

I weave *Naaxin* robes . . . the chiefs' robes or ceremonial robes [also known as Chilkat robes]. In the past, only high-ranked people would wear these robes because they showed the wearer's crests. I feel really fortunate to continue this art. I think there are fewer than six people who know how to weave these robes. I started out in an old style, a geometric style, but I was really challenged by the shapes and designs of the formline art, and I liked the different colors that are included.

In formline art, there's always an ovoid or a U-form. When I first learned the style, it wasn't difficult to get the ovoid, but it was connecting all the pieces to have them work perfectly together that was the trick. My first robe took me two years. It takes a lot of commitment and sustained passion to stay with the big projects. I'm still working at these shapes, to make them as good as my ancestors ever did.

For years I lived on the east coast, on Martha's Vineyard—another island— where I was a professional watercolor artist. When things changed in my life and I wanted to go home, I went home to Masset, my mother's and grandmother's village. There are so many people my age that are coming back to the traditional arts. And I did too. I came home to weave.

I come from a family of weavers. My sisters, grandmother, mother, aunts, cousins . . . they're all weavers of cedar bark and spruce root. It was my mother who first went into the textiles. She loves a challenge and so she started weaving the formline art in wool. With basketry techniques there are only geometric designs, so when she first started, I remember her saying, "Evelyn, this is so exciting, I'm working on a circle. It's just like falling in love."

In the old days, the women's weaving designs were dictated by pattern boards that the men painted. Nowadays, no one is designing the chiefs' robes. So I go back to robes that are in museums. I wouldn't copy someone else's crest without the proper protocol. Many families didn't survive the epidemics that ran along the coast, so we could probably never find out who originally owned some of the older crests.

So I feel it's okay to use those designs. I feel good about those real old robes—they were made by geniuses.

My first robe was a copy of one at the American Museum of Natural History in New York. I visited the museum one day and I just looked at it and looked at it. As I got further and further into the design and I could see that one element worked so perfectly with the placement of another element, it made me realize that the designer—the man who painted the pattern board—must have worked closely with the weaver. There are so many details about weaving that a designer would need to know, like the width that a three-strand braid makes or the width that three of them make. It's unfortunate that today there aren't artists who work with the weavers to create *Naaxin* designs. When it comes time for me to weave an original design, I'll try to do it. That's not traditional, but I'll try.

I weave for myself . . . for the joy and challenge of it. And I sell my weavings, so all the objects—the aprons, the leggings, the robes, the tunics—go away from me. And that's pretty traditional. In the past the women wove for their chiefs; they wove for their high-ranked people and their artwork would go away from them.

When a chief or high-ranked person commissions me to make something for them, I know that they will dance it. And when a collector commissions something, I know it's going to hang on a wall, but I approach it the same way. I want to have a consistent quality to my work. I want to use the best material, make it as strong as it possibly can be. Because, even if a collector buys it now, someday it may dance.

Chilkat (*Naaxin*) Robe. Evelyn
Vanderhoop (Haida). Merino wool,
yellow cedar bark, sea otter fur.
1997–1999. Width, 63". Private
collection

Opposite page:
Evelyn Vanderhoop in a Chilkat
tunic with sea otter fur collar.

NATHAN JACKSON

Tlingit
Sockeye Salmon Clan
Ketchikan, Alaska

In our society, there are two sides—the Eagle and Raven. And within that is your clan lineage. Mine is the Sockeye Salmon clan. Your clan lineage follows your mother's side and represents the area that you're from. Among our people you couldn't marry somebody from the same side, you had to marry somebody from the opposite side. In a potlatch, all the people from the same side sit together. The people usually wear their crest, whether it's Frog or Sockeye Salmon or Bear. All the clan symbols are part of the environment.

When I was a youngster, I was being raised a fisherman. Seasonal fishing happens only during the summer months, and you can make quite a bit of money. One day I was disk-sanding the bottom of a boat preparing to go fishing and some of the jellyfish powder and copper paint got into my lungs. They thought I had tuberculosis because I started coughing up blood. I ended up in the hospital and was there for 55 days. While I was there I carved small miniature totem poles. That's how I got into carving. And that's how I started on my trek, I guess you'd call it, to understanding quite a bit about Northwest Coast art.

Over the years I've looked at the old pieces, and I try to imagine how the artists handled them. If you look at the work of these good artists that have already paved the way, it's like you're looking over their shoulders. And it's really exciting to see the treatment that they could do and how they handled each piece.

Symmetry plays an important role in Northwest Coast art, in everything from a totem pole to the smaller things, such as jewelry. The oval shape has symmetry to it. In the old days, they'd use cedar bark templates on the bentwood boxes, for instance. And it was kind of like using the French curve. Instead of using a pencil, they would lightly mar the wood around the template. If you look closely, you can see that in the older pieces. There are a lot of little tricks that we can learn from the old-timers, just by looking at the older pieces.

There are pretty strict guidelines in Northwest Coast art, especially in two-dimensional art. There are standard elements in the designs, and you go from there to create a style that's identifiable as your own. Depending on how well the artist understands the art, it's okay to experiment. But it's best to stay within the limits of the art form so that you're not producing something foreign. The art relates to clan crests and to peoples' identities. My being Tlingit, I try not to do something that's Kwakiutl, or something that's from a different area. I try not to get into something that's too far-fetched. It's much better to stay within the framework of the clan crests.

When I'm coming up with a design, I experiment with drawings. Some people are fast with it; I take my time. It takes time to fit a piece of art into a space. I might have a whole bunch of ideas going in each drawing, whether it be symmetrical or asymmetrical. It can be hard when somebody orders a wedding ring; you have to fit the design into the ring. And then the next part is being able to engrave it. I used to carry around my jewelry with me, and when I wasn't doing anything, I'd start engraving.

It's encouraging when artists are willing to share wood and other materials. But there's also competition, and that's healthy. Any time there's competition, it challenges you. I've always said there's room for everybody in the arts. You should be able to work together, to enjoy each other's company and learn from each other. And that's what's important, being able to learn new things and new approaches. That's been going on forever. When the Tlingits picked up artwork from the Haida people, there was obviously somebody at that time who was willing to share.

I feel connected to the past because I am who I am—I'm Native, I'm maintaining the culture. What I do is a continuation of the past. I think perhaps that's the feeling a lot of the carvers get when they accomplish something. I'm happy about having my work in museums; it's a special opportunity. Because once I'm gone, that piece is going to stay on beside the old work. That makes me feel good.

Hairpiece. Nathan Jackson
(Tlingit). Silver, wood. Height,
2". Private collection

Opposite page:
Nathan Jackson in full regalia
including a Chilkat blanket,
beaded yoke, and headdress
with frontlet

KEVIN CRANMER

Namgis (Kwakwa̱ka'wakw)
Victoria, British Columbia

When my Uncle Roy initiated me for the *hamatsa* [the Kwakwa̱ka'wakw Cannibal Dance in which the initiate is ritually possessed by the cannibal spirit and then is ritually quieted and reintroduced to civility], he gave me the name *T's̱am K'wagal*, which refers to the sound that a *hamatsa* makes when he swallows.

Staying with the traditions and being able to create these things gives you a voice. It's not just a matter of learning the technical act of making art, you must learn the importance of it, and the meaning of it. As the years have gone by, I've begun to understand how important it is that, as an artist, I have a role to play in supporting the chiefs, my relatives, and the other families who are in the potlatch world. Our potlatch ceremonies are ways of recording important events in life. I have a four-year-old daughter and when she turns twelve or thirteen, I will have a feast to announce to our people that she's entering an important stage in her life; she's becoming a young woman.

I've been fortunate to work with relatives and other artists who were not selfish with their knowledge. Back when I was first learning to carve with my Uncle Tony Hunt, they were all at his studio— Calvin Hunt, Frank Nelson, Tony Hunt, Jr., Tom Patterson, John Livingston, Patrick Amos. I was lucky to have worked with the late Art Thompson from the Nuu-chah-nulth people. And I worked with Tim Paul, also Nuu-chah-nulth, on three major pole projects, one of which was for the closing ceremonies of the 1990 Commonwealth Games in Auckland, New Zealand.

Large projects like that usually require collaboration. It can take about three months to carve a pole and, during that time you're spending every day working side by side. Looking back on it now, I realize that you learn from these masters more than how to carve monumental sculpture, you learn a thing or two about how to conduct yourself. One of my uncles once said that you should conduct yourself as though the old people are still here.

The first pendant I made was a moon pendant with inlaid abalone. I made it for my mother's birthday because I thought it would be neat to try something small,

something she could wear. After my older sisters saw it, then everybody wanted one. That Christmas I was up until five in the morning getting the last one finished.

Our community big house burned down in 1997. People had many memories of being in there and seeing important events. So the community rallied to rebuild it. I wanted to be a part of the group that carved the big house. It didn't work out that way, but I really wanted to contribute in some way. In the big house there is a chief's chair where the host chief is given a place of prominence. I made a chief's chair, so I could give in some way.

I'm never more gratified than when I'm able to make something for our ceremonies. It's nice when galleries call and ask you to express yourself artistically, because you know your work is appreciated. But for me, I'm more gratified when I'm able to make something for a family member and see it danced. In the old days, and still today, when a chief is going to potlatch and if he needs something to be made for that special day, it's a real honor to be asked as an artist to make that object. That's a real acknowledgment of your abilities.

It's important to teach, to pass along your knowledge. I remember when I was thirteen or fourteen at Uncle Tony's work-shop I'd ask Tony, Jr. about an angle of a mask, or how to design something. I'm sure there were times when he'd be impatient because he had his own things to work on. But he'd always make time. Much later, I was working with a young carver, and the same thing was happening. He would come over and ask questions . . . "How does this look?" "Do you think I should round the end a bit more?" "How do you think that nose looks?" One time I was really frustrated about being interrupted because I was so involved with what I was doing. But when I looked at his mask to help him, it all came back to me—this was exactly what I used to do to Tony, Jr. And I just started smiling. It would have been really awful if he hadn't had the patience with me. So I realized, you have to do this in a good way. You have to be patient. Circles of life, I guess. They come around after a while.

Pendant/baby frontlet. Kevin Cranmer (Kwakwa̱ka'wakw). "When my son was born I wanted him to have a frontlet, which is a dance headdress. Because he's just a baby now, it's a baby-size frontlet. A full-size frontlet is usually about seven inches high by six inches wide. So when he grows out of this, he can wear it as a pendant if he chooses. When he gets older, I'll make him a full-size frontlet." Wood, abalone, paint. 2003. Height, 3". Private collection

Opposite page:
Kevin Cranmer wears a cedar bark neck ring that is indicative of someone who has been initiated into the *hamatsa* society.

CHRISTIAN WHITE

Haida
Yakulanaas Raven Clan
Old Masset, Haida Gwaii (Queen Charlotte Islands),
British Columbia

My islands—Haida Gwaii—are beautiful, pristine islands. Our beaches are nice and sandy with certain areas that are full of seafood we gather in season. There are towering spruce trees, hemlock, cedar, yew, and alder; the trees grow right up to the edge, the high water mark, at many spots. The waters around our islands are abundant with halibut, salmon, cod, and many other sea creatures like the killer whales, humpback whales, gray whales, porpoises, seals, and sea lions. Every day I see dozens of ravens and eagles and seabirds flying about. Every once in a while I'm delighted to see flickers; flicker feathers are treasured by the chiefs of our people.

In the wind and the waves you can hear songs from our ancestors. One time my father and I were carving late into the night. There was no radio playing, no traffic. But we started to hear singing and drumming. So we went to the back door and listened. Within a moment it faded out, and we heard the waves coming in on our north beach. My father said to me, "Our ancestor spirits are with us." That had a lot of meaning for me.

I have two traditional Haida names. One, *Sakiidtsangwaay*, translates as "Voice of Gold," and the other name, *Kilhlguulaans*, means "Headdress on the Sea." *Sakiidtsangwaay* comes from my grandfather and was given to me during a special occasion up in Masset. *Kilhlguulaans* was a name my father coined for me, and it was presented to me at his memorial potlatch.

I mainly carve in argillite, a black, carbonaceous shale found on Haida Gwaii. I've been carving it since I was about twelve years old. As my father moved on to other mediums, I picked up his tools, made a few attempts, and knew that the stone was a good way for me to express my art. We get the stone ourselves and carry out maybe 100 pounds on our backs for several miles. I cut it up into usable pieces, and put aside the larger pieces for sculptures and the smaller pieces for jewelry.

The Haida have been carving argillite for 300 years. Originally they carved ceremonial objects used by the shamans such as pipes and amulets depicting creatures from Haida stories. Argillite carving continued through the time of the banning of the potlatch. They were thought of as curiosities for the tourists, but for our elders, it was a way of carrying on the culture and passing things down to the next generation.

As I was growing up, some of the most valued possessions of the women were pieces of jewelry. The jewelry was another thing that never really stopped; it's continued on right through to the present. These pieces of jewelry—the bracelets, the necklaces, the earrings—were more than adornment. They were a way to display a person's crests. They would be passed down from generation to generation, or they were presented as gifts. The jewelry was a way of continuing the culture in an Anglicized world. It was acceptable to the missionaries so it became one of the "legitimate" ways of carrying on our traditions. Even today the jewelry is much valued by our own people, for wedding rings, for graduation presents, and also to display the crests.

I create a lot of jewelry for sale to collectors and galleries. I like to show my art to the world, and I like to teach about Haida culture. I'm able to tell a story with the jewelry and reach a different audience than I reach with my sculpture. And I like to have my work alongside artists from other Native cultures that have their own styles. Their work can be quite different than mine, but there are similarities in our traditions. It gives us a chance to get together and share.

Each time I hear a Haida story I'm inspired by a new part that I've never understood before. There's a constant renewal of ideas for me. And that's all part of the creative process. There's so much involved in the art, even though I've been working in the form for about twenty-five years now, I'm always learning something new. I'm grateful to my grandfather and to all our elders who have passed on the stories and traditions and encouraged us to keep up the art.

Beaver pendant. Christian
White (Haida). Argillite,
abalone, two shades of
fossilized ivory. 2003.
Width, 2¼". Courtesy
Spirit Wrestler Gallery

94

COREY MORAES

Tsimshian
Raven Clan
Seattle, Washington

When my son turned one, we had a small feast. We had given him a baby name in the traditional language. By having people over and gifting them, it legitimized his acceptance of the name. Gifting like this, like the potlatch, is payment to witnesses to validate that an event occurred. He was born on September 12th, the day after the World Trade Center disaster. We named him *Gwis Gwaask'm Laxha*, which means that sunlight that first comes through after the storm clouds break, because he was our light in that dark day.

As far as I know, there weren't any artists in my family. When I was about twenty-five, I started to look back at my own culture, in an exploration of who I was. So I did research in museums, galleries, and books. And I had a moment of epiphany—the old pieces spoke to me in a certain way. I felt a connection between the design and me, and I felt compelled to research it. It's my hope that every time I create a piece, it will live on long after I'm gone from this earth.

It's amazing what has been created with basic elements—the ovoid, the U-form, and tertiary spaces have been the basis for countless creatures, poles, and masks. Every day I come up with new ideas, and it all stems from these same basic elements. In some respects I think the medium—wood or gold—dictates which direction you're going to go with the formline. But there are elements in my work that show up time and again. Over time, that has developed into my own style. And it was like that in the past. Some of the old masters' names have been long forgotten, but you can still identify them by their own way of doing the formline and the carving.

In the Northwest cultures, it was the artist who brought the family's rights or privileges into the public's eye. If someone paddled up to a village in a canoe, they first saw the poles that told the stories of family fishing rights, hunting rights, histories, and legends. You could look at a pole and know the family's history.

It's the same with the jewelry today. Native women are interested in obtaining things that display their crest. The non-Native buyer wants something of beauty, something that speaks about their tastes and how they want the world to see them. When I'm creating a piece that doesn't stay within the Native community, it's like I have an unspoken dialogue with the buyer. The ovoids and the U-forms are like an alphabet, and the more that you use them and see them, the more they become like sentences and phrases and paragraphs and stories. The knowledgeable buyer is going to see this unspoken dialogue that I'm doing in the piece. In turn, a collector who buys a piece of my jewelry finances my freedom to research the art form and therefore, more accurately represent our iconography back to the community.

I get my greatest satisfaction from the pieces I make for ceremonies, pieces that will be used in the potlatch. One of my favorites is the baby regalia I did for my son. When I was making the regalia, people would say, "Why are you putting so much work into that? He's going to outgrow it right away." I want him to realize as he gets older that his father put care and attention into that regalia because the art form is so important.

Once we stop having the drive to continue our art form and our language, the culture is going to disappear. But I don't think that's going to happen anytime in the near future. When the potlatch was prohibited, a number of instrumental master artists continued the art form. In the early sixties, the generation before mine, artists picked up the art form again and relearned it. Now, I see people my age who are driven to continue it. The culture was almost completely lost before, and we can't lose it again.

Bracelet. Corey Moraes (Tsimshian). A rendering of a traditional paddle design becomes abstracted when wrapped onto a bracelet. In this piece Moraes reexplores the techniques of oxidizing and brush-finishing first brought into Northwest Coast jewelry by Bill Reid during experimentations in the 1960s. Silver. 2003. Width 1½". Courtesy Legacy Limited

DEMPSEY BOB

Tahltan-Tlingit
Wolf Clan
Terrace, British Columbia

I was lucky. My grandfathers were song composers and singers, and they were artists and leaders. They told me the history, and I listened. They knew I was going to do something with that knowledge.

In my art, I do everything. I make pieces for our people and for commissions. Large pieces and small pieces. . . in bronze, wood, ivory, and gold. I got into jewelry because I like small things. I've been trying to master the sculpture and put it into jewelry, finding my own style. But you have to come from understanding your culture and history. Then you can truly innovate. You can't innovate from nothing. . . it's still nothing.

My inspiration comes from my people and our history, from the animals and stories. For me, it's critical to live with my people and culture, because wherever you live, that's who you are. Your strength comes from the people and the land, and it's all connected. The land is strong. When I look at the landscape, I see designs in the rocks, and the trees, and the water. That's how our old people were too; they saw designs in the snow and the rocks and the forest. We're from the wolf clan. I like the wolf image, and it's the hardest one to carve. But I also like the stories of frogs from my grandfather, and I love carving frogs. The designs just come out. I think a true artist doesn't really know how it happens. You don't say to yourself, "Well, today I'm going to be creative." It doesn't work that way. You have to live it, and it will come out. It has to flow out of you.

Traditionally our bracelets were carved out of mountain goat horn. Then we got silver and gold coins, but we had no store, so we made bracelets out of them. We made earrings, pendants, things that were valid to our culture. That's how it evolved. We got different materials, but we were trying to save the art form too, so we adapted it to these new materials. We were always pushing the art, pushing the limit. One time I used a mirror on one of my pieces, and this guy said, "Hey, that mirror's not traditional." I said, "You know what, if the world lasts another 100 years, that's going to be a traditional mirror. And you're not going to be here to argue about it. I'm not either."

Even the fact that we're doing it still today has changed it. When I was in Toronto doing a lecture I was asked if I still used stone tools. I said, "I didn't come here in a canoe; I came here on a jet." Near my village they've found carvings that were over 10,000 years old. The people are still there and we're still carving. But we live today; we don't live years ago. If the art's not changing and evolving, it dies. So when people ask, "Is it traditional or is it contemporary?" I tell them that everything that was ever done, even the most traditional piece by today's standards, was at one time contemporary. It's the use of the design over time that makes it traditional. And not everything necessarily becomes traditional; only the great pieces have the chance of becoming traditional. You learn the rules so you can make them your own. It sounds easy, but it's the hardest part of the art.

There are some things we don't do with the art, out of respect for the ancestors. You have to know there are rules, forms. For example, there are things we only put on grave houses, but some young people don't know yet that you don't put those designs on things that will belong to other people.

In a way, artists were like the leaders in our society because they made the culture visible. Art lifts people's pride. Art makes you see who you are. It reflects the culture, and culture is what you do, where you live, what you believe.

Opposite page:
Frog necklace. Dempsey Bob (Tahltan-Tlingit). Dempsey Bob delicately carved the frogs of slightly graduated sizes and used the lost-wax method to cast each in 22-karat gold. Across a moonstone, two frogs are connected by their tongues, symbolizing communication. 1995. Length, approximately 16". Private collection

Left:
Dempsey Bob wears a woven Chilkat design headband and tunic trimmed with beaver fur.

98

DOROTHY GRANT

Haida
Brown Bear House: Raven Clan
Delta, British Columbia

In addition to being a clothing designer, I'm a collector of the arts, particularly jewelry. Being a Haida woman, it's important to have jewelry. It signifies a lot in your life—your status, your identity. We all love to have lots of bracelets when we go to functions or momentous occasions, because it's a show of love. Jewelry makes me feel empowered.

I'm a basket weaver, and I do some jewelry, but my main medium has been fabric. I started out making ceremonial regalia, such as button blankets, dance aprons, and basketry hats. My grandmother taught me basketry. At that time, in 1981, there weren't many women my generation who did weaving; it was mostly the grandmothers, the elders. But it's an art form that has been revived in the last twenty years. Now there are hundreds of weavers.

From those traditional wearable arts, I was inspired to create something new. The button blanket is a recent art as far as tradition goes. It's a ceremonial blanket that evolved out of European trade items—the Hudson Bay blankets and pearl buttons from China. After making them for many years, I had the idea of doing wearable art, things that had sleeves as opposed to a square blanket. Beautiful clothing that people could wear to feasts or potlatches. So it was born out of that ceremonial aspect.

The art that I put on the clothing is traditional formline art. It's something that I studied for many years, so I have great respect for the forms. I think that Haida art is one of the most elegant forms. It looks fluid and free, but it has a structure with a set of rules. I manipulate the designs onto the clothing so that they work with the body.

What I've tried to do over the last fifteen years is build a bridge of awareness between cultures through clothing. I've carefully kept my business small, so I could foster it in the right direction, keeping the integrity of the art. I sell my work to people from all walks of life—Native people, non-Native people, professionals, art collectors. By purchasing it and wearing it, they're making a personal statement. Because clothing *is* a personal statement. Whether you're buying a designer suit or something from the mall, it's a personal statement about who you are. When people buy my clothing, it's a statement about their alignment to Haida culture, their acceptance of it. And it allows them the experience of wearing art as opposed to looking at art. It's a really good thing to bridge our cultures like that, through clothing.

Opposite page:
"The Raven Takes the World," Haida wedding dress. Dorothy Grant (Haida). The dress is made of white deer hide and silkscreened with a Haida design, "Raven Takes the World." Raven, the Transformer, is depicted holding the four corners of the earth with his human hands. The dress was made in honor of Dorothy's mother, Eleanor Judy Morrison. The edging of the bodice is beaded with mother of pearl beads and glass trade beads, and the three-tiered body has hand-cut fringe. 1994. Length, approximately 49". Private collection

The dentalium headdress, by Marianne Jones (Haida), was commissioned by Dorothy Grant in 1994 to match the wedding dress. It was inspired by the headdresses worn by Salish tribes. Dentalium shells, amber beads, blue glass trade beads, and mother-of-pearl. Private collection

Left:
Dorothy Grant wears a hat, coat, and necklace of her own design.

100 WILL BURKHART

Tlingit
Eagle Nest House: *Kaagwonton* Clan
Sitka, Alaska

I carry on the heritage of being a carver. I work with silver and gold and also large carvings, totem poles. When I was very young I was always hanging around my grandfather's shop. My mother was an artist also; she painted a lot on his projects. And once you start hearing all the stories, it takes you away, and before you know it you're doing artwork.

Alaska can be hard, harsh to you, life and death situations. But it can also offer so much, the fish, the hunting, just the raw beauty of the area. I think everything comes together like a painted mosaic in the artwork; it all comes to your environment, your surroundings. I think our people express it, and all the creatures and special events, with art.

I've done the jewelry a lot longer than the wood. I'm more comfortable with it, although there's so much to be said about wood. If I had the chance, I think I'd work with metal all the time. I'm from the Eagle side, from the Eagle Nest House, so I have the right to use those animals that represent that side of the tribe. And then there's the Raven side. And sometimes you have to get permission from certain people before you can use certain crests. So you have to know your history, and who to ask, and how to ask.

I've worked on large totem pole projects where I was the head carver. And in a small community there are so many people from different clans that represent the whole area, and to keep all those people happy you have to know the history of both sides so you don't offend anybody. When you're doing the art, you are part historian; you have to know all the rules. And that goes along with the form line. That's the responsibility you have when you take on an apprentice; you teach them about things that you can and can't do. It's a rigid art form, but once you learn it, it's not.

I've done a lot of projects, and most have been affiliated with the tribe, which has been fortunate for me because a lot of people don't have that opportunity. In the Sitka area, I've worked on projects that meant more than being in the marketplace.

They were for a specific reason and meant a lot more than monetary values.

I think it's really important to make my own tools. How you're going to approach a certain piece depends on what kind of cuts you want. Sometimes I'll make one tool for one specific purpose on a certain carving. You learn how to shape and grind and temper and then sharpen. That's half the job, learning how to make your tools.

I strive to make something better than I did the last time, or come up with a special idea. When you're asked to do something . . . and maybe you've done that crest before . . . it never gets boring because I always try to make it better.

One of the hardest things I've ever carved was a 36-foot canoe. Basically, it takes over your life. I have the utmost respect for the canoe makers in the past. It's a lost art. How they even came up with how to do it is amazing to me.

Jewelry has always been important. They didn't have silver and gold in the old days, but they always adorned themselves with certain things, objects they held dear, things of value that they traded. The jewelry is more than a piece of adornment. It represents the clan crests, particular stories, a particular hero in a story, or some event that happened in the past. I think I'm doing something for the future because I'm perpetuating the art.

Eagle hair clip. Will Burkhart (Tlingit). Silver. 2003. Length, 3½". Private collection

102   NICK GALANIN

Tlingit
Sitka, Alaska

I remember countless nights of my father working quietly at his bench, and it always intrigued me to see the work he created, to learn how important it was to him, and to observe the use of his tools. Being in his shop was like being a kid in a toy store. My father [Dave Galanin] and my uncle [Will Burkhart] allowed me to work with their carving tools and answered my questions. Growing up, they had watched their grandfather, George Benson, working on large projects for the community in his shop.

The art has always been an important part of our communities. When you see the old photographs, the art forms were everywhere. It's a language, and it's a tool, and it's beautifully powerful. To explain Tlingit art briefly isn't easy. When I look at an older piece that's well done, I get a great sense of joy, an uplifting feeling. The forms are full and alive with a breath of life. I only hope to translate that strength in my own work.

The strength of a piece often comes from its concept; the medium then follows. There is great joy in working in all scales and mediums, and you have to be equally sensitive. There are subtleties you've got to pay attention to in order to make the piece effective. I've always thought that it's the same no matter what you're doing, whether you play music, or dance, or make art. The working process is the same—if you pay attention to the subtleties, the piece can be understood.

I'm enjoying pursuing my own ideas. I've done small commissions for the community and, for me, that's where the most joy comes from. Because that piece takes on a life when it's used and when it's danced. To see it in a context that has inspired artists for thousands of years is excellent.

But I've also wanted to pursue new ideas to grow as an artist. I've been to Europe to see museum collections. In London, I did a course in contemporary jewelry design and silversmithing. I had just finished a few big Northwest Coast projects, and had put a lot of energy in that direction. I wanted to continue with that in London and try to share it. But at

the institution, it was hard. I was taking something so literal, from such an established art form [Northwest Coast art], and trying to combine it with their criteria for the course work. It didn't work. I ended up running the two alongside each other. It was frustrating for me as an artist, but it was a valuable experience.

I will be doing a master's course in Indigenous Visual Arts in New Zealand for two years, working with Maori artists. I won't practice their art form, although I'll learn about it. I'll bring my own Tlingit art form and history down there, and will do contemporary work with heavy foundation or influence from the Tlingit. I'm excited to see where it goes and to learn how they've handled change in their culture and society.

The line between traditional and contemporary is blurred. Any culture that's living or breathing is going to move forward, and change is undeniable. It's important to understand the history and to ground myself in that foundation before trying to expand too much. On the other hand, as an artist, I hope to offer something different and new. It's a fine line to walk. People have preconceptions about what traditional artwork is or what Tlingit art should look like. Hopefully I can educate through my art form, and see what's possible.

Copper sun mask. Nick Galanin (Tlingit). To create this mask, Galanin started with a flat sheet of copper and used a Japanese technique of hammering to raise up the metal. The face has a matte patina contrasted with a textured and polished finish around the edge. Copper, abalone. Height, 5⅜".
Private collection

104

VICTORIA MOODY

Haida
Raven Clan
Skidegate, Haida Gwaii (Queen Charlotte Islands),
British Columbia

In 2001, six poles were raised [at the new Qay'llnagaay Heritage Center in Skidegate], one for each of the old Haida villages. Each pole had a master carver and two apprentices. Percy Ellis and I were the apprentices on the pole representing the village of T'aanuu. On that pole the master carver, Ron Wilson, let me carve a portrait of myself transforming from a human into a shark. I did that because my grandfather, Chief Nathan Young or *Git_kun*, had passed away. I thought carving the pole would be a healing process for me. He was huge part of my life. And it has helped; when the project was finished, that was the end of my mourning. And it was a celebration to raise the pole. If my grandfather were alive, I would have presented my cedar bark robe to him because he was a chief and a very regal man.

There is a rebirth going on right now of something that we almost lost. My vision of helping revive the cedar bark weaving began with my wonderment at the fact that the Haidas had only cedar—they made everything out of cedar. I thought to myself: If they could figure it out back then, why couldn't I figure it out with all the technology that we have today? And things just exploded. Within a year I had accomplished three major projects, including the Transition Robe. I took a class with two weavers, April Churchill and Evelyn Vanderhoop, and learned how to do the Raven's Tail [a geometric style of weaving in mountain goat wool that predates the Chilkat blanket]. And, that's why I put the Raven's Tail on the "Transition Robe."

I call it the Transition Robe because it reflects my transition into doing this ancient technique of weaving with twined yellow cedar mixed with mountain goat wool. The Transition Robe has in it bark from all six poles, and it was actually a three-year plan to make it. When they would bring the logs in for the poles, I took strips of bark from each one and put them aside especially for the blanket. And I pounded the bark for a year, preparing it for the robe. It's the first cedar bark robe that's been woven here in probably 200 years, and the only one that many people have seen

with their own eyes—at least in Skidegate. Nobody remembers seeing a piece like this, and no one knows when the last one would have been done. I wanted to see how cedar bark and wool could be mixed and it was a perfect marriage. It was a major breakthrough for me as a weaver, but it wasn't an original idea. This kind of work was done for thousands of years. Cedar was used for everything the people needed.

All kinds of things went through my head as I was making the robe—things like how they must have traded in the old days, because our islands don't have certain resources, and they're very isolated. Even today we are isolated. The older people used to have to travel and trade to get certain valuable goods, like eulachon grease or the mountain goat wool to incorporate into their clothing. So the people would go to other tribes and trade for the things they didn't have. The wool was wonderful because it was light but strong, and it wasn't as scratchy as the bark. Depending on the amount of cedar you use, a robe can be quite heavy, especially when it gets wet. They were on the sea a lot, and so ponchos would be woven with two or three layers to protect the person who wore it and to them keep warm. One layer was an insulator, and the other one was the outer shell. Sometimes the layer against your body had your crest woven into it. Other people wouldn't see the crest, but it was there to protect the person.

I've been so sick the last few years with fibromyalgia that I haven't been able to work since the pole and the Transition Robe. I think it's important for people to know that that disease is out there. It's one of those taboo things; people don't want to believe you're ill because it's invisible. And you're in constant pain all the time. But I'm feeling better and starting to weave again. The last few years have been a real test though. The best medicine is indigenous —body, mind, and spirit. A well-known shaman showed me this.

I needed something special to wear for the T'aanuu pole raising, so I made a poncho. I used the spider web pattern and went by what I thought would be the right measurements for my shoulders. The collar is sea otter fur. And the zigzag pattern I put there to represent waves, because our pole was going to be raised right beside the beach. The cedar bark is blended with merino wool, and the bottom fringe is twined rope. On the hat there's a painted spider web design and deer hooves hanging off the brim, like teardrops. I collected those myself, because we eat a lot of venison. An ermine skin hangs from the back of the hat. I save most everything; there's not much waste of anything. That's part of the way we are.

We use eagle down in our ceremonies as a blessing. When we raised the T'aanuu pole, we danced around it, and we took the eagle down and splashed it against the pole. Some of the eagle down sticks to the pole, and some of it floats up. That's sort of the final touch and also a blessing.

"Transition Robe." Victoria Moody (Haida). Victoria Moody created this magnificent robe using bark from each of six totem poles carved for the Qay'llnagaay Heritage Center in Skidegate, British Columbia. The first such robe seen on the Queen Charlotte Islands in 200 years, it was "danced" by Victoria at a rally in protest of excessive logging on the islands. Red cedar bark, merino wool, sea otter pelt, mountain goat wool. 1999–2001. Length, 7' 7½". Private collection

Opposite page:
Victoria Moody at the celebration of the T'aanuu pole raising. She wears a cedar bark poncho and has painted her cheeks to represent her transformation from a human to a shark in honor of her grandfather. She wears a small labret, a traditional Haida woman's form of adornment.

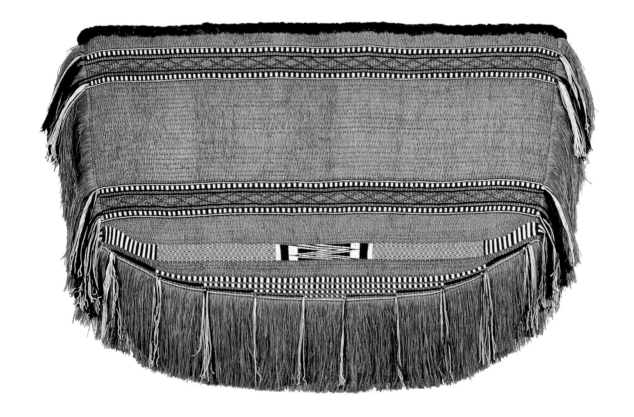

106

MARVEN TALLIO

Nuxalk and Heiltsuk
Grizzly Bear, Eagle, and Killer Whale Clans
Vancouver, British Columbia

My family name, Tallio, is traditional. It's from Taleomy, a village in Bella Coola, the Nuxalk Nation, where my father is from. My mother is from Bella Bella, or the Heiltsuk Nation. I grew up in North Vancouver, but I visit Bella Coola and Bella Bella quite often.

One mask that I really like is the Bella Coola Thunderbird Spirit Mask. I think that one really inspired me to continue with my art work. I've seen it danced, and it's quite powerful.

There's a group of us, my friends and I, who carve quite a bit together. We're each well-known artists now, but we all started quite young, maybe nine or ten years old, just to make some extra money for ourselves. I learned by watching the older people. At first I carved just more or less what I liked to see, to try my own different style, things I saw in books or different pieces that caught my eye. I did a lot of eagles.

I like to go free and do designs I like and whatever it takes to get me working. I was doing some polar bear pieces; they were nice little realistic pieces, not traditional native style. I think it's up to the individual if he wants to experiment with different new types of material, maybe add in some new stories . . . you know, our life and times, in this day and age. So that's where I like to take my art, but also keep the traditional art in there.

I carve wood and do jewelry. Usually when it's for a wood or a large project, I plan it out on paper. But when it comes to jewelry I just put the project on my block and draw out the design freehand. If I like it, then I start carving.

I've got three crests. On my Bella Coola side, it's a Grizzly Bear; and for the Bella Bella side, it's Eagle and Killer Whale combined. I get a lot of my ideas from the older pieces I've seen, like the bentwood boxes, just looking at them and going through the whole design.

For me right now, the marketplace is going very well. I treat what I'm doing as my job, but I enjoy doing what I do. I chose to be a full-time artist, and I like to be my own boss. The income is good.

My grandfather was a functional kind of artist. He made canoes and spoons and different things that were for function, not for show. My dad is a well-received artist right now, and I've worked with my uncle who took over my grandfather's chieftain name in Bella Bella. We had a memorial feast, a potlatch feast for him. So I've done some dance masks for him, and some jewelry. In potlatching, everything comes together. Watching my pieces being used in the dance brings them to life.

108

DAN WALLACE

Lek-Kwil-Taich (Kwakwaka'wakw) and Haida
Kolus and Double-Finned Killer Whale Clans
(Kwakwaka'wakw) and Eagle Clan (Haida)
Vancouver, British Columbia

My traditional chieftain name is *Gi-Gamie Kin-Kwus*. It was recently given to me, at my young age, because of the passing of my uncle who was the chief. Because my blood comes from two sides—Lek-Kwil-Taich and Haida—I've got the right to work in these two art styles. I feel privileged that I'm allowed to do that and I think my artwork reflects that.

Growing up on Vancouver Island gave me a good opportunity to witness our ceremonies. I watched my grandfather and my uncle carve, so that's where I get most of my traditional knowledge. It's a really good base. You have to know what the art form is about and why we have it . . . this is who we are; this is *our* identity. It's a way for our people to restake our claim in who we are. When our potlatch ceremonies were outlawed and people were put in jail within our own territories, even then, my family never stopped potlatching. I have family that died in jail because of that law. But we're still alive today and benefit from such a strong tie to our culture.

My grandfather said that art's been in our family as far back as he can remember. He was raised traditionally until he was taken away to residential school. His grandfather carved, and his grandfather's father carved. Our family has always made their own things, and they've always helped out other families, too. If another family needed something for a ceremony, we would carve a piece for their own story, the story that belongs to them.

My grandmother told me that one of her uncles was the first to introduce metalwork to my grandfather's village. He did engraving on silver dollars and made a living on it, and he also contributed to the ceremonies, making sure that people, especially all the grandmothers, walked around proud, wearing wide bracelets. Today when we adorn somebody with jewelry—our grandmothers or our mothers—we're raising their status and their wealth in a visual sense. It's building us back up. I like to see the old ladies walking into a ceremony wearing their bracelets, their arms all dressed up. You can tell that they just feel good. They know who they are.

It makes me feel so good to see them wear the jewelry with pride. I like decorating our people.

I look back at Charles Edenshaw and his work, and I couldn't imagine myself doing jewelry like he did. Today we've got the jeweler's block, a nice bench, a nice light, and we can sharpen our gravers any time we want. He'd have to hammer out his silver by hand, and that probably took a couple of days just to do that. And then he'd start the engraving and would work almost freehand. I look at some of the old pictures of potlatches. They would have sometimes twenty small poles with bracelets stacked up. I'm just amazed at the work those older guys put in to make all those pieces.

I try to incorporate an ancestor's figure or face on all of my pieces, because I want to remind myself that I wouldn't have this today if it weren't for my ancestors. So I pay respect to the art form and to my own people and make sure that I always recognize it.

I prefer to carve wood only for ceremony, that's why I'm glad I found jewelry too. It's a more contemporary art form that is affordable for a lot of people.

Most of my inspiration comes from knowing my family stories. I also help out other families who want to have their stories on art. They share their story with me so I can put it on a bracelet or a pendant. When I make jewelry for commercial reasons, it relates to the same thing. It feels good that I can do a piece of jewelry that can relate to somebody's own ways. Maybe I can help somebody express their love more visually, or help get someone recognition where they should be recognized.

The responsibility of my chieftainship is not just to take care of my own family. I have to keep my eye out for the whole village. It's really humbling. How do I bring something good to our village and our people? We're coming from an imposed dysfunctional past, and we have to relate really good connection stories to break past and shatter that dysfunction. I have family members who are on the same wavelength, and that's good because ten years ago, even five years ago, there wasn't as much healthy support as there is today.

I want to build on to what I know. I want to take jewelry to another level of excellence. My mother, in her generation, was deprived of traditional knowledge. But I can see emotions beginning to come up; she's walking around with more pride. Now she can say, "That's my son. He's the chief of our family now. Look at this piece he made for me." You can see the pride beginning to go back to where it belongs, and helping the healing begin for my family and my people.

Rattle pendant. Dan Wallace (Kwakw<u>a</u>ka'wakw and Haida). Silver, wood, abalone. 2003. Length with clasp, 3¾". Private collection

ROBERT DAVIDSON

Haida
Eagle Clan
Vancouver, British Columbia

When I first started carving, I worked in argillite. From the early 1900s to the 1950s, the majority of the work being produced was in argillite, which is a type of black slate that's very soft and carveable. After European contact, the economy changed drastically. The sea otters and other resources were drastically depleted, so other economies began to develop, and argillite carving was one of them.

At that time too, the missionaries discouraged the Haida people from following our beliefs and traditions. In order for the Haida to embrace Christianity they had to give up many of their Haida values and that meant their carving, their songs, their dances, their names, and their tattooing. Those people still carrying tattoos on their bodies became ashamed of them. There are stories of women wearing gloves to hide their tattoos. Silver bracelets replaced tattooing. The missionaries felt they were doing the right thing, but there was no regard for any of our values. In fact, there was competition between the missionaries and the shaman, because the shaman held a lot of power and authority. So the missionaries would do things to discredit the shaman.

It was a powerful transitional time. The Haida had to let go of their totem poles too. I think the last totem pole to be carved and raised in Old Masset would have been about 1880 or 1890. Many of the existing totem poles were sold to explorers, and many of them are now housed in museums around the country. They were sold, chopped down, or left to rot. Through the new diseases such as smallpox and tuberculosis, the population dwindled to about 5 percent of what it had been. Children of the survivors were taken away from their families and moved to schools in a completely different part of the country. Those children, when they finally could go back home, were no longer part of the community. It is the art that has helped to reconnect my generation and my parents' generation to the values of our ancestors.

I find it very exciting today to see so many artists wanting to express their feelings through our highly developed art forms. I feel there's a blossoming, and, at the same time, it's my responsibility as an established artist to feed back into the learning process. And I'm even more committed today than I was twenty years ago. It's up to people who are established in the art form to nurture this blossoming, this revitalization, and to maintain the standard.

Northwest Coast art is not a limiting art form, but it is a very challenging art form. Once I started to understand the principles of the art form, I felt like it was my challenge to expand on that knowledge. I think this happened with the artists of the 1850s. Based on my observations of objects that were collected in the nineteenth century, there is a definite progression of the art to about 1880–1890. Certain artists went outside of the mainstream and continually expanded on the art form, and jewelry was one of the mediums they used.

It's part of being human to expand and go beyond what has already been established. But people who choose art as their medium of expression have to have an understanding of the principles of the art form, like knowing a vocabulary or the letters of the alphabet. The art form—how the ovoid works, how the U-shape works—is my vocabulary. Because I come from that school of thinking, then the art form becomes my language. Right now I'm challenging myself to go beyond where I have been already. At certain points in my life I look back and I can see where I've just been making variations of variations, and I have a choice of continually doing that or I can expand my understanding of the principles.

I raised a totem pole in my family's village of Old Masset back in 1969 because I felt there was a gap and a separation of cultural values. I was brought up seeing only miniature replicas of our past in argillite and in the engraved silver bracelets and pendants. That was the extent of art in Old Masset, and in many of the villages up and down the coast where the ceremonies, the songs, the feasting, and the potlatching were all outlawed. I came to the city and saw all the art objects housed in museums—the masks, bowls, canoes, totem poles. I never saw any of that in Old Masset, and when I went back home, I thought: "Wow, there's none of our art here." After several trips home and seeing that difference, I made a promise that I would carve a totem pole and present it to the village.

It took years of continuing my practice as an artist to realize the responsibility I have, the responsibility that was being taught to me by my uncles, my grandmother, my grandfather, my dad, and my mother and aunties. What's exciting now is that my cousins are asking me to talk to their sons. And so the gift that my uncles gave me, I'm able to give to my cousin's sons.

Northwest Coast art has a certain charisma, a certain magic, and once a person is exposed to Northwest Coast art, they almost become addicted. I think owning the jewelry or the masks or the graphic arts gives people energy. There's a pulsating energy that comes from the Creator and also from the maker. It's almost like our hands are connected to the supernatural world. The Haida have a strong connection to the supernatural world.

Jewelry keeps the economy going. Art was always a commodity. For example, one of the best places to find good cedar logs was in Masset Inlet. So Masset Inlet became like a canoe factory and box-making factory of Haida Gwaii. The mainland people highly prized the Haida canoe. The canoes became sought-after products, and thus the trade was quite strong. That's what held us together—the trading and the demand—the demand for boxes, the demand for our art. Because there was a demand, the art flourished; it kept developing. In the early 1900s, the demand for canoes was no longer there, but those people who were skilled canoe makers adapted again, and they became wooden boat builders. They had an amazing understanding of the wood and the ability to steam-bend it.

In Masset, it seemed like every decade there was one person who maintained the skill of engraving silver or gold. When I was a child there was only one person I can think of, his name was Art Adams, and before him it was John Marks. It was in the 1960s and '70s that more people picked up the technique of engraving, and today there are more engravers than I can name. Artists now have access to study museum pieces and attain the standards of our ancestors. It's exciting for me to see the younger generation picking up an interest in the art and expanding on it. It's really great to go to the different galleries now and see who is doing what and who is improving. It's an exciting time.

Bracelet, "Big Thunder, Little Thunder." Robert Davidson (Haida). 22-karat gold. 1991. Height, 1". Courtesy of Gallery of Tribal Arts

Opposite page:
Robert Davidson in his studio

THE SOUTHWEST

"To put a timeline on a piece of artwork is impossible. You might say that a piece took a week to make. But you've got to consider that that one week is like traveling in time. All the things that you've learned from your grandmother, grandfather, mother, relatives . . . are in that work. All that time is in that one piece." —Phil Loretto

DANCING FOR RAIN UNDER A TURQUOISE SKY: THE SOUTHWEST

Kari Chalker

Across the arid Southwest, the earth is stacked in angular tiers. Over eons, layers of sandstone laid down as sea floor or blown in as sand dunes have been carved by wind and water into canyons and mesas. Volcanic eruptions piled up extensive mountain ranges, isolated snow-capped peaks, and jagged rock formations.

Summer thunderstorms track across open miles inundating narrow swaths of juniper, prickly pear cactus, and snakeweed while leaving nearby areas parched. Arroyos and gullies can remain dry for weeks, months, or years at a time, before suddenly being flooded by a torrential storm far upstream. Summer's heat stresses thirsty plants and people, and winter rain and snow soak the earth for another growing season. Views stretch for uninterrupted miles, and the horizon is punctuated with identifiable, familiar landforms, marking neighboring communities, trails, or places of spiritual significance.

Here life succeeds along a narrow margin. For the people who have hunted game in the foothills, gathered medicinal plants in the mountains, and farmed corn and beans in canyon bottoms and on mesa tops, success requires specialized knowledge and deep spirituality centered on the need for water. Homes are located near springs or streams, and beautiful pottery was made to store precious water. Prayers, in the form of dances performed by masked beings adorned with shell and turquoise, call for rain.

The People

From about 10,000 BC to 7,000 BC, the Southwest's earliest peoples were PaleoIndian big-game hunters of mammoths and giant bison. As the climate changed and these Pleistocene mammals died out, people of the Archaic period (6,500 BC to 1,000 BC) adjusted to hunting smaller game such as elk, deer, and rabbits, and they gathered seeds, greens, and roots. However, little evidence survives to tell us what the PaleoIndians and Archaic people wore or what they believed.

By about 2,000 years ago the people of the Southwest obtained agriculture with corn (maize), which had been domesticated in Mesoamerica, as the principal staple. As people came to depend upon farming, they developed particular sets of architecture and tools specific to their region and resources. Based on these particular adaptations, three broad cultural groups have been defined by archaeologists: the ancestral Pueblo (Anasazi), the Mogollon, and the Hohokam. The ancestral Pueblo, characterized primarily by distinctive black-on-white pottery, occupied the Colorado Plateau of northern Arizona, northern New Mexico, southern Utah, and southwestern Colorado. The Mogollon, characterized by brown pottery, primarily occupied the mountains and basins of western New Mexico and the eastern edge of Arizona. The Hohokam lived in the lower desert basins around the current cities of Phoenix and Tucson, making painted, buff-colored pottery and watering their crops with elaborate irrigation canals fed by the Salt and Gila

Top:
Arid layers of sandstone carved by wind and water, pockets of desert scrub vegetation, and occasional high mountain peaks watered by isolated rain and snow showers characterize many parts of the desert Southwest.

Bottom:
The angularity of the Jemez Mountains and flanking mesas is echoed by the architecture of Jemez Pueblo. 1899. Courtesy Peabody Museum, Harvard University, photo N33836.

Rivers. The Hohokam probably contributed to the ancestral Pueblo population, although they are believed by some archaeologists to be the ancestors of the Tohono O'odham (Papago) and the Akimel O'odham (Pima). The two cultural groups referred to as Mogollon and ancestral Pueblo were both likely the principal ancestors of today's Pueblo Indians.

Earliest archaeological evidence of a Navajo ancestral presence in the Southwest dates to about AD 1500. The early Navajos and Apache were Athapaskan speakers who migrated south from modern-day Canada. The Navajo and Apache made their living hunting, gathering, and raiding until the late 1800s. The Navajos also adopted many traits from the Pueblos, Spanish, and Mexicans. From the Pueblos it appears the Navajos borrowed corn growing and weaving. Further, it seems likely that the Pueblo belief in katsinas, or spirit beings, inspired the Navajo belief in their own spirit beings, which they call *yé'ii*. As the Europeans brought in sheep, the Navajos took on sheepherding as well, and adapted the Pueblo weaving techniques into their own exceptional blanket and rug styles in wool. From the Mexicans they learned ironworking and eventually silver-smithing. Over time, with much industry and talent, Navajo farmers, herders, and artisans made these techniques and traits very much their own.

Each of the groups, Pueblo and Navajo, has its own specific origin histories that tell of having lived in and climbed up through successive worlds to this current world. Although Pueblos were considered a sedentary people—and indeed, many Pueblo village sites have been occupied for hundreds, even a thousand years—the process of migration features prominently in Pueblo oral histories. Great spirit beings instructed the people to wander, and they lived in many different places in search of a "center place," where life would be in balance. Ancient spirals and other rock art symbols etched on canyon walls tell of these migrations.

In 1540, Spanish explorers under Francisco Vázquez de Coronado followed ancient trails north and encountered the Zuni people. They were disappointed not to find rumored gold and silver. Even so, new Spanish incursions were not far behind, and in 1598, Juan de Oñate and his soldiers founded the first Spanish settlement at San Gabriel del Yunque, near San Juan Pueblo at the confluence of the Chama River and the Rio Grande in northern New Mexico. The search for silver and gold continued and to that end the Spaniards brought with them bellows and other tools necessary for processing metal, teaching some of the Pueblo men how to work iron.

The Pueblo people along the Rio Grande were forced to provide labor for Spanish interests and to donate much of their harvests, making it increasingly difficult to provide for their own communities. In 1680, all of the Pueblo Indians, from Pecos in the east to Hopi in the west, carried out a detailed plan to rise up in revolt against the Spanish and forced them to flee south along the Rio Grande to El Paso.

But by 1692, the Spanish renewed their forces and, under the command of General Diego de Vargas, they reentered the upper Rio Grande area. From that time on Pueblo life was irrevocably changed. The mission churches that had been

Bracelet. Lucy Year Flower (Pojoaque Pueblo). Under a band of turquoise mosaic are appliquéd a water serpent, clouds, lightning, and spirals. Formerly a potter, Year Flower uses classic pottery images in her jewelry. Turquoise, silver. 2002. Width, 1". Collection Schaaf

Opposite page:
"Corn Dance" silkscreen, 1976. J.D. Roybal, San Ildefonso Pueblo. Accompanied by a drummer and singers, male and female dancers dressed in regalia dance in a group prayer for rain. Permanent collection, Indian Pueblo Cultural Center Museum, Albuquerque, New Mexico

This page, top:
Yé'ii (spirit being) bracelet. Carl and Irene Clark (Navajo). The design, blending a *yé'ii* figure and a rug pattern, was created from 7,000 pieces of stone to form a micro-mosaic. Irene tufa-cast the bracelet including a hidden image on the inside of the band (not shown) of Arizona's San Francisco Peaks with cloud, rain, and a corn plant. Silver, Mediterranean and Pacific corals, lapis lazuli, jet, mother-of-pearl, sugilite. 2003. Width, 1¼". Courtesy Michael Bernstein and Gene Waddell

This page, bottom:
Pendant. Duane Maktima (Hopi and Laguna). Gold, turquoise, ivory, and jet. Ca. 1990s. Height, 1¾". Collection Schaaf

Opposite page:
Ancestral Pueblo petroglyphs pecked into a sandstone wall date prior to AD 1300. Spirals are considered by many Native Americans to be symbols of migration.

This page:
Tablita headdress. Zuni Pueblo. *Tablitas* are ceremonial head-dresses worn by dancers throughout the Pueblo world. They are flat pieces of wood often cut into stepped or terraced shapes that represent clouds. They are painted, frequently with water symbols, and usually topped with feathers. Wood, cloth, pigment, hide, string. Ca. 1915. Height, 26¾". Collection American Museum of Natural History, 50.1/9014

Opposite page:
Palhikwmamant katsina doll dance group. Ernest Moore (Hopi). This award-winning set of twenty-four katsina dolls (only five dolls shown) represents a katsina dance featuring "Nectar-drinking Butterfly Maiden" katsinas with warrior-guards, clowns, and a chorus of Mudheads. The group is led by a "katsina father" (in red shirt). The *Palhikwmana* katsina (center) wears an elaborate *tablita*. Wood, paint. 2003. Height of Mudhead (far left), approximately 13½". Collection American Museum of Natural History

Top:
Turquoise pendants and beads, a jet frog with eyes and collar of turquoise, and a necklace of thousands of jet and spiny oyster shell beads are some of the remarkable ancestral Pueblo jewelry found at Pueblo Bonito. Collection American Museum of Natural History, H/10426, H/3764, H/3871, H/9233, H/5149, H/5138, H/5133

Bottom:
Hohokam shell jewelry dating between AD 1100–1500. The Hohokam were master carvers of shell jewelry. Massive quantities of raw shell were imported from the Pacific coast and traded through Hohokam territory (the desert basins around modern-day Phoenix and Tucson) up to Pueblo groups in the northern Southwest. Shell bracelets and beads are found in archaeo-logical sites across the region. The necklace is made of olivella shell beads with a cut shell pendant inlaid with turquoise and argillite tesserae. Frogs and bracelet are carved Glycymeris shell. Diameter of bracelet on right, 2⅛"–2¼". Collection Arizona State Museum, The University of Arizona

Six cylinder jars from Pueblo Bonito. Pueblo Bonito was one of many sprawling, multi-room buildings in northwest New Mexico's Chaco Canyon. At its architectural peak in the twelfth century, Pueblo Bonito stood five stories high. Although these cylinder jars were unique to Chaco Canyon, they reflect a deeply rooted emphasis on and preference for geometric shape and design. Collection American Museum of Natural History, H/3521

A bolo tie entitled "Twin Towers" (left) by Mary Tafoya (Santo Domingo Pueblo) and a cross pendant (right) by Joseph Chama (Santo Domingo Pueblo) use ancient mosaic-based aesthetics to express new ideas and beliefs with new techniques. Length of bolo tie, 2¾". 2003. Bolo: serpentine, jet, spiny oyster shell, turquoise, pipestone, lapis lazuli. Cross pendant: gaspeite, clamshell, melon shell. 2000. Collection Museum of Native American Jewelry, Albuquerque, New Mexico

Thunderbird necklace. Artist unknown (Santo Domingo Pueblo). Necklaces of this type are also known by the misnomer "Depression" necklaces and were made from the late 1920s to the late 1950s. Throughout the time of their manufacture as tourist items, low-cost materials such as bone, gypsum, and plastics were used for the mosaics in addition to natural turquoise, and the thunderbird pendants were strung with glass, bone, or gypsum and occasionally glass trade beads rather than shell (*heishi*) beads. They were made before the pueblo had electricity and so were constructed completely by hand. Collection Museum of Native American Jewelry, Albuquerque, New Mexico

Katsina bracelet. Lee Yazzie
(Navajo). In this tour-de-force
piece, Yazzie has painted with
stone a realistic image of a
katsina dancer in motion.
Bisbee turquoise, jade, coral,
mammoth ivory, Acoma jet,
ironwood, serpentine, 14-karat
gold. 1980–1983. Width,
3⅛". Collection Donald Mundy
and Tanner's Indian Arts,
Gallup

Top:
A Zuni jeweler uses a pump drill to create beads. American Museum of Natural History, 280300

Bottom:
Navajo mother and child at Ganado, Arizona. Photo by Joseph K. Dixon, Wanamaker Expedition, 1913. American Museum of Natural History, 317002

built in each pueblo were reestablished, and many Pueblos took the name of their patron saint. Since that time Spanish villages and the Pueblos have existed side by side, and their mutual influence over the centuries has given northern New Mexico its distinctive character.

Today's Pueblo and Navajo People

Collectively known as Pueblo Indians, the inhabitants of the stone and adobe pueblos along the upper Rio Grande and west to Zuni and Hopi speak several distinct languages and differ in architecture, ceremonialism, and material culture. However, they have many similar characteristics that include making pottery, farming corn, and living in rectangular, contiguously built stone or adobe villages (in Spanish, "pueblos") centered on plazas.

Spirituality is not a separate body of thought and practice; it permeates all of life. For these farmers in the desert, prayer for rain is a primary focus of ceremonialism. All of today's Pueblo Indians believe in katsinas, benevolent spirit beings that visit the people as both clouds and masked dancers. Katsinas can bring rain, provided that people have concentrated on thoughts of goodness and balance and have followed proper protocols and rituals through elaborate ceremonial dances.

Pueblo dances are strictly choreographed ritual events sometimes involving hundreds of dancers, filling the plaza with motion. Movements are subtle and constrained, each person matching in rhythm and action the dancers next to them. Drummers and singers keep the base tempo as attendant priests oversee protocol and maintain overall decorum, sometimes adjusting an individual costume or retrieving a dropped necklace. Elaborate costumes of embroidered kilts, body paint, shell and turquoise jewelry, dewclaw rattles, bandoliers of olivella shell, and flat painted headdresses called *tablitas* contribute to an abundant mass of color and sound. Everything about these ceremonial dances—the songs, regalia, and movement

Top:
Detail of finished *heishi* neck-
lace beside the raw material,
olivella shells. Necklace by
Martine Lovato (Santo Domingo
Pueblo). Collection Museum
of Native American Jewelry,
Albuquerque, New Mexico

Bottom:
Inlaid shells. Ava Marie Coriz
(Santo Domingo Pueblo). (Left)
The artist kept one half of this
spiny oyster shell in its natural
state while inlaying the other
half. (Right) A fully finished
inlay piece is part of a series
entitled "Gifted Hands." Spiny
oyster shells, turquoise, jet,
mother-of-pearl. 2001. Height
of shell on left, 4¼". Collection
Museum of Native American
Jewelry, Albuquerque, New
Mexico

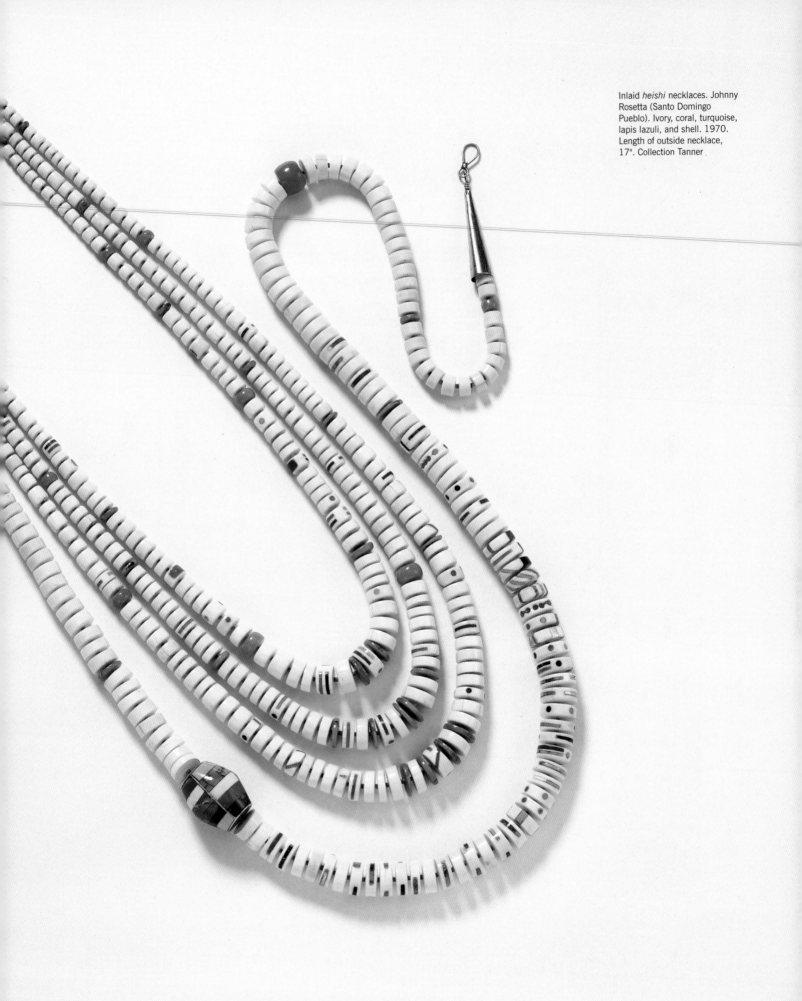

Inlaid *heishi* necklaces. Johnny
Rosetta (Santo Domingo
Pueblo). Ivory, coral, turquoise,
lapis lazuli, and shell. 1970.
Length of outside necklace,
17". Collection Tanner

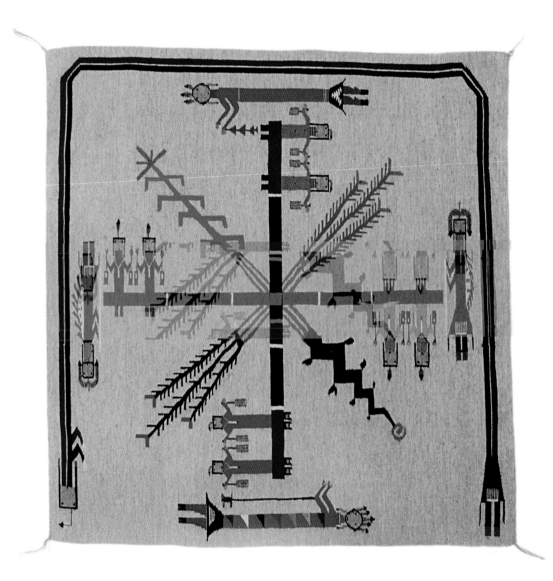

A modern-day Navajo rug
depicts a traditional sand-
painting. Karrie Tellman
(Navajo). Wool. 21st century.
Width, 47¾". Collection
American Museum of Natural
History, 50.2/6843

Historic Navajo bowguard (*ketoh*) of cast silver set with turquoise. A bowguard's original purpose was to protect the wrist while using a bow and arrow. Today, bowguards are worn as part of ceremonial regalia and for special occasions. Silver, turquoise, leather. Length of silver, 2¾". Collection Eleanor Tulman Hancock

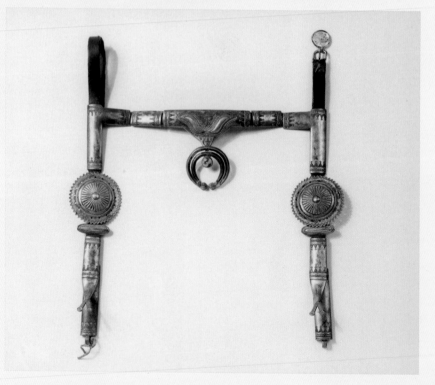

Top:
A Navajo silversmith sits at an outdoor work area near Bluff, Utah. A child operates the bellows on a small forge used to melt silver. 1897. American Museum of Natural History, 125040

Bottom:
Elaborately decorated horse bridle with a *naja*, a crescent-shaped central ornament. The naja was brought to the New World by the Spanish who had adopted it from the Moors during the Moors' occupation of Spain. The Navajo may have adopted the naja directly from the Spanish or indirectly from Plains groups who used similar adornment. Silver and leather. Ca. 1900. Width, 15½". Collection The Heard Museum

—constitutes a communal prayer. At Zuni and Hopi ceremonies, katsinas dance as the people respectfully and prayerfully watch. Along the Rio Grande, where Spanish missionaries forbade traditional practices, the Pueblos continued the rituals covertly. Among the Rio Grande villages today, the secrecy continues, and the katsina ceremonies are extremely private.

Today there are eighteen Pueblo villages along the Rio Grande and its western tributaries, the Rio Puerco and the Rio Jemez. In eleven of the villages, the people speak three different but related languages of the Kiowa-Tanoan language group: Tiwa (at Taos, Picuris, Sandia, and Isleta); Tewa (at San Juan, Santa Clara, San Ildefonso, Pojoaque, Nambé, and Tesuque), and Towa (Jemez Pueblo alone). At Santo Domingo, San Felipe, Cochiti, Santa Ana, Zia, Laguna, and Acoma, the people speak the Keresan language. Two Pueblos lie farther west, across the Continental Divide: Zuni Pueblo, whose members speak a language unrelated to any other living group; and the Hopi, who live in twelve separate villages and speak a Uto-Aztecan language related to tribes to the north and south.

At Hopi, the katsinas arrive from their home in the San Francisco Peaks near Flagstaff to live with the people for half of the year. Arriving at *Soyalangw,* the Winter Solstice ceremony, and departing around July during *Niman,* the Home Dance, the katsinas bring blessings and reminders of proper living.

At Zuni, the early winter *Shalako* ceremony is one of the most impressive ceremonies. At newly built houses throughout the community, 12-foot-tall, bird-like Shalako katsinas dance back and forth throughout the night, snapping their large, articulated beaks, while Mudheads, distinctive katsinas with red body paint and knobbed heads, dance in attendance. Drummers and singers maintain a powerful rhythm, while visitors come and go through the night, sharing a feast of mutton stew.

The Rio Grande Pueblos have numerous ceremonies throughout the year, some timed with and in celebration of Roman Catholic events. Each Pueblo celebrates its patron saint's day, and there is much activity around Christmas. Among the Tewa and Keresan villages, society is divided into two halves, or moieties. The Winter and Summer people (Tewa) and Turquoise and Squash People (Keresan), dance in alternate groups in the plaza to pray for rain, to celebrate the patron saint, and to thank the spirits for a harvest.

Traditionally, the Navajos live spread out across the landscape in matrilineal extended-family groups or "outfits." The traditional home is the hogan, an octagonal or conical structure constructed of logs or stone and sometimes plastered over with mud. Today many Navajos have opted for the convenience of conventional housing or mobile homes, but often a hogan is maintained for the elders or for ceremonies. The Navajo reservation is the largest in the United States, covering much of northeast Arizona, northwest New Mexico, and a small part of southern Utah. The Navajo population is the fastest-growing of all Native American groups, numbering almost 300,000.

Navajo belief and ceremonies emphasize individual health and prosperity. Medicine people communicate with the supernatural Holy People through elaborate ceremonies known as chants, sings, or ways, as in the Blessingway or Nightway, in which the *yé'ii* figure prominently. Sandpaintings are temporary representations of holy beings or supernatural events, created by medicine people on hogan floors with dry, powdered minerals. These sacred paintings aid in the healing process.

Closely related to the Navajos, the various Apache groups (Jicarilla, Mescalero, Chiricahua, Western, and Lipan) all speak similar Athapaskan languages. Unlike the Navajos—whose economy was dominated by animal husbandry (sheep, goats, horses, and some cattle) by the nineteenth century—most Apaches traditionally retained a hunting-gathering lifestyle, though the Western

This page, top:
A Navajo woman silversmith works inside a log hogan, filing cast silver conchos. Although it was not common for women to work silver, female silversmiths began to earn money from their craft by the early 1900s. Photo by Laura Gilpin. A Navaho Girl Silversmith [Pine Springs, Arizona] P1979.128.134. Gelatin silver print, 1952. © 1979 Amon Carter Museum, Fort Worth, Texas, bequest of the artist

This page, bottom:
Ambrose Roanhorse with his class at Fort Wingate School. Many fine jewelers studied silversmithing at this school east of Gallup, New Mexico, including Kenneth Begay, Lee Yazzie, and Jesse Monongya. Photo by Laura Gilpin. Class in Silver-Smithing, Fort Wingate Vocational School [New Mexico] P1979.128.410. Gelatin silver print, January 25, 1955. © 1979 Amon Carter Museum, Fort Worth, Texas, bequest of the artist

Opposite page:
Navajo squash blossom necklace with a cast naja. The squash blossom necklace was developed during the 1880s, and its distinctive flaring bead was likely based on Spanish-Mexican decorations that were inspired by pomegranate blossoms. Each bead was formed by doming two pieces of silver into cup shapes and then soldering the halves together. The Navajo word for the squash blossom literally translates as "bead which spreads out" (Adair, 44). This particular necklace was said to have been ordered by Chee Dodge from his close friend Slender Maker of Silver and was worn by Chee Dodge's daughter, Annie Wauneka (Lauris Phillips: personal communication, 2004). Silver, turquoise. 1885–1890s. Total length, 28". Collection Lauris Phillips

One of the most distinctive pieces of Southwestern jewelry is the concho belt. The concho, from the Spanish word for shell, was adopted by the Navajo from Plains Indian hair adornments. The earliest belts, dating before the 1880s, were of simple silver round or oval plaques decoratively stamped along the edges and having an opening through which a leather strap could be laced. When metal stamps came into use in the 1880s, decoration of each concho became more elaborate and included repoussé to create patterns of relief. At this time, a metal bracket was soldered to the back of each concho for attachment to the leather. Between the 1880s and 1890s, silversmiths began to set turquoise in the center of each concho, and often an additional decorative piece of silver was placed between conchos (Adair, 30–32).

a) 1868–1870s. Length of concho on right, $3\frac{11}{16}$". b) 1880s. c) 1880s. d) 1925–35. Collection Lauris Phillips

a

b

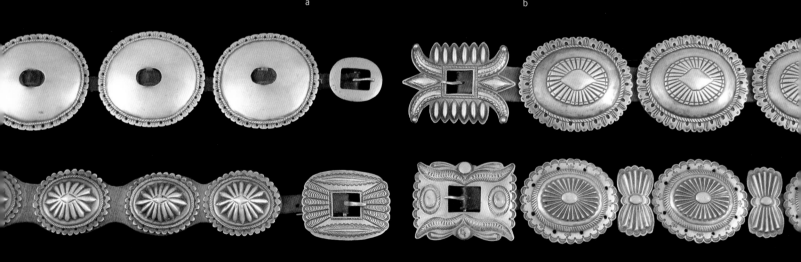

c

d

Three Navajo silver bracelets.
a) 1895–1900. Height, 1⅛".
b) 1900–1910. c) 1890s–
1910. Collection Lauris
Phillips

a

b

c

Bracelet. Fred Peshlakai,
(Navajo). Fred Peshlakai
learned the art of silversmithing from his father
Slender Maker of Silver, one
of the earliest silversmiths.
Peshlakai was the first
silversmith to sign his work,
and that was usually at the
request of a customer, a trader,
or for a juried show. He was
known for his use of excellent
turquoise, traveling to mines
to personally select stones,
which he cut and polished
himself, a rare practice for
silversmiths. For about twenty
years, Peshlakai ran a shop
in Los Angeles in an area
specializing in Mexican tourist
crafts, and through this period,
his jewelry developed a
Mexican character (Lauris J.
Phillips: personal communication, 2004). Silver, turquoise.
Width, 1⅜". Collection Lauris
Phillips

Apaches especially also took up corn planting. Apache ceremonies are typified by the *Gan,* or Mountain Spirits, and by the female puberty rites.

Art Style

In the Southwest, which includes vast territories and diverse peoples, there is no cohesive art style to parallel the strength and unity of the Northwest Coast's formline art. Styles have varied through time from region to region and from group to group. However, it can be said that there is an emphasis on geometric shapes and patterning that echo the angularity of the landscape itself. In prehistory, styles reached across broad areas and tended to change slowly. As the Pueblo people drew together in the 1400s to live where they do today, communities developed their own identifiable styles influenced by their particular histories, beliefs, and lifeways. More recently, the idiosyncrasies of historical influence such as the trading post system and the marketplace created by Southwest tourism influenced even more distinctive styles. This holds true throughout the arts—basketry, pottery, carving, weaving, and jewelry.

The History of Southwestern Jewelry

Turquoise and shell have been important in Southwestern jewelry and ceremonialism since antiquity. Archaeological evidence shows that shell, including Olivella, Glycymeris, and Conus, was imported from the Pacific coast along ancient trade routes. Usually arriving as raw material, it was worked by grinding, polishing, incising, and drilling with stone tools. Ancient Southwest jewelry forms included beads, pendants, bracelets, rings, earrings, and hair ornaments. Mosaics were created by gluing pieces of turquoise with pine pitch to wood, shell, and clay. Turquoise is found throughout the Southwest, but the most spectacular collections were discovered in Chaco Canyon, a shallow, sandstone drainage in what is today northwest New Mexico. In excavated rooms and burials at Pueblo Bonito and other large sites in

Chaco Canyon, enormous quantities of turquoise were found in both raw and finished states, suggesting that Chaco was a production and redistribution center for the nearest source, the Cerrillos mines one hundred miles to the east, south of current Santa Fe. Turquoise and shell beads were sealed up in wall niches in the kivas (ceremonial rooms), evidence that their presence and use had a sacred significance beyond mere beauty. Long into historic times, the Cerrillos mines remained an important source for turquoise, the major material for jewelers at Santo Domingo and other Rio Grande pueblos.

Use of and references to shell and turquoise throughout Pueblo and Navajo beliefs indicate these materials' major significance in cosmology and spirituality. Ancient Hohokam shell jewelry carved into elaborate water forms such as lizards and frogs suggests significant symbolic connections of shell to water. Today at Zuni Pueblo, ground turquoise is added to cornmeal for use in prayers. And a passage from the Navajo creation myth connects natural materials to the mechanics of the supernatural world: "Along the circumference [where the sky meets the earth] . . . sixteen poles leaned toward a distant point in the sky where they all converged. Four of those poles were made of white shell. Four were made of turquoise. . . . Four were of haliotis [abalone] shell. And four were of red stone. It was along these various poles that [the Sun] made his way each day. . . ." (Zolbrod, p. 212–13).

With the exception of rare copper bells traded up from Mexico, metals such as brass, copper, silver, and gold were not used by Native peoples until the arrival of Spanish and Mexican colonists. From the late 1600s to the mid 1800s, the social environment throughout the Southwest was unstable and dangerous. Mexicans, Navajos, and other tribes, including those from the Plains, raided each other for goods and captives. The Navajos had been noted wearing silver, likely acquired from Hispano settlers or Plains tribes, since the late

a

b

c

d

e

f

g

h

Navajo silver pins showing
an assortment of decorative
techniques including stamping,
repoussé, and setting
turquoise. a) 1890s–1900.
Length, 1⅞". b) 1925.
c) 1890s. d) 1930s. e) 1880s.
f) 1930s. g) 1880s. h) Fred
Peshlakai, 1940s. Collection
Lauris Phillips

Opposite page:
Three pins (top to bottom)—
Sun Face, Dan Simplicio;
Butterfly, artist unknown;
Knifewing God, artist unknown.
Zuni Pueblo. At Zuni, jewelers
have developed several identifiable styles including the
popular mosaic work. Today
depictions of everything from
spirit beings to birds, bighorn
sheep, and cartoon characters
can be found crafted in turquoise, shell, jet, and other
stones. Mosaic work began in
the 1920s and was inspired
by prehistoric mosaic work
discovered by archaeologists
at the ancestral village of
Hawikku. Two mythological
beings often depicted are
Knifewing God, a winged
figure who can swoop down
to carry off young girls, and
Rainbow Man, who is associated with rain and the colors
of the heavens (Ostler, 88).
All are of silver, jet, turquoise,
shell. Width of Sun Face, 3".
Collection Eleanor Tulman
Hancock

Top:
Quail concho detail. Dennis
and Nancy Edaakie (Zuni).
This single concho is one of
many that make up a bird
concho belt. Delicate pieces
of stone and shell are inlaid
into silver to create a realistic
portrait of a quail. Silver,
turquoise, abalone, coral,
jet, shell. Diameter, 2⅛".
Challis L. Thiessen Collection

Left:
Rainbow Man pin. Attributed
to Leo Poblano (Zuni), father
of Veronica Poblano, (see
p. 186). Silver, turquoise,
shell, jet. Ca. 1930s. Length,
3¼". Collection Lauris Phillips

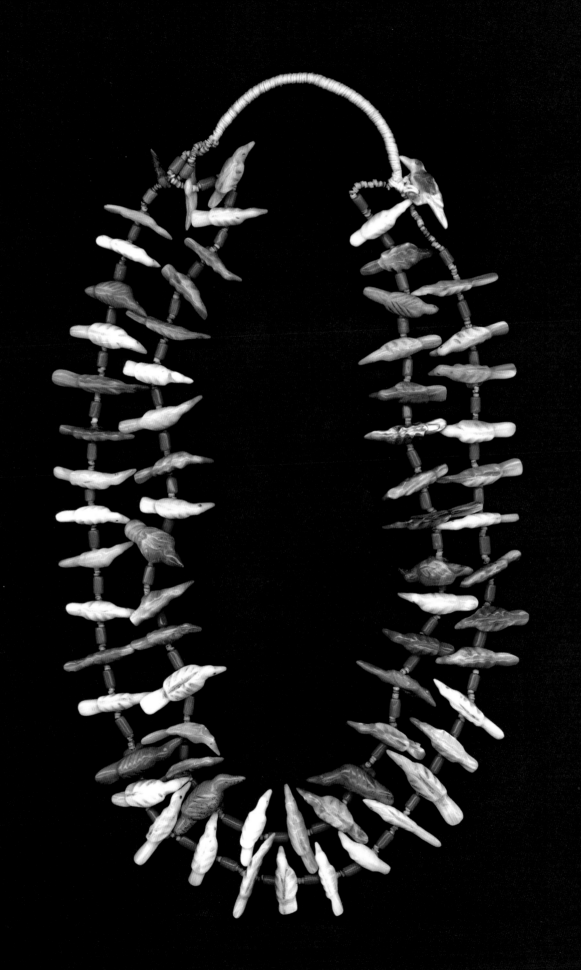

Opposite page:
Bird fetish necklace. Leekya Deyuse (Zuni). Leekya was considered one of the best carvers of stone and shell fetishes and was the first modern carver of fetishes for necklaces. Strung with coral beads, sixty-nine birds were individually carved and hand-drilled, a remarkable amount of work. Known as "perched birds," each sits on a small tab of stone through which a hole could be drilled more easily. Today, with electric drills, a hole is drilled through the body of the fetish. Abalone, shell, and coral. Ca. 1945. Length of each bird, approximately 1¼". Challis L. Thiessen Collection

This page:
Copper bracelets and bow-guard, some of the first pieces done as part of the G.I. Bill jewelry classes at Hopi. Bowguard (right) decorated with clouds and details of rainbird eyes, wings, and tails, is by Valjean Joshevema, 1949. Bowguard width, 2⁹⁄₁₆". Bracelet (left) is by Starlie Lomayaktewa, Jr. Ca. late 1940s. Bracelet (center) is by Franklin Namingha, Sr. Ca. late 1940s. All, collection Schaaf

eighteenth century. But it was not until 1850 that a Navajo man named Atsidi Sani, literally "Old Smith," learned metalwork. Grey Moustache, a silversmith taught by Atsidi Sani and a relative of his by marriage, tells how it first happened: "My grandmother told me that [Atsidi Sani] learned how to work with iron before [silver]. He learned how to do this from a Mexican by the name of Nakai Tsosi [Thin Mexican] who lived down near Mt. Taylor. . . . In those days the Navajo bought all of their bridles from the Mexicans, and Atsidi Sani thought that if he learned how to make them, the Navajo would buy them from him" (Adair, p. 4).

Atsidi Sani taught his sons and neighbors ironwork. In 1864, under political pressure, the United States army rounded up most of the Navajos and marched them to Fort Sumner along the Rio Grande in New Mexico, a tragic event known as the Long Walk. During their internment from 1864 to 1868, many Navajos died of disease, malnutrition, and, it is said, of heartbreak and hopelessness. Upon their release, they returned home, took up metalwork again, and Southwestern Indian jewelry as it is known today began.

Early Navajo silversmiths used American and then Mexican silver coins as their raw material, hammering them or melting them down to form bridles, bracelets, buttons, and earrings. Some early forms, such as the concho, were influenced by the Plains Indians who wore similar adornments of German silver (an alloy of silver and nickel) in their hair or as long "drops" from their belts.

The Navajo silversmith Grey Moustache remembers the early days of jewelry trade between the tribes: "The Hopi and the Zuni used to trade the Navajo turquoise and shell beads for silverwork. I used to make [bowguards—wide, braceletlike wrist protectors] for the Zuni, and I would trade one of those for a necklace of shell beads. I went down to Zuni several times each year to sell my silver. I had several friends there in the village. . . . I think those Zuni Indians got their turquoise out of old ruins. They had dark blue

stones that were finer than the stones you see nowadays" (Adair, p. 9).

A few years after the Navajos returned from Fort Sumner, Atsidi Chon, a silversmith from the Ganado area of Arizona, taught a Zuni man named Lanyade his techniques. Before the arrival of silverworking, Zunis had been well known for carving turquoise and other stones into small representations of animals called fetishes. Beginning in the 1920s, the two skills were combined to create jewelry of stone set in silver, depicting certain images such as the Knifewing God.

At Hopi, the first man to learn silversmithing was Sikyatala, who learned it by watching the Zuni silversmith Lanyade, during a visit Lanyade made to Hopi. At the pueblos along the Rio Grande, some individual artists also took up silversmithing, favoring things like the double-barred crosses with simple silver beads, which often represented rosaries (see page 181). However, silver did not have the same level of popularity along the Rio Grande that it did among the Navajo, Zuni, and Hopi. At Rio pueblos like Santo Domingo, artisans continued the ancient practice of making ground and polished turquoise beads and shell beads, which came to be known as *heishi*, the Keresan word for shell. The early silverwork from all groups included similar forms and styles, and it may be impossible to distinguish a given piece of this period as Zuni, Navajo, or Hopi.

In the 1880s, the railroad opened the west to tourism. People on the way west were fascinated by the desert expanses and by the Native American cultures. At the same time, traders and Native American craftspeople recognized a new way to earn cash by selling authentic items, formerly for personal use, as tourist souvenirs. Tourists saw the Native-made baskets, pottery, rugs, and especially jewelry as fascinating objects to take home to demonstrate one's interesting adventure in the "wild west."

The Fred Harvey Company, which facilitated tourism in the Southwest with its comfortable train

Top:
Following World War II, the G.I. training program for veterans helped sponsor a silversmithing course for veterans at the Hopi pueblos that began in early 1947. Out of this program came many new designs and techniques, most notably the overlay technique now considered so characteristically Hopi. Instructors Paul Saufkie (left) and Fred Kabotie (right) encouraged jewelers to look to traditional Hopi designs for inspiration. Courtesy of the Hopi Tribe Cultural Preservation Archives.

Bottom:
Bracelet and ring. Paul Saufkie (Hopi) and Fred Kabotie (Hopi) collaboration. According to scholar and owner Gregory Schaaf, with these pieces "they were trying to come up with a style of jewelry that would separate them from the Navajos and the Zunis. The bracelet features silver appliqué (on the side) and an area of Zuni-like stone mosaic. This bracelet was made during the time of the veterans classes." Silver, shell, turquoise, jet, and coral. Ca. late 1940s. Bracelet width, 1". Collection Schaaf

dining cars and its hotels, had made Indian silver available by buying pawned pieces from the traders for resale to the general public. But tourists tended to want jewelry that was lighter in weight than the heavy pieces the Navajo smiths made for themselves and for the Pueblo people. So in 1899 the Fred Harvey Company ordered lighter-weight silver made especially for the tourists with pre-cut stones ordered from a turquoise mine in Nevada, and Indian jewelry became a commercial enterprise.

So great was the popularity of Indian jewelry that by 1910 imitations were already being made by white workers in a Denver factory. The interest in and demand for Indian jewelry has continued steadily. Tourists today can buy jewelry in trading posts and galleries throughout the Southwest, and at more informal locations like roadside stands and the *portal*, or porch, at the Palace of the Governors on the plaza in Santa Fe, New Mexico. Juried shows—including Gallup Intertribal Ceremonial and especially Santa Fe Indian Market—continue to fuel an interest among collectors and to strengthen a commitment by many artists to create top-quality, high-end jewelry.

Today's Trends

Whereas the jewelers of the early 1900s showed great workmanship and developed beautiful styles based on traditional forms, beginning in the 1950s, individual craftspeople increasingly moved beyond convention to establish jewelry as a medium for personal creativity. Kenneth Begay, Charles Loloma, and Preston Monongye, among others, began to produce works that represented their own creative visions. This new, "contemporary" jewelry increasingly stretched the genre boundaries of local traditions. Exotic materials such as gold, ironwood, corals, sugilite, lapis lazuli, opals, and diamonds became part of the palette, but still the best work remains recognizably rooted in its original cultural forms, imagery, and in its emphasis upon the importance of high quality.

Today's Southwest jewelers—indeed, all Native people—live to varying degrees in two worlds: the world of traditional life and the modern world of a cash economy. Among the Pueblo Indians and Navajos, traditions and the arts were significantly altered by European colonization, but they maintain an unbroken tie with a rich past. Jewelers are significant contributors to that flow of knowledge. As Mike Bird-Romero expresses it: "I hope the young people that are coming up see older things and have the same impressions that I have. I hope they get the same kind of positive feelings from the old things so they can go forward and keep doing their best."

Necklace. Morris Robinson (Hopi). Silver and turquoise. Ca. 1940s. Pendant length, 1¾". Collection Schaaf

THE SOUTHWEST "PAINTERLY" STYLE AND ITS CULTURAL CONTEXT

Peter M. Whiteley

Looking at Native North American arts of the Southwest and Northwest, broadly speaking, we see a contrast between a "painterly" style, and a concern with colors on surfaces, in the former, versus an emphasis upon "carving" in the latter. Even the language Northwest Coast artists use to describe making jewelry—that they are silver or gold "carvers"—shows the sculptural emphasis of their work. These two different artistic approaches reflect certain generalities about personal and cultural identity in each area.

In her well-known book *Patterns of Culture*, published in the 1930s, Ruth Benedict famously contrasted Native Southwest and Northwest cultural styles as "Apollonian" and "Dionysian," respectively. Based on a psychoanalytic model of archetypes, such terms seem dated now, and the broad-brush psychological approach to culture-and-personality that preoccupied Benedict, Margaret Mead, and their mentor, Franz Boas, has receded from anthropological inquiry. Their old-fashioned character notwithstanding, Benedict's observations retain significant value.

Concentrating in the Southwest on Zuni Pueblo, but with Hopi and all the other Pueblos included by implication, Benedict emphasized the reserved style and conformism of the Apollonian sensibility. In contrast, the Kwakwaka'wakw of Vancouver Island embodied a Dionysian exuberance in their cultural forms, notably the potlatch. Benedict's ideas may plausibly be extended to the variation in artistic styles that we see between the two regions. These contrasts are not hard and fast, but rather pertain to general tendencies or orientations. If a Pueblo person is performing in a dance, for example, whether it be a social dance (like the Corn Dance of the Rio Grande Pueblos, or the Butterfly Dance at Hopi) or a religious ceremony (like a katsina dance), the dancer seeks to do what the script tells him to do. If you are dancing in a line, you want to maintain exactly the same tempo and perform in an identical way to the person in front of you. By doing so, your conformity with the group produces an overall intent toward ritual harmony and an image of collective beauty. In other words, beauty lies in the group working together. Hopis refer to this by the term *namit-nangwu*, which means "all our hearts working together in unity."

For the Pueblos, just as in the Northwest and in many other indigenous communities the world over, you are born into a community, and you grow up with people you will know until you die. As in any human community, conflicts arise— between families, individuals, or clans—and often play a significant part in ordinary social life. In a ceremony, on the other hand, the central desire is upon each person setting all conflict aside, and using his/her higher being to unite for the benefit of the community and indeed of the whole world (ceremonies not being parochial in their intent). Before a public ceremony, Hopis gather together to meditate, smoke, and pray in the kiva. In doing so, they seek to unite their thoughts and their hearts, so that the ceremony will succeed in producing the desired benefits—especially rain and snow so that

Corn Dancer-Early Morning Katsina bolo tie. Edward Beyuka (Zuni Pueblo). This ceremonial dance figure displays elements of a Zuni Corn Dancer and a Hopi Early Morning Katsina, with variations added "perhaps out of respect for sacred images" (Gregory Schaaf: personal communication, 2004). Silver, turquoise, coral, jet, mother-of-pearl, shell. Ca. 1970s. Height, 6" long. Collection Schaaf

the crops will grow, all creatures may drink, and all of life be sustained.

For the Pueblos, there is a deep sense of belonging to the community and attachment to a particular place. Hopis and Zunis, for example, both consider that they each live at the "center of the universe." The world is definitively ordered, by the four directions, the zenith, the nadir, and the most central place of all, the heart of the village in the plaza. Each of those directions is associated with the ordering of seasons, of celestial phenomena, topography (especially sacred mountains), flora, fauna, insect life, and minerals. And each direction has a specific color attached to it. So, for Zuni, north is associated with yellow, west with blue, south red, east white, the zenith multicolored, and the nadir with black. This general idea of direction-color association is something that all the Pueblos share, although the specific color-direction correlation varies among Pueblos. Pueblo people thus live in a highly ordered and structured cosmos. All ritual activities are performed according to a calendar determined by phases of the sun and moon. In this way, the community itself is harmonized with the larger organization of the cosmos.

The conformist, collectivist style in the Pueblo Southwest contrasts significantly with Northwest Coast ritual, noted for its exuberance and its celebration of individual status and achievement. Among Northwest Coast cultures, rituals concentrate on individual titles, ranks, names, and privileges. They are intended to broadcast the virtues and social standing of a particular individual and his or her family as these have been passed down from past to present. That kind of emphasis reflects a more rigidly hierarchical society, with ranked statuses from aristocrats and nobles, down to commoners and slaves.

This sense of individual title and rank is expressed in Northwest Coast cultures in many ways, including a "ritual forging of identity" onto the body.[*] Initiation ceremonies the world over frequently entail modification of the body, by cutting, burning, or perhaps penetration (e.g., of the nasal septum) by a bone point. We know that in the past, Northwest Coast people, especially the higher ranks of society, wore ornamentation that involved penetration of the body, by labrets, nose-rings, and especially tattooing. For Northwest Coast people, tattooing thus literally inscribes or "carves" individual identity—as part of a family, rank, or clan—onto the body (see Martine Reid's essay).

Archaeological and ethnographic evidence suggests that Pueblo peoples typically did not tattoo themselves. However they did, and still do, *paint* their bodies, their pottery, and their kiva murals, and weave color into their ceremonial clothing. In certain kinds of rituals, Pueblo performers paint themselves elaborately from head to toe, in multiple different, well-defined colors. The colors chosen are associated with the purposes of the particular ceremony, its time of year, the directional orientation, and so on. When painting on the body—whether the red and yellow of the Hopi *Wuwtsim* society, gray for the Antelope Society, blue and white for certain kinds of katsinas, or reddish brown for the Snake Society— each color has its significance and ritual value.

This system of colors comprises a language in itself, in which there are various media of communication—such as via the seven colors of corn that Hopis grow, the colors of different bird feathers, of flowers, or clouds, or of butterflies. Moreover, certain colors are associated with seasons. Some Hopi winter katsinas wear turquoise-dyed moccasins. You will never see summer katsinas wearing those turquoise moccasins, because the color is associated with the season and its particular ritual foci. Similarly, the Rio Grande Keresan Pueblos (like Santo

* The phrase is taken from Fitz John Poole, who uses it to describe the intent of ritual initiation in Papua New Guinea.

Top:
Kiva wall paintings like this one from the fifteenth-century ancestral Hopi site of Awat'ovi represent some of the first known depictions of katsinas. According to J.J. Brody, "The circular face, headdress, and staff held by the figure identify him as the *Ahul* [katsina] who appears at the *Powamu* ceremony to symbolize the coming of the sun" (p. 90). The katsina wears a beaded necklace and possibly armbands or body paint. A corn plant grows to his right. Courtesy of Peabody Museum, Harvard University, photo MR 266

Bottom:
Parrot bracelet. Manuel Hoyungwa (Hopi). Silver. Ca. 1980s. Width, 1⅝". Collection Schaaf

Top:
Replica painting by Paul Kay of a kiva wall painting at the fifteenth-century site of Pottery Mound in New Mexico. This female figure wears a style of dress still worn by Pueblo women today in ceremonies. "She stands framed by a terraced rainbow and has a macaw in her right hand and a painted bowl on her head. Dragonflies in the background, which symbolize water, suggest an outdoor environment" (Brody, 129). Courtesy of the Maxwell Museum of Anthropology, University of New Mexico, 76.44.744

Bottom:
Ho-ote Dance. Fred Kabotie (Hopi). Fred Kabotie (father of Michael Kabotie, see p. 176) was a painter, teacher, and designer. He painted many murals including one inside the Grand Canyon's Watchtower, designed by Mary Colter, architect for Fred Harvey. Watercolor. Ca. 1925. Collection Amerind Foundation, Inc. Photo courtesy Amerind Foundation, 2027 Amerind Foundation, Inc., Dragoon, Arizona, Accession No. 2027

Domingo) divide their whole society into two moieties, Turquoise and Squash (each with its own kiva), that run parallel to the similar division of the Tewa Pueblos (like San Juan) into Winter and Summer moieties. The "winter" value of turquoise and the corresponding "summer" value of red-yellow/squash are thus part of a symbolic language that cuts across all the Pueblos, even through their major ordinary-language differences.

Just as in speech constructed in ordinary conversation, ritual expressions of symbolic value through colors are transitory and linked to particular performances. In the kiva mural paintings of the 1400s, at pueblos like Pottery Mound or Awat'ovi, elaborate images of supernatural figures were painted in multiple colors (see pages 151 and 152). At the end of the ceremony for which the mural was painted, the images were covered over with whitewash. Then, the following year, as the time came for that ceremony to be performed again, the images were painted anew, and again covered over once the ceremony was finished. In the same way, at some Hopi villages today, all the plaza houses are whitewashed on the outside before the summer katsina ceremonies. If you ask, "Why do you do that if you are asking for rain?" the Hopis reply that they are "challenging" the clouds—which manifest the spirits of the ancestors and katsinas simultaneously—to bring their rain and wash off the newly painted walls. The same principle applies to the body paint of the dancers: the challenge is to the rain to come and wash off that beautiful, but temporary, ritual identity.

The regularity of the seasonal calendar has its counterpoint in the transitory quality of each ritual engagement: the entire emphasis is upon process and productiveness, rather than stasis and completion. The year itself changes and moves through phases with the seasons and the moons. For people following the ritual cycle, it is as if one's ceremonial identity shifts with those cycles too. One maintains a clear identity as a member of a clan, moiety, etc., but ceremonial identities

and roles attached to performances are impermanent. I think that emphasis on impermanence—upon the creative act of painting brilliance and meaning in an only transitory, evanescent manner, including onto the body—is pervasive in Pueblo consciousness.

The general contrast in the ways Northwest Coast peoples and Southwest peoples see the world and their place within it can also be seen in forms of personal names. In the Northwest, the social emphasis upon individuality is tied to the system of ranked statuses. Those statuses run through the generations, and individual identity is subject to reincarnation. In Tlingit thought, for example, one may only receive a name if the person who previously held it has passed away. People look for certain traits in a baby to see if that is the right person to inherit the name and its identity. It is as if, in the Tlingit world, there is a set dramatis personae, who, as individuals, reappear every generation or so onto the stage continuously acted on by the living.

At Hopi, on the other hand, names are not inherited and there is no parallel sense of reincarnation. Each name is a new poetic composition, and one received several names throughout life—each one "painting" a new identity-image onto the person, and displacing the former identification. Very often, Hopi name-images refer to color or to the appearance of color in motion. For example, Sakwwisnöm, a woman's name, literally means "blue in a line woman." The name refers to the appearance of shimmering color in a line of greasewood bushes blossoming in the valley, as seen from the top of a mesa. While English tends to focus on things, objects, and entities, the Hopi language emphasizes outlines, shapes, colors, movements, and processes. Everything about Hopi, from names to everyday conversations, picks out the colors of the world, their movement, shimmer, transformations at different times of day, and at different seasons of the year. Again, a name like Puhuve'yma, literally "newness going along," refers

Tufa-cast necklace with pendant. Preston Monongye (Mission Indian-Hopi) and Jesse Monongya (Navajo-Hopi). Bear paw and Long-Haired Katsina imagery merge in a pendant that dangles from a deeply textured cast and inlaid crescent. For the Hopi, the Long-Haired Katsina's beard and flowing hair symbolize rain. 1977–1978. Pendant length, 2½". Private collection to a butterfly newly emerged from its chrysalis going along with freshly decorated, colorful wings.

Since meaning in the Pueblo world is created through the dialogue and counterpoint of colors, images, and cycles, we begin to see why Southwest jewelry is characterized by this "painterly" aesthetic. In the Southwest, color is a primary mode of visual expression. In the instance of Hopi silver overlay, where color is absent, the painterly approach may still be seen in the juxtaposition of light and dark, background and foreground. This contrast is a strong principle that runs throughout pottery designs, murals, and textiles too. The popularity of silver among Hopis—and indeed, until recently, a relative distaste for gold—indicates an aesthetic value placed upon mirror surfaces that reflect the colors of the world. The use of silver in jewelry represents a definite innovation, a painting with reflected light. But in retaining the same aesthetic principles as occur in Hopi weaving, basketry, or pottery, the transfer onto jewelry is simply a translation of preexisting artistic forms into another genre.

In Pueblo jewelry, when the artist uses particular symbols from the natural word—animals, footprints, insects, water forms, and lightning— the image represents an excerpt from a story. If a Hopi artist uses the image of a particular species or element—a reed, bear, badger, the sun, a spider, a butterfly—it has specific associations, with both clan identities and mythological narratives. The reed, for example, is the element through which Hopis ascended into this current "fourth world" or phase of life, from below. Any image of a reed that an artist of the Reed clan depicts on a piece of jewelry always has a broader resonance: the reed is never merely a picture of a reed, but the reed-image itself evokes a multi-layered metaphorical context. Similarly, any reference to a butterfly also refers to the Butterfly clan, to the "butterfly maidens" (the term for adolescent girls characterized by their "butterfly whorl" hairdos, representing the stage of life before adult

womanhood), and to the process of pollination and fertility in plant cultivation. All natural species and the celestial elements are, as the French anthropologist Claude Lévi-Strauss famously put it, "good to think." The ordered and classified natural world serves, like the colors of this defined world, as a fund of metaphors for expressing meaning and value beyond their immediate context.

Perhaps the most emphatic expression of the painterly style is Zuni stone inlay. The works of master Zuni inlay artists, like Dan Simplicio, Leo Poblano, Dennis Edaakie, and Frank Vacit, "paint" representational colored imagery onto a silver background. And with some formal differences, this same style in the use of color and imagery reappears strongly in the work of Charles Loloma, Preston Monongye, Lee Yazzie, Jesse Monongya, and the many artists each has influenced. Jewelry produces somewhat greater permanence—as on a bracelet or necklace—than the older artistic genres. But just like a name or a dance, the jewelry often excerpts an image or condenses a story from the vast array of poetic and dramatic imagery of nature and the supernatural world that continues to animate Pueblo and Navajo sensibilities in the twenty-first century.

SOUTHWEST MASTERS

KENNETH BEGAY

Navajo (Diné)

Born in 1913 in a remote part of the Navajo Reservation, Kenneth Begay was raised in the traditional Navajo way. Kenneth's son Harvey Begay remembers, "My grandfather was a medicine man who specialized in the Beauty Way. As a child, my father helped him as a 'gofer' and did not go to school until he was twelve years old. Even when our family lived off the reservation, my father would keep jars of native herbs and other ceremonial objects. He used the herbs when family members got ill, and he always used the same medicine man for the healing ceremonies, Mr. Black Hat, who had been an apprentice of my grandfather's."

Kenneth attended the Fort Wingate Indian Boarding School near Gallup, New Mexico. He had already learned black-smithing from an uncle back home. At school he continued with a blacksmithing class and took an interest in their silver-smithing class as well. The teachers at Fort Wingate, one of whom was Fred Peshlakai, recognized that Kenneth had unusual abilities and fostered his talent.

For a short time after graduating, Kenneth made jewelry for tourists at the Grand Canyon. But once he married and had children, the family wanted something more stable, and they moved to Flagstaff where Kenneth worked for the Babbitt Brothers shop. While in Flagstaff Kenneth met John Bonnell, and with Kenneth's cousin, Allen Kee, the three men started the White Hogan, an Indian craft shop eventually located in Scottsdale, Arizona.

While working with the White Hogan, Kenneth refined a distinctive and innovative style based on clean lines, boldness of form, and repeated motifs to create elegant patterns. He was a master of silver flatware and beautifully decorated silver boxes. As early as 1951, Kenneth brought nontraditional materials such as ironwood into his jewelry palette.

Kenneth Begay taught silversmithing at Navajo Community College from the late 1960s to the early seventies; one of his students during that time was James Little. Through his innovative styles and great creativity, Kenneth opened new avenues for jewelry as an art form. Kenneth Begay died in 1977, but his influence continues in the generations of silversmiths who have been inspired by his work to pursue their own creative visions. His contributions to the art form have led many to call him the "father of contemporary Navajo jewelry."
KARI CHALKER

Silver bowguard. Kenneth Begay (Navajo). The traditional bowguard takes on a new look with Begay's simple, elegant style and innovative approach of repeated polished swirls. Length, 2¾". Collection Dr. and Mrs. E. Daniel Albrecht

Opposite page:
A 1974 photo of Kenneth Begay outside a ceremonial hogan he built near his modern home twenty miles southwest of Ganado, Arizona, on the Navajo Reservation. He is pictured standing within several hundred feet of where he was born and is now buried.

160   PRESTON MONONGYE

Mission Indian and Hopi

Preston Monongye (1927–1987), of Mission Indian and Mexican heritage, was brought to the Hopi Reservation as a young boy. Adopted into the Monongye family, he lived the Hopi way and participated in traditional Hopi ceremonies, frequently mirrored in his art. Involved in the Katsina Society, he incorporated much katsina imagery in his work. Described by Indian arts trader Joe Tanner as a "great warehouse of ideas," Preston Monongye was a sculptor, painter, potter, and jeweler. "Our art, as in non-Indian art, takes form from what we see today," said Monongye. "We may use old techniques, along with old designs taken from potsherds or pictographs, but then we re-design them or add innovations of our own and we have 'the new Indian art.'"

Apprenticing with his uncle, Hopi silversmith Gene [Nuvahoyiwma], at the age of nine, Monongye helped melt down the silver Mexican pesos and American coins then used in Southwestern silverwork. When he began making jewelry after World War II, it was Indian arts trader Roman Hubbell who encouraged him. Artistically and technically innovative, Monongye was best known for his tufacast silver jewelry combining a variety of finishes in bold designs and colors. Although capable of fine stone inlay, Preston preferred to concentrate on metalwork, and have the stones set by others. Some of his finest collaborative efforts were achieved with Lee Yazzie for Joe Tanner in Gallup, New Mexico. . . . Monongye's son Jesse Lee [Monongya] also assisted his father with stone inlay. LOIS S. DUBIN

Excerpted with permission from "North American Indian Jewelry and Adornment: From Prehistory to the Present" by Lois S. Dubin.

Bracelets. Preston Monongye (Mission Indian-Hopi) and Jesse Monongya (Navajo-Hopi) collaboration. These bracelets show Preston Monongye's heavily textured style and his inclination to have others do the stone inlay work. In both bracelets, Jesse Monongya did the lapidary work. (Top) Jesse describes the geometric design as "the spirit going upward with prayer." Turquoise, coral, Acoma jet, shell, silver. 1967–77. Private collection. (Bottom) The design represents stylized corn. Turquoise, coral, jet, shell, dolomite, silver. 1976–77. Width, 1½". Collection Mary Ann Abrams

Opposite page:
Preston Monongye at his workbench, 1975. Photo courtesy Heard Museum

Charles Loloma (1921–1991) grew up with traditional Hopi parents. As a member of the Badger Clan, Loloma (Hopi for "Many Beautiful Colors") was involved in ceremonial life in his village of Hotvela at Third Mesa. Trained in painting at Hopi and in ceramics at Alfred University in New York, Charles turned to silverwork in the 1950s, combining elements of his Hopi background with a contemporary sense of aesthetics.

As a boy, Charles watched his grandfather pour molten silver into sandstone molds to create buckles, conchos, and bracelets. Charles saw beauty in the roughness of the local sandstone and later incorporated texture into his designs by casting pieces in tufa-stone molds and purposely not buffing the final piece smooth. Echoing local rock formations and mesas, he used vertical slabs of turquoise, coral, and ironwood to construct bracelets and pendants. One of his trademarks was to use casting imperfections to his design advantage, allowing an unintentional hole to become the focal point of a piece.

Loloma's jewelry illustrates his remarkable ability to blend traditional and contemporary aesthetics. His patterns recall the geometric richness of ancient pueblo walls and sandstone mesas chiseled by geologic time. Yet Loloma also believed that jewelry was meant to be worn and must work with the body. His sense of balance therefore extended beyond aesthetics into weight, proportion, and comfort.

A secret inner composition, known only to the wearer, is a mark of Loloma's work. Though not visible when worn, an interior mosaic is just as meticulously crafted as the exterior design. Robert Rhodes, an educator and the husband of Verma Nequatewa, who is Charles' niece and was his assistant for twenty-three years, explains: "Charles used to talk about the inside inlay of a bracelet or the inlay on the back side of a pendant as 'inner gems.' He said that what is inside a person is often different than what shows on the outside. The inner gems of jewelry play to the inner gems of a person. We don't always have to show everyone all of what we are. We can share these elements with those we wish. But even if we never show the inside, we know beauty is there and it makes us better."[1] LOIS S. DUBIN

Excerpted with permission from "Jesse Monongya: Opal Bears and Lapis Skies" by Lois S. Dubin.

1. Robert Rhodes, letter to the author, August 1, 1994.

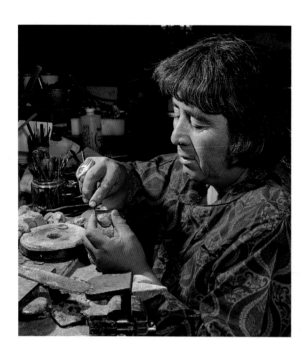

162 **CHARLES LOLOMA**

Hopi

This page, right:
Bracelet. Charles Loloma (Hopi). In this tufa-cast bracelet, Loloma used a flaw in the casting process as a window to reveal the inlaid interior of the bracelet. Loloma's niece Verma Nequatewa (see page 174) often collaborated with him, doing the inlay on this and other pieces. Turquoise, coral, lapis lazuli, silver. Early 1970s. Height, 1⅞". Collection Hopi Tribe

Height bracelet. Charles Loloma (Hopi). Always one to push style boundaries, Loloma took the idea of inlay with stone to the extreme, setting vertical columns of ironwood and stone at varying heights, echoing the angular Southwest landscape. Turquoise, ironwood, coral, fossilized ivory, silver. Ca. 1970s. Height, 3". Collection Daune and Austin Turner

SOUTHWEST CONTEMPORARY ARTISTS

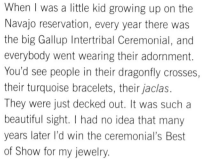

166

JESSE MONONGYA

Navajo (Diné) and Hopi
Water Flow Clan
Scottsdale, Arizona

When I was a little kid growing up on the Navajo reservation, every year there was the big Gallup Intertribal Ceremonial, and everybody went wearing their adornment. You'd see people in their dragonfly crosses, their turquoise bracelets, their *jaclas*. They were just decked out. It was such a beautiful sight. I had no idea that many years later I'd win the ceremonial's Best of Show for my jewelry.

Being raised by my grandmother, I learned so much about the turquoise and how it was part of the Navajo prayers. The turquoise is just not skin deep. As my grandmother would tell me, it's the center of our hearts and our souls. Things that are blue are associated with the water and with the cleansing of our soul. Even with the sweat lodges, they are more than just for hygiene, they are spiritual. It's a cleansing of the spirit. When I was growing up, the elder Navajos were so disciplined with the ceremonies. And I always respected that. I think a lot of my strength comes from that, from growing up with the discipline of the elders.

I went to boarding school, where I got kicked out of silversmithing class. I was messing around with the torch too much, heating up my friends' seats, stuff like that. I didn't know my dad, Preston Monongye, until after I came home from the Marines and Vietnam. Then I looked for him and found him. I didn't know he was a famous jeweler already. I'd watch him work, doing his silversmithing, but at first I didn't really have any interest in it.

Then I had a dream that my mother found me—I never knew my mother either—but in my dream she found me and told me that I would become a famous jeweler. It was like a lightning bolt hit me. And I looked at my dad's work again, and it seemed like I knew what I was doing already, right off the bat. So I worked with him a while, and then I started entering competitions, and I won . . . beat my father and some of the other big-name guys. So that's how it started. My dad influenced me a lot. He was a true artist; he could design anything. I admired that. He wasn't a good father, but he was a great artist.

My grandmother had taught me at an early age to pray every morning. She used to wake me up at five in the morning, get me out—the wind blowing, snowing, whatever —and take me out to pray with her. So one day, I was maybe thirteen years old, I said, "Grandma, I got an idea. Why don't we pray inside where it's nice and warm?" Of course, it never worked out that way.

You see a lot when you live like that . . . the sunrise, the stars, the moon. I was raised in a log hogan. It's shaped like an octagon, and on top there's an opening for the smoke to go out. At night I used to look out that hole and see the stars, the Big Dipper, and shooting stars. When you're on the reservation, you feel like you can touch the stars because they're so close and they're so bright. We slept on sheepskin bedding on the floor. And you never get away from the wonderful smells—of the earth, and the pine, and the cedar bark that we put between the logs. I always thought it was a beautiful way to live. That's all in my work.

When I first started with the jewelry, I reached back to my grandmother's teachings about the prayers and the four sacred colors. I like those colors so I use a lot of turquoise, and yellow, black, and white. I would dream the colors, and I would wake up in the middle of the night and draw it out.

And then I started dreaming big-time— 18-karat, 22-karat. I wanted to move on to really good, expensive materials. It took a long time to establish that. My customers are part of what pushed me. They've requested the best of stones from all over the world, like Lander Blue turquoise, opals, Tahitian black pearls, and diamonds.

I make a lot of jewelry with images of Monument Valley. It's fascinating to me . . . the color in those rocks changes from early morning till night. I think what brought me to Monument Valley was that it was a challenge. It was a challenge for me to try to match what God mastered and to match those color combinations. And part of being able to do that was getting successful enough that I could afford to buy the most expensive corals—orange, angel-skin color, and dark red. There's such a range of color

Turtle bracelet (two views, this page and next). Jesse Monongya (Navajo-Hopi). In this example of jewelry engineering and use of the finest materials, the turtle revolves and its hinged shell opens (see next page). 18-karat gold, coral, lapis lazuli, turquoise, dolomite, opal, Acoma jet, shell, malachite. 1997. Diameter of turtle, 2". Private collection

Turtle bracelet (this page and previous). Jesse Monongya (Navajo-Hopi). The turtle's hinged shell opens to reveal an inlaid Sun Face and an image of the Hopi Two Horn Priest Katsina in gold overlay. 18-karat gold, coral, lapis lazuli, turquoise, dolomite, opal, Acoma jet, shell, malachite. 1997. Diameter of turtle, 2". Private collection

in the corals from the different continents that I can pretty much match the landscape, and it's a challenge for me.

I'm a nostalgic person. I have goats and sheep in my backyard in the middle of Scottsdale. They remind me of things that were instilled in me as a little kid . . . we had about 400 head of sheep and goats and horses, and we'd take them all up into the Chuska Mountains when we'd migrate in the summer. It was a beautiful life, an awesome life. We hunted deer and wild turkeys, and we never wasted an animal just to be killing it. If you stay with the traditional ways, it brings so much to your life. The old ways, the prayers, thinking about the sacred colors—it all makes you more balanced in the world. For me and my art, it's important to reach back to my tradition. I don't think I'd be a complete artist unless I had learned to pray with the older people and to respect the way they think. If I didn't have the traditional upbringing, the colors wouldn't come to me and I don't think I'd be a jeweler today.

In the old days, the Navajos did squash blossom necklaces and different kinds of silverwork. So that was identified with the Navajos. The Zunis did stone inlay pictures of hummingbirds and cardinals and sun gods. The Hopis did all the overlay in the silver. So at that time, everybody was identified with a certain style. When people saw my work in the late 1970s, they would say, "Your work looks like Zuni. Are you Zuni?" And I'd say, "No, I'm Jesse Monongya." What had happened was Preston Monongye, Charles Loloma, Kenneth Begay, Lee Yazzie—all these great artists—had changed the whole scene around so that it was your own identity that people saw. They saw you as an individual artist. Because of them, the art gave me my own path.

And the art has kept me alive. I lost my daughter, Stephanie, a year ago, and the whole world seemed to be black. Things got dark, and finally now that cloud is starting to leave. But one thing I had to do again was to get up early in the morning, and go out and pray again. It's really helped me to rebound and create good pieces

again. And I have so many collectors who are really friends. I have orders for jewelry that will probably last me another twenty years because they knew I was hurting, and they understood that I needed to work.

I've always felt that I was given this opportunity—this ability. Knowing that I have a purpose in life is what's kept me going. A lot of time I get sidetracked, and it's my art—my jewelry—that brings me back to focus. Because of that I can always go back to the center and pick up the pieces again. To be able to create things has helped me reach the inner soul of myself and has kept me alive. I don't know where I would be if I didn't have this art.

Reaching out to other people, other clans, and other tribes, and respecting their ceremonies and appreciating what they bring into the world, that's important. When we met the Northwest Coast people of the Haida Nation, we didn't really know anything about them other than what you can learn reading books and magazines. But when they came down to visit us in the Southwest, it was like finding a friend that you haven't seen in a long time. Right from the start we felt we had something in common. The market for Northwest Coast art is not as big as ours in the Southwest yet, but their artistry is amazing. There's so much talent built into the Haida Nation, it's incredible.

While we were there, there was a funeral, a memorial service for one of the elders. We were made to feel welcome as special guests, and it was just a breathtaking experience. What's etched in my mind forever was the way our Haida friends went through their grieving process. The deceased belonged to the Eagle Clan, and they carved a mask that looked just like him but with a beak. This masked person danced and walked around between the loved ones. The dancing and the feasting and the celebration with your family and your tribe around you is such a beautiful way to accept the sadness and to release his spirit.

For us to come together like that was one of the finest moments among tribes. How the Great Spirit works, how God

brought us together to enjoy each other's culture and each other's art was just amazing. Now we know each other and we have faces to put with the voices. We can remember how they smile, how they laugh—knowing these people this way is worth more than money can buy.

170

ANGIE OWEN

Santo Domingo Pueblo
Santo Domingo Pueblo, New Mexico

Jewelry-making has been in our family for generations. My grandpa used to mine his own turquoise at the Cerrillos mine. He left behind a bucket-full for us to work with. From the stories that were told to us, the men would go in a group to mine the turquoise. They would camp out until they had gathered enough, and then they would come back and split it up among the men.

My parents both worked in shell and turquoise. My father traveled to Navajo-land to do business, and my mom was constantly doing jewelry. In the summer-time, it was a mixed job; my father would farm, and my mom worked right along with him both as a jeweler and as a farmer. I used to sell our family's jewelry under the portal in Santa Fe, so I could help out while my mom was at home making jewelry.

Santo Domingos always used their own materials. They never sold the raw mate-rial. And for shell, there was always some-body bringing it; there was always a trade route. Today, we have lots of choices for stones and shells. Every Monday and Tuesday dealers come and there's a market here at the pueblo. If they know you use good materials, they come looking for you.

The Navajo people were our biggest customers. We used to make *heishi* and turquoise *jaclas*. They were popular items for the Navajos and always in demand. We made wonderful *jaclas*. While my dad was gone my mom would work for other people in the village who either didn't have the time to grind or didn't know how. My mom did work for at least four people. She would get five dollars for doing maybe twenty strands. But it was still five dollars, which was a lot of money back then.

There are many stages to making *heishi*. In the old days, my parents would take an olivella shell and tap it to split it. Then they cut the olivella pieces into squares and drilled the squares in the middle. If it had large corners, those were clipped; if they're small, you don't need to clip them. Then they strung those drilled pieces on a wire, and ground them all on a flat stone, until eventually it's round. Today with lapidary equipment, the process is

basically the same, and it's still a long process, but it does go faster. You can take the string to a grinding wheel and a sander and then a polisher.

One of the disadvantages is that with the modern equipment now, we're com-peting with the Philippines. They're copying our style. Some traders are taking our necklaces to the Philippines and China to copy, making the beads there and bring-ing home the finished product. It's hard for my people to compete, especially those people who rely on just the beads. Buyers can avoid the imports if they buy from a reputable person. If it's inexpensive, it's imported, and if it's expensive, then it's handmade. My people are having a hard time competing with the import business, and I wish the federal government would get stricter. I would guess ninety percent of us at Santo Domingo are self-employed and working on jewelry and pottery. So the imports make a big impact on our people being able to make a living.

Instead of doing beads with my folks, I asked my father about doing mosaic, which was what my mother used to do. She used to do the Depression necklaces. Out of that, I started making the herring-bone inlay. That's a style I originated and keep doing, although I do a lot of different styles. All my brothers, their wives, my sister—they're all doing mosaics, and each of us has our own style.

My bracelets actually start with a large shell. I shape it into a bracelet and then I clean it so the epoxy sticks. When I'm picking the stones for the top I decide if I want colors in it or if I want it plain. Sometimes if the stone is really nice, then I don't want to take away from it by putting many different colors with it. It takes me probably a good three or four days just to sit and cut the stones to have enough materials to cover one project. And you can't just stop to cut because then you lose your concentration on the size you are cutting. Then I decide which pattern I want to do. I start from the middle or down in one section, and I work from each side. When one side is dry, I turn it around and work on the other side. I use all shell for the base because I want it to be traditional, and I don't want to take away from the stone. I feel that silver is too flashy.

Now my grandkids and grandnieces and grandnephews work with me, especially in the summer. My door is always open and whoever walks in the door that wants to learn and work with me, can. If I'm grinding they know they're expected to grind. Right now most of the grinding is done by my grandkids. Even the major pieces. My grandson Corey can do a major piece and I don't have to worry about him grinding away too much. I'm teaching him to finish off the bracelet the way that I prefer. And he's getting there. He's good. The discipline is there and that's what it takes.

I love making the jewelry. Once you decide what you want to do, then you want to see it finished. You have to have the passion and love for it otherwise things just don't come together. You have to put your whole heart into it. They tell you if you're not in a good mood, don't try and create something; it's just not going to come out. They teach us at home to enjoy what you do, what you create, and that way the person that becomes the owner also enjoys it . . . as it was meant to be.

Turquoise mosaic bracelet. Angie Owen (Santo Domingo Pueblo). Turquoise, shell. 2003. Width, 2½". Private collection

172

LEE YAZZIE

Navajo (Diné)
Gallup, New Mexico

I sign my jewelry "Lee Yazzie" but my full name is Lee A. Yazzie. The "A" doesn't stand for anything; it's just that when I went to boarding school, there were so many Lee Yazzies that they put the "A" in there to distinguish me from the others. I was born in a small community called Vanderwagon, south of Gallup, in 1946.

The last thing I ever wanted to be was a silversmith. For many years, I thought it was a curse because it's the only thing that I knew. I watched my parents trying to make a living with jewelry, and I just didn't feel there was anything in it for me. I wanted to be an accountant. I wanted to work for a big firm. I had really high hopes when I was a little lad out there herding sheep. Sometimes you would lay under a cedar tree and see the sheep grazing and maybe a couple of horses out yonder. And you look at the sky, using your imagination, you see the clouds moving and you see different figures. Then you see the contrail of a jet plane and you wonder, "How high is it up there? What's out there? How does everything look from there? Will I ever get the chance to go that high?" And I thought, "No, that's probably not for me." I enjoyed the environment I grew up in because we had a big space, it was our playground and we could discover whatever was out there. But I had this big dream of getting my family out of poverty. We lived in a small hogan, and I have seven brothers and six sisters. I always dreamed that someday I could buy my family a nice home.

My father was a medicine man and did ceremonies for people who were ill. I have a lot of aunts and uncles on my father's side. Some that belonged to the Christian religion used to tell my father that he was doing the work of the devil. I didn't understand what it meant. So, in my own way, I started to search. If there was a truth, I wanted to find it. The way that I see things and my work is that we are all God's children, every one of us. The most beautiful thing is our spiritual being, and that's where my creativity comes from. I humble myself before my maker. Then I say to myself, "What beautiful thing can I create today?"

I always see beauty in the eyes of people or in their faces, and I ask myself,

"How can I enhance this beauty with what I can create, and do it in a way that is different?" I don't want to be better than somebody else; I just want to do the very best I can. Today, even though I accomplish some unique pieces, I don't ever think I'm better than somebody else. When that happens, you lose good energy.

In one of my pieces, I depicted the journey that I am on in this life, and also the fact that I'm guided in this journey by a deity. And so I put a deity with a face, and then I put another small round head to show that I am the offspring of this deity. I put a line that shows my beginning, and also the death of my being here. I have this arrow that goes into infinity, and that shows that gods live forever. So one day we ourselves will be gods if we have proved to be deserving of such blessing, if we do all that we're set out to do in this world.

I feel blessed that I have a lot of ideas, a lot of designs that I haven't even made yet. And they are still coming. It's just like the energy and the light that comes from the sun. If we can harness it, it will be for our benefit. When I see designs floating around, I have a way to harness that design so I can get the blueprint and then get my faculties in order so I can execute that design. When someone buys my jewelry, they don't know how much of me they buy, because of the challenges that I go through in making that piece.

I owe a lot to Gene Waddell, who has been a silent partner of mine. We've worked together and he's been supportive of me for over thirty years. Our friendship and mutual respect have allowed me to create the things I create.

My mother was an excellent silver bead maker. I always had a great admiration for her. When I get depressed and think, "Why am I doing this? There has to be something easier I can do," I see the image of my mother working on her bezel and burnishing the stone. She had this favorite black velveteen blouse that she used to wear. Over the years, it got worn and frayed on the sleeves. When I see her, she always turns to me and smiles, and that smile gets me to accept what it is that I'm doing, and accept who I am. I'm glad that I am a silversmith.

Buckle. Lee Yazzie (Navajo). Owner Gene Waddell is a friend and business partner of Lee Yazzie and part-owner of the Lone Mountain turquoise mine in Nevada. The buckle's large center stone was mined in 1980. Waddell asked Yazzie to make a buckle with the stone almost twenty years later, and, according to Waddell, Yazzie "outdid himself." Silver, Lone Mountain Spider Web turquoise. 2000. Width, 2⅜". Collection Waddell

174　VERMA NEQUATEWA

Hopi
Badger Clan and Butterfly Clan
Hotvela, Hopi, Arizona

With the Hopis, they say that we're all artists. They say it's just the way we are when we're born, because even when a child is in the womb, and the mother goes to ceremonies and to the night dances at the kiva, there's something already developing in that child. I do believe that before we're born, we've got something. Later, you just have to find ways to get it out and keep doing it to get good at it. Most of the Hopi people have artists in their families. My brothers and my son carve katsina dolls. My sisters are basket weavers.

I worked with my uncle Charles Loloma for a long time, side by side. He taught me so much . . . that you have to be positive to be able to create good jewelry. If you're not in a good state of mind, it shows up in your jewelry. Creating a piece has to come from the heart. It's not a surface thing.

Instead of criticizing, my uncle always talked about the positive. So he was a good collaborator on some of the pieces. Sometimes he'd form the piece for me to inlay, and I'd create the stonework. From the beginning I would listen to why things work certain ways. And then sometimes I'd have my own suggestions. As I got better, I got stronger and more daring in some ways. At first I was creating dainty little pieces. He was creating a masculine kind of jewelry, because he was so daring. Some pieces of jewelry would be so very sculptural. Sometimes we would tease him and say, "Who is going to wear this? It's so tall!" He'd say, "Somebody will!" He was always so sure of himself. He said a piece should be enjoyed from all sides, each side as beautiful as the outside.

The most important thing that I learned was about the stones themselves, how to work the stone and study the stone. You look for which side of a stone talks to you, for the right shape in it so that you can use the most in the stone instead of grinding it away. Sometimes you can leave some sections of the stone rough, to show it for what it is. Actually, I don't create the jewelry. It's like the beauty of the stones directs me how to use them. The stones are actually my bosses.

My uncle taught me about shape and form, line and height. And he taught me about working with the colors . . . which stones work together. For example, putting lapis with a light turquoise will make the turquoise more blue, more intense. If you put that turquoise next to a white ivory, sometimes the ivory will kill it, and the turquoise color will wash out. It's really important too to have space in a piece. It's the hardest thing to do, to make a piece simple or subtle. I try to make a piece clean and so beautiful that it hurts.

For me, being an artist and being Hopi, it's important to be part of our ceremonies. I never really moved away from home. My family is responsible for certain things, and I have to help out with all of that. Even if I'm in the middle of doing jewelry, I leave it aside and do the ceremonial things. I feel that's part of why I do jewelry and how I create. Helping with the ceremonies gives me more energy to be able to get back to creating.

For the ceremonies, wearing jewelry is important. You'll see people wearing turquoise necklaces that come from either Santo Domingo or Zuni. Most of the Hopi jewelers don't use much inlay or turquoise. We all trade back and forth. So the jewelry is being shared from New Mexico to Arizona.

Being an artist means you are able to create to the utmost. There are really no limits. Some people are just craftsmen who create without thinking . . . a mass production type of thing. And there are really fine craftspeople whose work is refined. But with the true artists there are no limits at all. They're creating and trying new things and going different directions.

Maiden ring. Verma
Nequatewa. Fossilized ivory,
turquoise, coral, 18-karat
gold. 1993. Length, 2⅛".
Collection Dr. and Mrs. E.
Daniel Albrecht

MICHAEL KABOTIE

Hopi
Snow Clan, Water Clan
Songòopavi, Hopi, Arizona

I suppose my arts came into being because drawing and painting were the two things I could do well. After I dropped out of the University of Arizona, I was a poor dishwasher and a poor encyclopedia salesman. The start of my art journey was my first one-man show at the Heard Museum in Phoenix in 1966.

Back in high school I was a troublesome student. I was taken out of carpentry class, put into auto mechanics class, but I didn't know anything about automobiles. So they put me in home economics, but I had too much fun with the girls and got into trouble drinking vanilla extract. At that point they put me into my father's [Fred Kabotie's] art class where I couldn't get into trouble. They were doing jewelry and silversmithing. After that, I didn't do any more jewelry until the late sixties. Although I've been making jewelry since then, I consider myself more a painter than a jeweler. Painting is a more fluid medium for me. Metalsmithing is more technical and more restricting.

Back in 1973, I helped found an art group called Artists Hopid. It was one of the first Native American art movements that was reservation-based, not city-based, not Santa Fe-based. We researched the graphic traditions of our tribe and reinterpreted them on canvas. One objective was to document Hopi history and values for posterity, so we painted two murals at the Hopi Cultural Center Museum.

In 1999, the Museum of Northern Arizona in Flagstaff asked if I would be involved in their mural project, examining and reinterpreting the kiva murals of the ancestral sites of Awat'ovi, here at Hopi, and Pottery Mound in New Mexico. Kiva mural style has hard outlines, so it translates very well into Hopi overlay jewelry. For my jewelry, I've modified the basic overlay technique into three layers, and sometimes I use lifters so the designs float away from the background. I call those my floating designs.

Art historians and scholars put labels on artists and art: "That's contemporary; that's traditional; he's idiosyncratic." I just slice through those labels and do my thing. My inspirations are the rich traditions of our Hopi arts and crafts. These traditions don't die; they re-emerge in various forms. Sometimes I use the format of the Hopi migration stories. I also employ concepts from Buddhism and the Alcoholics Anonymous Twelve-Step process. For me they all parallel the journey to the shadow side where creativity resides, and that's what art is. Art talks across cultural boundaries. So I employ those concepts and themes, but still use the vocabulary from the Hopi murals, which is flat, two-dimensional.

Hopi is not compartmentalized; you're connected in all ways to your "living room"—that's what I call my Hopi Mesas. So the agricultural values, dancing in the plazas, the landscapes around me, how they're identified, and the spirits embodied in these landscapes and in the plants and animals—all of those things are influential to me in my artwork. Rituals, ceremonies, songs, storytelling—all of these are part of the Hopi educational system, plus hard work. You don't go to government school to learn these things, you learn them in the kiva, and are initiated to be part of the ceremonies and the sacred knowledge.

But contradictions exist. Sometimes Hopi people are put on a pedestal, considered innocent and highly spiritual. But what the outside world doesn't know is how many of us fall off, and how many don't want to get back on. Hopi is just like any other society. We have people fighting each other, loving each other, honoring each other, dishonoring each other. We have rap singers, artists, writers, poets, traditional dancers, non-traditional dancers. We're very human.

Traditionally, Hopi is a communal concept because living out in that harsh environment you have to be interdependent, not only on other people, but also on nature. For example, the Spider Woman is a very important part of my life . . . the wisdom keeper, the grandmother figure, the female figure. She was an integral part of my growth. I remember my grandfolks telling me the stories about Spider Woman and the Twin Heroes. These are universal, archetypal symbols. When I became an alcoholic and wanted to get out from my disease, there was Spider Woman in my mind; she spoke to me. She became my strength and my courage to pull myself into the world of sobriety. The Twin Heroes are the mischief-makers, they're the tricksters, and always manage to find themselves in trouble. They have to humble themselves to ask for help, and Grandmother Spider Woman scolds them and says, "You managed to get yourself into this, you find the solution." When I was an alcoholic, I was the trouble-maker, and it was the Spider Woman who came to me and said, "There's a solution. Go find it."

I treat the whole idea of jewelry as a journey, because it is, in many ways, reflective of life. All of art is, but jewelry is the most dramatic. In creativity you have

to get acquainted with the raw and the savage. That's what initiations are all about. That's what the Twelve-Step program is about, and that's what Buddhist concept is all about—you have to journey within to meet the raw and the savage self, then return with renewed awareness. Jewelry work is like that because you have to deal with your emotions, with your expectations, with your perfectionism, and with your skills. There's usually a big gap between what you think and what your hands can do. You beat up on your material, bang it around, scratch it, cut it, torch it, throw it into acid, and bang it around some more, file it some more, and then, at the end, you have this beautiful piece. And that's what life is, and it's quite violent. When I tell people, "Jewelry is one of the most violent

art forms," they say, "Oh, no, can't be." But we need to see the other side of life, and art leads us into that area. Too many times we live in the light, and we're like little moths. We keep bumping against the light, and we get blinded by it. I think we need to get away from the light, and appreciate the shadow side also, and blend them together. I say, "Bring light into the dark, mix it well, and bring it back out as art."

Individually, we all go through the journey of forming ourselves. If we put the responsibility on ourselves for positive change, there's a solution and there's something that you can do. That's when we go through the hammering process. That's what the life process is all about. Jewelry is a metaphor of that journey and in the end, we honor ourselves with the jewelry.

Silver kiva mural. Michael Kabotie (Hopi). Blending imagery from kiva murals at Awat'ovi and Pottery Mound, Kabotie has brought together in three-layer silver overlay some of the most compelling imagery in the Pueblo world. Each of the six panels can be detached and worn as a pendant. 2003. Height, 3". Collection Dr. Edwin L. Wade

Opposite page:
Michael Kabotie wears (as a pendant) one panel of his silver kiva mural.

178

HARVEY BEGAY

Navajo (Diné)
One Who Walks Around Clan and Mexican Clan
Steamboat Springs, Colorado

I was born on the western edge of the Navajo reservation, a place called Tuba City, Arizona. My sisters and I grew up off the reservation, but we spent most of our summers with our paternal grandmother, doing all the things that Navajo families do in the summertime—herding sheep, hauling water, going to summer ceremonies. We were not given Navajo names largely because of what my mother experienced in the Indian schools where it was heavily ingrained in them not to speak the language, not to follow the traditions of their tribe. So that's what my parents chose.

My father [silversmith Kenneth Begay] was trained as a blacksmith in an Indian school, but he became interested in their jewelry program, so he tried his hand at it. He had unusual abilities and a vision far beyond what most silversmiths had at the time. He knew how to manipulate silver in any way, produce any form he wanted, and he became well known for his unusual jewelry. My father's volume of work was enormous, just amazing. I've been working for over thirty years, and I don't think I've done half of what he did in his short career of thirty-five years.

But as I was growing up I was unaware of my father's talent. I started working with him when he was in Scottsdale at a time when the Indian jewelry market was booming for everybody. I was a junior in high school at the time, and I stuck with jewelry long enough to pay part of my way through Arizona State University. But when I graduated in 1961, I thought, "Wonderful. I don't have to do this anymore!"

After college, I joined the Navy and was assigned to a pre-flight class in Pensacola. I was the only brown kid there, and that was true for the rest of my military and civilian life before I became a jeweler. But I didn't think too much about it because I was heavily involved in flying. I was in a fighter squadron that flew F-4s based aboard aircraft carriers. It was exciting to be flying the hottest jet in the military inventory. I figured I was probably the only Navajo to fly in North Vietnam in a warplane at that time.

When I came back, I got married and lived in Phoenix. Airlines were not hiring, but McDonnell Douglas was hiring flight test engineers, so I sent them a quick resume and in 1966 we moved to St. Louis. We test-flew production F-4s destined for the United States Navy, Air Force, and Marines. All this time my father was asking me, gently, "Would you consider coming back and working with me?" I just sort of humored him and never really committed to anything. But by 1970, production of the F-4 was on a rapid decline, so I quit, took my father up on his proposition, and we moved back to Navajo-land. It didn't work out. Living back there was somewhat of a culture shock for me, and especially for my wife—she's non-Indian. So instead we found a place in Steamboat Springs, and with little money and high hopes, we opened a small shop at the base of the ski mountain and called it "The Navajo Craftsman." I guess because I was Navajo, because of the name, and because of the quality of the stuff we were carrying, it became successful right away. And then two years later, Indian jewelry boomed again. We didn't know it was going to happen, we were just fortunately placed. While this was going on I wanted to get back into working with my hands, with the metal and my tools.

Once I started back on my path, I didn't have much influence from my father. My techniques and designs were essentially his, but I got frustrated so I began experimenting on my own with different techniques, mostly fabrication where you build things out of sheet and wire into whatever form you want. When I look back, I can see the progress I was making, but at that time I felt like I was coming up against a wall. I felt like a little kid again, doing the same thing my father was doing. I couldn't get past that wall for a long time. I wasn't sure I had any design capabilities or craftsmanship. As I look back now, I know that I did, but I just wasn't confident in what I was doing.

While I'd been exploring new techniques, I saw magnificent work by Pierre Touraine and asked if I could work with him. For about a year and a half he showed me how to get a higher quality product than what I was doing, and also encouraged me to learn how to work with diamonds. Then he said, "Harvey, you don't need me anymore." At that time Lovena Ohl saw my work and asked me to be in her Scottsdale gallery. As it turned out, it was what I was destined to do.

Once I started working with Pierre and Lovena, and as I began designing things that were similar to my father's but differ- ent, I gained confidence. I favored pottery and Navajo rug designs, but in a way that hadn't been done before. Or I'd see an interesting curvature or angle, and I'd say "That would make a nice bracelet." So my inspiration comes largely from things I observe and can translate into jewelry form.

The unfortunate thing about the boom in Indian jewelry is that there is so much counterfeit Indian jewelry now available. Nobody knows the difference. Sometimes even I can't tell the difference. The Indian jewelry market has been so exploited, especially in places like Albuquerque and Gallup. A lot of what is sold as Indian jewelry isn't even made here in the States, and it hurts all the Native craftsmen and jewelers.

Necklace and earring set. Harvey Begay (Navajo). Begay's inspiration for this set was the feather motifs used by famous San Ildefonso Pueblo potters Maria and Julian Martinez on their highly polished black pottery. Turquoise, 14-karat gold. Ca. 1991. Total length, 22". Private collection

180

CIPPY CRAZY HORSE

Cochiti Pueblo
Cochiti, New Mexico

I was born at Cochiti Pueblo to Terecita and Joe H. Quintana. Except for a few years in the military service, I have always lived on my reservation.

In a way, I got into silversmithing by accident. After I was discharged from the Navy, I got a job with a construction business at Cochiti, on the dam. While I was working up there I got injured on the job and almost lost my leg. The people in the company gathered up about $600 for me, and I put it towards getting my equipment—my acetylene torches and my files, my shears. I started making silver chain and gradually progressed to more challenging items.

My mother's advice came back to me. She used to say, "Go watch your father do silverwork, for some day that may help you." I'm glad I did that because my parents were both good teachers; they were a good team and made beautiful jewelry.

I've carried on the style that my parents do . . . simple and clean. I start from scratch and do all my own work, from start to finish. I melt silver into an ingot, then hammer and roll it to the desired thickness. From there I do chisel work and sometimes stamp work to create what I call "Pueblo style." My version of the difference between Navajo and Pueblo jewelry is that the Navajo style is more heavily decorated—there is not much silver left unstamped—while the Pueblo style is a little more plain.

Through no fault of their own a lot of the younger people have a hard time speaking our language, maybe because we, as young parents, never recognized the importance of making the time to teach them as our parents, and especially our grandparents, taught us. Some of the elders from Cochiti Pueblo realized that our language was being lost and decided to start a language program that seems to be working well.

I've tried to teach my own kids, in my own way, just like my grandmother. She never forced anything on us. She would just sit around the fireplace and talk about things that were done, why the ceremonies are done. I used to watch her pray, and I'd ask, "What are you saying?" And she'd explain to me. I'm glad I asked, and I'm glad I listened, because what I am today, is through her teaching.

I'm proud of my children; they have participated in tribal ceremonies without any urging. All I have to say is, "There's going to be a dance," and they'll say, "I'm ready, I've got my costumes." And they'll be out there. Our ceremonial dances are prayers. My children know that when they dance it is for people everywhere, young and old, for good health and peace.

I made a necklace about fifteen years ago and entered it in the competition at Santa Fe Indian Market. Well, lo and behold, it got a blue ribbon, and I sold it to someone from Texas. I thought that was pretty nice because it went to a good family. Later I started thinking about it, though, because we don't have any of the beautiful pieces my parents made. And I didn't want it to be like that for the family. So I asked to buy it back for my daughter, and the people were nice enough to sell it back to me. So now it's in the family, and I hope it stays in the family.

Double-barred cross necklace. Cippy Crazy Horse (Cochiti Pueblo). Old-style crosses like these were popular among the Pueblos. Crucifixes and religious medallions were introduced by Franciscan missionaries in the sixteenth century. Today, the Rio Grande Pueblos practice Catholicism while retaining traditional religions. Contemporary iconography of crosses and double-barred crosses merges pre-Columbian imagery of dragonflies with Christian symbols (including the heart at the base of the cross). Silver. Ca. 1988. Pendant width, 2½". Collection Erly Crazy Horse

182

EDITH TSABETSAYE

Zuni
Zuni Pueblo, New Mexico

I learned silversmithing from my parents, Joe and Susan Tsabetsaye. Later they had jobs, but even then they did silversmithing. I started at twelve or thirteen. My oldest sister, Jane, her husband Lawrence Basslente, and my uncle, Raymond Gasper . . . we were a big family and we all worked together to keep the family going, to buy groceries. I helped without anybody paying me. We just helped to keep everything going.

But after eighteen years, after I'd learned all this soldering and lapidary work, I already had my first child. My mom got a job as a head cook at Zuni Elementary School and that's when she said that now I'd be on my own to support my daughter and myself. Most of the people were doing the bigger stones as cluster-work or petit-point. I thought, "I need to do something different so that it will help me out in the long run." So I decided to do needlepoint, and I bought my tools. But the tools from the store weren't exactly what I wanted, because I wanted to make the tiniest needlepoint. So I had to make changes and file the tools down to make my work easier.

My jewelry is all traditional, and I only use the top-grade turquoise. I used to work with Lone Mountain turquoise, but it became rare. So later on I switched to Sleeping Beauty turquoise. Those two kinds of turquoise are harder and don't break as easily. And they don't change colors. They're a lighter color . . . when it's light, it gets prettier as you wear your jewelry. Turquoise is very important to the Zuni people. It's just part of our life; it's what we work with and what we pray with. The tiny bits of turquoise left over, they don't throw them away. They put them in the cornmeal to pray with.

I was married for eleven years and had three children. I was working as a food handler at the Indian Health Service hospital here at Zuni, sometimes going on the early shift at five in the morning. Babysitting was hard to get, so I decided to go back to what I had already started. I just wanted to stay home with my children and do my jewelry. I wanted to work steady on my own and make a career out of it.

I worked harder on my designs and did my grinding over and over. I wanted to make my stones look better or different than any other needlepoint maker. So I changed my grinding to a high dome where the stone is rounded on the top. I didn't want my work to look flat and show only from the top; it should show from three dimensions. It took a lot of patience, but I just had to do it. After I finished my grinding and silverwork part, and designing and polishing and matching it up and setting the stones, then—sure enough—the stones weren't just showing from the top; you could spot them from a distance. When somebody wears my jewelry, I can easily tell.

Our first year at Santa Fe Indian Market there wasn't even a booth. We just had a space, and we had no table or chairs. We bought some pillows at the dimestore, and we found a cardboard box. There was a rug in our vehicle, so we put it on top of the cardboard and displayed our work on it. That's the way we started at Santa Fe. But I got tired of travel; with family it was too much. It wasn't easy for me, but I kept trying and trying . . . I had hopes and dreams for a good life for my children. And then my name did become recognized so I really didn't have to travel much anymore. My children went to private school in Santa Fe, then on to college in Las Cruces. They don't make jewelry, but two of them, Tiffany and Bart Gasper, are well-known katsina doll carvers; Carlotta is a teacher and Chad works for the Institute of American Indian Arts. I changed my children's names to their great-grandpa's—Gasper. Henry Gasper was well known in the pueblo. He was the first elected governor and I wanted his name to be carried on.

It's very important to me to stay living at Zuni, because there are religious things that happen all year round. I do a lot of that . . . I can't drop it and go away during ceremonies. That's the way I was brought up . . . and it helps me, too, because, whatever sacrifices I make, I will be gifted, receive something back. My mother used to tell us, "No matter what you are doing with your work, just put it aside for a little while and take part in all these religious doings, what's going on, the cooking and baking and feeding. You can always go back to what you were doing." And it does work, because somehow I always manage to catch up on my time. It always pays back.

I was always very much in love with my work. I think that's why I couldn't hold on to a job . . . because my mind was always on my jewelry making. I made a career out of it. I got my soldering from my parents—they won awards too—and I do appreciate what I learned from them. But it's time that I say that I did this and it came from me. After I changed to needlepoint, I made my own way to where I am now. I appreciate all the buyers and those who represented my work. I am grateful to them.

Needlepoint concho belt and raw turquoise. Edith Tsabetsaye (Zuni Pueblo). Lone Mountain turquoise, silver. 1970s. Length, 32". Collection Tanner

Opposite page:
Edith Tsabetsaye wears the first necklace she made (circa 1962), an example of the cluster-work style that she learned from her parents and for which they won many awards. Edith soon created her own award-winning needlepoint style using smaller stones and shaping them to create a three-dimensional effect.

184

PERRY SHORTY

Navajo (Diné)
Shiprock, New Mexico

I was working at the silver counter of a store in Gallup, selling materials to artists, when I first decided to become involved in jewelry. I saw folks come in and sign their checks and that was literally part of the reason I got into it. I wanted to make a few extra dollars, so I decided to try it.

I knew I didn't have a chance if I tried to compete with the contemporary artists. To make sure I had a chance at some success I chose the old style because it wasn't very common back then. Although my first motivation was money, as I have worked over the years there is a certain integrity I want to keep. I don't want to compromise. I've seen artists sell out by making mass production pieces, and they lose the quality. I didn't want to go down that road, so more than anything I try to keep the integrity of the old style.

But I'm not a traditionalist in any way. I grew up in a Christian home. My mother shielded us from getting involved in the tradition and the religion of the Navajo. I don't speak Navajo, but doing the jewelry made me want to learn. I took some classes and I'm learning. I can read Navajo, but I can't carry on a conversation yet. Not that I feel disconnected; I'm proud of being a Navajo. If I can say that I make a contribution to Navajo culture, it would be my jewelry making.

There are phases in the old style. In the first phase, the pieces are not as elaborate. They're simple, almost crude, and that was because of the limited resources and tools that smiths had in the early days. There's a second phase where they began to get more intricate, with cut-outs, for instance, and soldering was introduced. The trader had a lot to do with things at that point; he helped them get things they didn't have access to—better materials and tools. And then there's the "classic period," from around the late 1920s and early 1930s. That's the style my jewelry falls into, where it's very elaborate, a lot of wires and drops and stones. I've tried to use the old, rarer stones that were used a lot back then.

I've been working with coin silver lately, melting down old coins into an ingot. Then I hammer it down. Depending on how thick the ingot is or what stage it's at, I cut strips and make wires or just continue to flatten it out into a thin sheet and use it for the bezel and appliqué work.

In the jewelry world today, I think there's a rush to come up with the ultimate design that's so different and complex to make people want what you're making. In the market, most folks are moving forward in this way. But I've found my niche, and that is to make old-style jewelry. And, if anything, I've regressed from making the elaborate classical style jewelry back down to the first phase jewelry. I've gone as far as trying to melt coins down with hot coals, using bellows. And I wonder as I'm working if this is what the early smiths felt like —wondering, what can I do with this chisel, and how can I apply it to this piece of metal? Making their own stamps and things like that.

So I've studied a lot of old jewelry. I have a knack for the old . . . to incorporate what I've seen and studied. It's almost like I have a file in my mind of designs and patterns from the old phases. And the creative part is taking one design that was used during this period, and then another one, and putting them together to make a piece that will work.

I've learned that human nature likes decorated silver. One of the philosophies in Navajo culture is that they like to adorn themselves. That's why they have their saying "walk in beauty, walk in harmony." So with that in mind, as long as I've made something that's nice and it flows and it pleases someone's eye, then I've done a good job.

Coin silver concho belt. Perry Shorty (Navajo). Shorty explains, "I don't know how many pounds of coins I melted for this belt, but once the silver was in an ingot form, I then hammered it on an anvil. It took so much hammering that the nerves in my hand tingled for almost a year. I'll probably never do a belt like this again, just because of the amount of labor involved." 2002. Average width of conchos, 3½". Private collection

VERONICA POBLANO

Zuni
Child of the Corn Clan and Coyote Clan
Zuni Pueblo, New Mexico

At an early age I started carving fetishes with my mother. I think we were one of the first families that carved fetishes as a source of income. Back in the 1950s, my father [Leo Poblano] also had another skill of doing mosaic inlay. He and my mother would design the inlay free-form and put it on the back of aluminum plates or copper backing. They'd take it to their trading post friends like C.G. Wallace and they would have someone else do the fabrication of the setting.

I know we all have a purpose in life. Mine is to finish my father's mission because his life was cut very short when he was killed fire-fighting in California. We were so young during that time, and my mother really suffered after his loss.

When I was maybe thirteen years old, my neighbors Madeline and Edward Beyuka introduced me to silversmithing. I used to go visit and watch them work while they did their lapidary. They did a lot of mosaic inlay work, creating all kinds of Zuni dancers and katsina figures. They made jewelry for sale, to support their families.

I started helping my aunt, Gillie Tsadiasi, make little Sun God earrings. I made the circular bezel for her and she would help me solder. The inlay has three different pieces—turquoise, shell, and coral. I pieced them together and shaped them into circles and set them in. The Sun God is a traditional design that Zuni people still use today, but it was simple enough for me to do, and that's how I started.

When my mother passed away, I wanted a new direction. My life wasn't going anywhere. I was a hairdresser by trade and worked for many years as a makeup artist. I'd always dreamed about living near the water, so, even though I didn't know anybody in California, I moved my kids to San Diego and eventually Solano Beach. I still did hair, but I think it was about a year after we moved that I decided to give up hairdressing and be an artist full time. We started doing street fairs and people noticed that I was doing something different with my inlay work. They started to seek us out. It was hard living there because it's so expensive, but we were able to do it and we enjoyed what we did.

When I came back to Zuni with my new works of art, people asked me, "Where did you go to train? Who taught you? You're better than you were before." And, you know, there wasn't anybody that taught me. I taught myself. Sometimes you've got to leave an area to find yourself, to find out what you really want to be in life. I'm proud of myself for doing that . . . and to come home and show my people what I have done with my creativity.

Everything that I use is natural. I don't use any synthetic or reconstituted material in my work And I'm very picky about my stones; they have to have a lot of color. I use stones from all over the world. There's one gem dealer who comes directly to us to tell us what's new for the year. We follow the fashion trends, and that's how our jewelry evolves every year. Spring comes, we use spring colors, and then the fall colors, they'll be darker. This is Zuni jewelry because it's made in Zuni, and I am Zuni and proud to be. But it's not traditional. My form of thinking, of creating, is far different.

I was never really a traditionalist, but as I grow older I realize that it's very important. I speak fluent Zuni, and so do my children, even though they don't speak it often. Our language and being a part of the culture is one of our greatest possessions. A lot of religious activities go on throughout the year in the village, and I'm always a part of that.

Zuni, and all the beauty around it . . . our history and knowing how we became people of the Southwest, makes you appreciate what you do with your hands, that your hands can create. I think eighty percent of the people in Zuni are silversmiths. I consider my people to be truly great artists, because each and every family in Zuni is talented. It's the Zuni way of life.

Anything is possible if you put your mind to it. My advice to young children, to the young possible artists, is to follow their dream. I became the kind of artist I am now because I never lost my focus on what I wanted to do. If you have a dream, continue to be positive and try to improve and you'll reach your goals. And don't forget where you came from.

Torque necklace. Veronica Poblano (Zuni Pueblo). "The inspiration for this necklace came from the trip to Haida Gwaii [the Queen Charlotte Islands] to meet Haida artists," Poblano said. "Seeing that area of the Northwest Coast brought me to a different level in my designs. When I came back from the islands, I realized my jewelry has to have some kind of movement. I could still feel and see the island—the water and the landscapes—and I began to use that imagination. With that inspiration, this necklace came about from the flowing aspects of the natural formation of the turquoise." Morenci turquoise and 14-karat gold. 2003. Total length, 10". Private collection

RAYMOND C. YAZZIE

Navajo (Diné)
Folding Arms Clan and Salt Water Clan
Pinehaven, New Mexico

Jewelry making was always in my family. My mother and father were silversmiths, and from a young age we all helped file or sand or do some part of the finish work. There are thirteen children in my family and I'm the second-youngest of the boys. I remember my mom always working on silversmithing; my dad would have to go off to work on the railroad. Back as far as eight or nine years old, I was already learning how to make things.

My brother Lee Yazzie did a lot for me through the years because of the way he trained me. When I was still really young, he was making jewelry for a shop in Gallup. I asked him if I could come in and learn from him. I think he already knew what potential I had. After working with him for about three years, at the age of fourteen, I got my first Best of Show prize. From there it just took off. Lee's tried to train a few others, but many people couldn't stay because Lee pushes hard, trying to bring out their potential. I'm glad I stayed; I almost didn't. One time I walked out because when Lee decided a piece wasn't good enough, he would take the stones out and make you redo it. And now, when I think back about it, I really appreciate how he pushed me. To cut stones like I do now, I give him credit for that. And I think our relationship became even better. To this day I feel like he's still watching me, and I ask myself if I'm doing the best I can. That's what I thrive on. I have a lot of respect and admiration for him.

My work is identifiable because I cut some of the smallest stones, sometimes to the size of a pinhead and still put a smooth polish to it. Through the years I had to learn how to hold the stones to polish them and how to use my fingers or even my fingernails.

None of my pieces are ever sketched beforehand. The design happens cut by cut. If there's one cut, one color or something that doesn't work in a certain area, I'll cut another piece. By the time I finish a bracelet I might have a hundred extra pieces that were cut and never used. So I do a lot of extra cutting, actually, to get all the colors right. I blend the colors from one side to the other and try to balance them all.

I put a lot of thought and energy into what I do. There are times, like when just a small quarter of an inch opening takes a week to finish, that I want to finish it sooner. I think, "Should I take a shortcut and use larger pieces because I'm the only one that's going to know?" But I can't, because I know that that's not the way it was supposed to be finished. I don't take shortcuts on anything. And when my customers get their pieces, they're really happy.

I'm hoping one of my kids will carry on what I've learned; I'd love to teach them. Cutting stones is an art, to get that smooth polish and to find the best area in the stone to show it off. I spend a lot of time thinking how to give life to a piece of turquoise or coral. What wants to come out of it? You have to study that in the stone before you get it to the wheel. When my son Christopher comes in and plays with stones on the grinder, I can tell by the sound of how he touches that stone to the wheel that he has the feel for it. He has the potential to be good at cutting stones. But I don't want to force him. I want him to come to me and ask if he can learn.

I owe so much to my wife, Colina. I really depend on her to help me with designs and inspiration. She's a large part of my success. And I still get my traditional blessings. It helps to make things flow naturally with my jewelry work, as it should. There are times that things fall out of place with my work, and that's when the traditional way comes in. I have a blessing or sing done to get it back into balance again.

"Blessings" bracelet. Raymond C. Yazzie (Navajo). "The turquoise in the Blessings bracelet came out of a collection from the 1950s. As I was working on the bracelet, images started showing up in the way I was laying the stones, and it reminded me of Dan Namingha's paintings, which I really admire. He includes a lot of abstract designs, and so his paintings became an inspiration for this bracelet." Constructed of 485 stones, the abstract design includes eight katsina images including a maiden katsina in the center. Several varieties of turquoise, black onyx, Australian opal, lapis lazuli, sugilite, 18-karat gold. 2002–2003. Maximum width, 1½". Collection Colina and Raymond C. Yazzie

Opposite page:
Raymond Yazzie wears a bolo tie created by his brother Lee Yazzie.

MIKE BIRD-ROMERO

San Juan and Taos Pueblos
Placitas, New Mexico

When I was a boy, I was always fascinated to watch the silversmiths turn something flat into something three-dimensional. In San Juan Pueblo we had some pretty famous silversmiths. I grew up with their kids, and when I'd go home with the guys to play, I'd see the father working on jewelry. Instead of going to play, I just wanted to stand there and watch him work. In junior high, you could take a course in jewelry-making. I've always been the type of person to look at something and say "I can do that." So I started making jewelry, including cloisonné. I thought it looked good, and apparently some of the teachers did too, because they would take some of the pieces for themselves and leave money so I could buy more materials. That's really where I started.

At the time that I was getting started, Charles Loloma and other artists were making contemporary jewelry prominent. Everybody was doing it, and that was the first style I worked in myself. After a while I decided I wanted to make more traditional jewelry. When I see older-style pieces, I see my mother. My mom used to have great old jewelry that she'd wear. Maybe that's where my romance with jewelry making comes into play. When I make things, I do it with the intention of my mother liking it.

I call myself a silversmith, not a jeweler, because when I started making jewelry, I learned the old techniques. In other words, I can make anything that I need to make. I don't depend on somebody else to cut my silver for me, melt my silver, make my castings, or cut my stones. I do it all myself.

Along with jewelry techniques, I learned about business from talking to more experienced silversmiths. One man I've always admired, Julian Lovato, gave me advice; "Always give your customer quality. Always use good stones. It's up to you as to how you do your business." And my mother was always my rock. She told me to always be mindful of how I handle myself. She would say, "You don't want to make yourself ineffective and price yourself out of the market. Set your pricing in such a way that you don't hurt yourself and you don't hurt your customer. It should benefit both of you.

I like to use old stamps on my pieces. The stamps tell a little story, so to speak, and those stories get incorporated into my jewelry. I've got tin cans full of stamps that were collected. My wife and I used to go to the old stores in Gallup. One of the little Navajo ladies who befriended us knew that I was always looking for stamps, no matter what condition they were in. Sometimes I've heated them up and reworked them so they're useable again. I look at these stamps and the pieces I made with them, and I think about the old smiths. I hope the young people that are coming up see older things and have the same impressions that I have. I hope they get the same kind of positive feelings from the old things so they can go forward and keep doing their best.

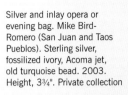

Silver and inlay opera or evening bag. Mike Bird-Romero (San Juan and Taos Pueblos). Sterling silver, fossilized ivory, Acoma jet, old turquoise bead. 2003. Height, 3¾". Private collection

192

VICTOR BECK, SR.

Navajo (Diné)
Manygoats Clan
Phoenix, Arizona

Although my mother and father weren't jewelers, they were collectors of jewelry. My father had a real eye for turquoise. He knew how to tell a quality stone, and he did a lot of business with the Zunis and the Hopis. Even though my father went through only the sixth grade, he was a tribal council delegate for twenty years. And my mother worked for the Bureau of Indian Affairs. They wanted to look nice and liked to wear the best quality jewelry. Turquoise has always been a gem for the Navajo. There are four sacred stones of the Navajo people—white shell, turquoise, abalone, and jet. Those four are part of our dress and customs and ceremonies. Those four I try to put into my jewelry.

I was a repo man for a while; I was a bank teller. But I found out what I wanted to be back in 1970. I was studying ceramics at college, but to get my degree, I had to take jewelry making. That's when I knew I wanted to work with jewelry. For a while I worked for another man who bought and sold Indian jewelry. For ten percent cash, I would go out on the road to different retailers with about $100,000 worth of inventory. One time I took a break and went back to Pinon to visit with my parents. While I was there, I had a dream that I went out to my pickup and all the jewelry was gone. When I told my parents about the dream, right away my dad said, "Let me go get the medicine man. Right today." My mom agreed, "Let's do it. Let's have a Blessingway ceremony. This shouldn't happen this way. If you're going to be working with jewelry, if you're going to be working with turquoise, you don't do it this way . . . just make money, make money. You have to stop and give thanks." So we had the ceremony that night, the next day, and the following night. After the ceremony, my mother said, "Victor, four days you be reverent. Don't go anywhere. Just stay home. Those four days you don't wash your body, you don't shave. Do nothing. Just be very reverent and think about your future." So for four days I sat, and I thought about my jewelry. And then it dawned on me. I said out loud to myself, "Why can't I learn it myself? Quality. Not quantity."

I'm a deeply rooted traditional person, but I'm also a Catholic. After my father died, I stayed in Pinon with my mother for a while, making jewelry, doing business there in my studio. One day the Father from the Catholic church next door came over and asked me, "Victor, these nuns in Donaldson, Indiana, want something for Our Holy Father in Rome. Would you be able to create something?" So I talked to the Mother Superior and she told me, "This year we're going to be making a pilgrimage to Rome to visit the Holy Father. We would like to take a piece that's made by the Native Americans. Can you make something that's befitting a chief? It can be a concho belt or a necklace, but the bottom line is it has to tell a story about your traditional ways."

I couldn't see the Holy Father wearing a big concho belt or a squash blossom necklace. So I prayed for what to do. I was driving along when all of a sudden it just hit me—a rosary. For our traditional ways, I use the four "our fathers" to represent the four sacred directions—the white shell represents the east mountain, the turquoise is the south, abalone to the west, and jet to the north. On all the beads in the ten Hail Marys, I put designs of the traditional Navajo weavers. And where you come back down to the Blessed Mother, I incorporated the white shell again because it represents the female figure. The crucifix had all turquoise, representing the male figure, and I added a touch of coral representing the blood. That's how I did the rosary. I recorded the story of it and the nuns loved it. So that rosary went to the Holy Father in 1978.

Being a Catholic, I have a lot of respect for their ways. The rosary had a lot of meaning for me. And from that day on, I've used the four sacred stones in a lot of my necklaces. And for each necklace, when I start working on the white shell, the turquoise, the abalone, and the jet, I do the traditional prayer.

After I did the rosary, people started coming around to ask me to run for tribal council. I was reluctant because I need my jewelry career. But at the same time, my people were in dire need of social and economic development for the community. We didn't have electricity, we didn't have a lot of conveniences that other communities had. So for four years I was a tribal council delegate, and I laid the groundwork for a public school and a big grocery store. Electricity came in; water came in. And I did the comprehensive plan so we could have development in business.

I've lived on the Navajo reservation the better part of my sixty-two years, but I lived other places too. When I was a kid, during the school year, I would go to school off the reservation. As I got into my career in the 1970s, I lived here and there, but my home base was usually Flagstaff. One of the four Navajo sacred mountains, San Francisco Peak, the mountain to the west, is nearby, and because of that, I always find peace there.

Even though I live in Phoenix now, the bottom line for me has always been "Remember who you are. Remember your prayers. Remember your traditional ways." At the beginning of my career, my father told me, "Son, don't just receive all of the time. If you overload yourself, it's going to get heavy for you, and you can lose your balance. So to keep yourself balanced, be thankful." Every four years I have the Blessingway ceremony for my creative ability and for my health. Also, each piece that I do, I pray for it, that it will find a good home, a good family that will take care of my little creation. That's my way of keeping balance with my tradition and my artwork.

Necklace, bracelet, ring, earring set. Victor Beck (Navajo). The necklace has eighteen strands of coral beads with turquoise, agate, onyx, 14-karat gold. 1993. Length of necklace, 18". Collection Edna Rober

194

GARY YOYOKIE, SR.

Hopi

ELSIE YOYOKIE

Navajo (Diné)

(Interview with Elsie Yoyokie)
Kiqötsmovi, Hopi, Arizona

When Gary was about eleven years old he worked for the Hopi Crafts as a janitor, sweeping the floors. He would watch the artisans, and eventually he tried to do some cutting in the silver. Gary worked there every summer through school, and that's how he learned the Hopi overlay technique. Gary and I were high school sweethearts, and we got married right out of high school. He went to college at Northern Arizona University in Flagstaff for law enforcement. We lived there for two years, and every summer and every semester break he would work on his jewelry. Sometimes he'd ask me to help him with certain things, and I started learning from him. First I just cleaned up the jewelry, then he asked me to cut designs. I started saying, I like this design or that design, and I started cutting them out myself. We started combining ideas. To this day, we share the work, and we share ideas.

I'm actually Navajo, and my parents live about an hour away from Hopi, at Low Mountain. I went to grade school at Hopi for eight years, so I was exposed to Hopi all of that time. And then I went to high school down at the Phoenix Indian School, and there was a mixture of tribes. So I got to know the other tribes, and I met Gary.

After the second year of college, Gary knew he didn't want to go into law enforcement and that he liked doing his artwork more than anything else. So we moved back to Hopi. My mother-in-law has a little *piki* house [a building with fire-heated stone for making piki, a flat, blue-corn bread], and she said we could use one area. Jewelry-making is messy with chemicals and noisy machines. But she reserved us a little area, and we started working.

We do the traditional Hopi overlay, and we also do contemporary. We have our own technique with texture that we came up with. People ask us how we do that, but it's a secret. We decided that it would just be our thing. A lot of times we blend it with gold or turquoise or coral. Sometimes we say to each other that we shouldn't have started it, because it's such a long process. But we also do the traditional two-layer overlay. And I think we're the only ones

that do three-layer bracelets. With three-layer work the second layer is cut out to show a design against a bottom one, then we add a third cut-out layer. With all the pounding when you're forming the bracelet, sometimes you leave hammer marks. So the third layer puts a clean surface on it.

The ideas for our designs come from everywhere. I might be cooking or Gary might be chopping wood, and, just out of the blue, you think of a design. A lot of it is from his traditions, designs that were handed down from generation to generation, things that Gary remembers from when he was young. He does a four-seasons design where he splits up the piece into four ways. I like to do insect designs, like butterfly, ladybug, or dragonfly. At first I liked them because they're pretty. But Gary said, "You know, those are water messengers, because they're the ones who tell us there's rain coming. When you don't see them, they've gone to find shelter, and that means we're going to have a storm."

Gary and I have been together so long, we connect with certain things. Gary will see something I'm doing and say, "Oh, that's cool," and then he'll make suggestions to improve it. We go back and forth. Sometimes, I'll tell him something's too busy, and he'll tell me when I'm getting too carried away. We tell each other honestly, and it makes our work better. It's just the two of us working so it takes a lot of time, and we just do one-of-a-kind pieces. We take a lot of pride in our work, and we try to get our jewelry the cleanest that we can get it. When we put our name on it, it means you're getting quality. We were invited to Japan to show our technique. People think we cut out the designs by machine because the cutting is so perfect. I think when people see how our work is made they begin to appreciate how much time it takes.

We've also made some pieces for our children, ceremonial pieces, and those will probably never be sold. They'll probably hand them down to their kids. And, those are for prayer purposes, which are always stored away; it's not for everyday wear.

My parents and grandparents are very traditional Navajo, but I've seen a lot of the Hopi traditional ways too. I have two boys who are active in their Hopi traditional activities. So, more or less, I carry things out like a Hopi lady. I got initiated, and I got a name, and I have a godmother at Hopi. Other than high school in Phoenix and the two years in Flagstaff, I've lived in Hopi all my life. I know who I am. I'll never be totally a Hopi, but living here with my husband and being a part of the community is good—whatever goes on, I participate.

We'll always be Native. You might live modern, but you need to have that traditional spirit. I have running water and electricity, and I live in a mobile home. I feel good living like that, because it makes life easy. I grew up in a hogan, and I know what that's like too. When I was small we had no running water, no power, just kerosene—traditional all the way down to the core. I like the modern conveniences that I have now, but at the same time I appreciate keeping our traditional values.

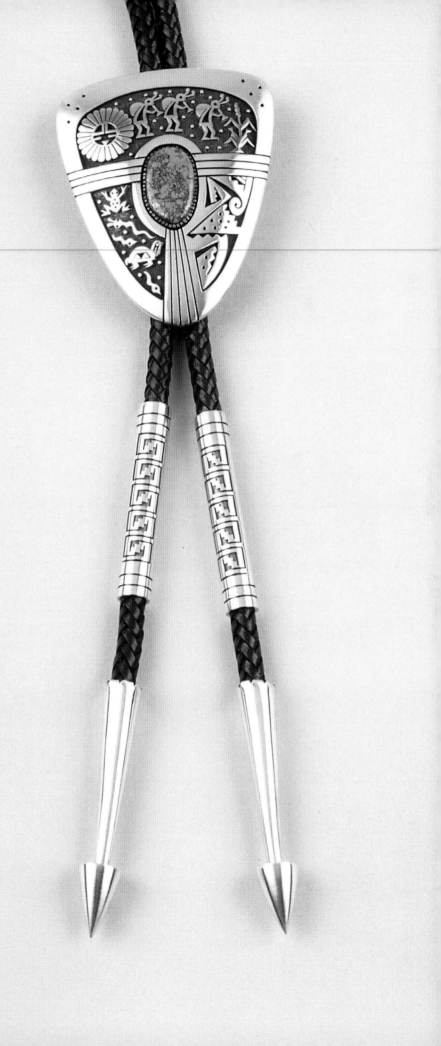

Overlay bolo tie. Gary Yoyokie, Sr. (Hopi) and Elsie Yoyokie (Navajo). Depicted in 14-karat gold against a silver background are (from top left) corn plant, grasshopper flute players with bags of seeds on their backs, water droplets, a sun symbol, geometric patterns representing lightning and storms, and water messengers including snakes, tadpoles, and frogs. The Morenci turquoise stone set in the center represents the sun. The Yoyokies' three-layer overlay with a stone set in a shadow box is part of their signature style. 1991. Private collection

196

VERNON HASKIE

Navajo (Diné)
Water Flows Together Clan, Towering House Clan,
Big Water Clan, Bitter Water Clan
Lukachukai, Arizona

One Christmas, my parents purchased Tonka trucks for my brother and me. I had already seen my father working, and I asked him, "Dad, why are you pounding on that metal so hard?" He told me, "Leave me alone, I'm making money." So I thought, "Well, I guess you can pound on metal and make money. This Tonka truck's made out of metal, I might as well pound it." And I pounded mine flat with a sledge hammer. My mother patted me on the shoulder and said "Son, what are you doing with your toy?" I said, "Leave me alone, I'm making money." So that's how it started.

Actually I started making things when I was nine years old. I had observed my parents making jewelry, so I challenged myself to make a pendant. My parents were away one afternoon and I just did it. I completed my first pendant on my own. They were both artists. My father would do the metalwork, and my mother would do the inlay. I learned some of the basic techniques and styles from my father. But I also saw Hopi overlay, the heishi-type strands of turquoise, the Zuni inlay. So I knew that there were more possibilities than just the style my parents did. When I started building on my artwork, I vowed never to get formal training, because I don't want to credit any institution or any other artist as being where I picked up my work.

The jewelers that I really look up to, like Jesse Monongya and Harvey Begay, are the ones who took Native American jewelry art into new directions. They expressed creativity that I had never seen in the pawn-shops of Gallup or in the trading posts.

A lot of the strength to learn jewelry came through prayers and ceremonies. They helped me to understand myself and my mental and physical capabilities more. And they helped me explore into the realm of creativity. Before I had many of these ceremonies, I was envious of what other artists could create. But the ceremonies opened a whole new world and I came to understand that creativity is endless. There's just so much out there, that to be able to get your hands on some of it is a blessing.

When I thought deeply about this, I knew all the designs and ideas that I have, I can't possibly create in my lifetime. That's how big creativity is, so I might as well pick out the best ones, the ones that are really vibrant and exuberant and come from my soul. I think the spiritual beliefs give you the encouragement to explore your mind, to open up and know that it's okay to experiment with extraordinary things that don't seem feasible. If you can make it, then you know your technique and your skills have become more honed.

In my culture, harmony and balance relate to the use of materials like turquoise, coral, silver, gold. These are all part of Mother Earth. When you use them and manipulate them, heat them, bang them, cut them, grind them, then you're kind of abusing Mother Earth. So what the ceremonies do is bring you back into balance and let her know that you don't mean to do these things.

When we have a Blessingway ceremony, there's a part where we have to take off some of our clothing—usually our traditional velveteen-type clothing—along with our jewelry. The clothes are set apart, and the jewelry is washed in a basket. And then we put our clothing back on, take our jewelry out of the basket, and we put it back on. It means that you went through a transition of who you were into a holy person. And when you're in that holy state, you're supposed to be humble and mindful of not making errors, like abusing animals or Mother Earth.

A long time ago wearing beautiful jewelry was part of courtship. You would try to adorn yourself to attract someone. And in the spiritual sense, the deities or the holy people identify you through your jewelry as well. They look down and they say, "This is a child of mine because he's wearing turquoise." There are stories behind white shells, turquoise, black jet, and the abalone shell. If you know the stories, it puts you in connection with the deities and then, when you do your offerings or your prayers, you're able to communicate.

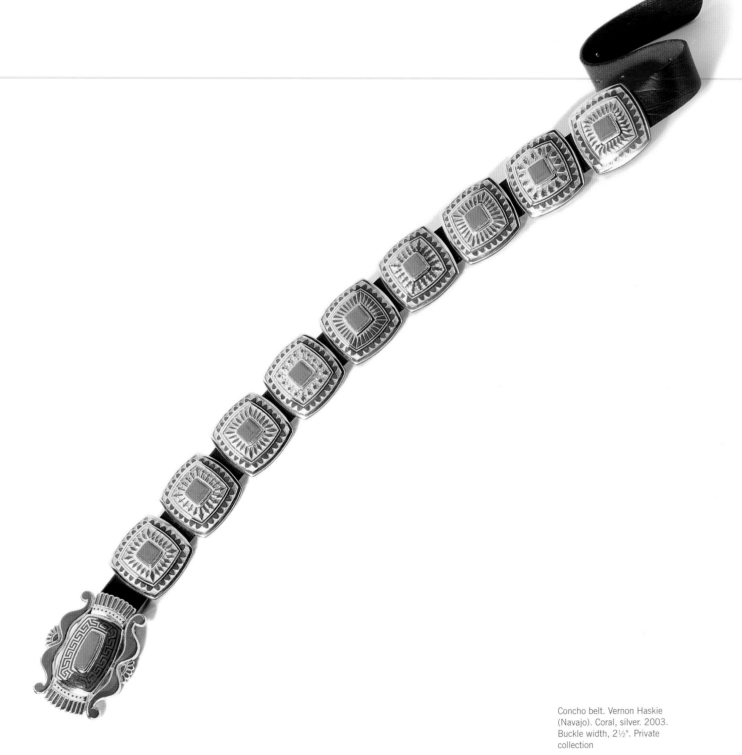

Concho belt. Vernon Haskie (Navajo). Coral, silver. 2003. Buckle width, 2½". Private collection

MARTINE LOVATO

Santo Domingo Pueblo
Albuquerque, New Mexico

I am *keewame'*, a Santo Domingo Pueblo man. My parents made jewelry the old way; they worked by hand, using a flat stone for grinding, sanding, and polishing. When I was growing up, we didn't have electricity around the village, and what interested me most was watching my parents make jewelry. I watched them and I learned. Nowadays a lot of young people in the village are not really interested in the jewelry. They'd rather watch the TV.

My mother made Thunderbird necklaces. These necklaces were made out of natural turquoise, old car batteries for black, and plastic spoons for red and white. The bead part of the necklace was made of bone or gypsum. Gypsum deposits are on our Santo Domingo land, and I remember my father carrying the heavy gypsum long distances on foot to our house. Like other children in our village, I'd go out looking for those spoons, picking up things for my mother and cutting them for her. She made the best Thunderbird necklaces in that way.

Ideas for my jewelry come into my mind from lots of places. I have dreams, and I walk in the mountains, in the fresh air, especially in the autumn, all those beautiful leaves falling down, different colors. I get up very early in the morning to pray. I see the Morning Star. One time it looked like there were different colors coming out of it. So that gave me the idea for the star bracelet.

It makes me feel good to see people wearing my jewelry. Because there is my handiwork, my professional work in that necklace. And in the village, a lot of Santo Domingo people wear my jewelry for our ceremonial dances, and that really fills me with happiness when I see them wearing it. Collectors worldwide wear my jewelry today. Each year people come to my booth at Indian Market in Santa Fe wearing necklaces, bracelets, or earrings of mine, and I'm so happy to see those pieces and the people who bought them.

I got a fellowship in 2001 from SWAIA [Southwestern Association for Indian Arts], and people from Santo Domingo Pueblo were really amazed. They'd say, "You're so talented. We didn't know you could make that kind of necklace." I'm not drinking anymore. This'll be about fifteen years. My family is really proud of me, and I feel so good about the changes that I made.

I used to work in silver but silverworking is not part of our Santo Domingo Pueblo history. I choose to follow the traditions of my people and work with the shells and the turquoise. In the [ceremonial] dances we wear necklaces made of these things. They're very traditional. I don't know how many years it's been going back—a long time. Turquoise is very important to our Pueblo culture. The true meaning of it is only known to a certain few people. We cannot tell this meaning outside of our culture. I can only say that it is very spiritual and inspirational and that we use it when we pray.

I used to go to Gallup to sell my jewelry to the Navajos. I would see other people from Santo Domingo there too, selling the *jaclas*. *Jaclas* are a little string of beads that are tied to the bottom of a longer string of beads. People still wear them that traditional way by tying the two strings together. I eliminated any string hanging or showing using one continuous thread so that it hangs beautifully with no gaps. So I set up my booth in the Gallup flea market; I took these new necklaces out there and I sold them all out. Now you see necklaces like this a lot, but I was the one that designed it like this first.

Now I'm using the finest materials that I can find, and I make my jewelry slowly and carefully, thinking it through and making it as beautiful as I can make it. To create one piece, it takes a long time. There's a lot of caution, there's a lot of things that go into it. Often, when I'm making a piece, I sing. Those songs are a prayer that remains in my jewelry and that is the gift of myself that I give to the people who wear my jewelry.

The jewelry I make is for anybody who wants to wear it. I like for people to wear it because it's coming from my heart, my hand, and my culture.

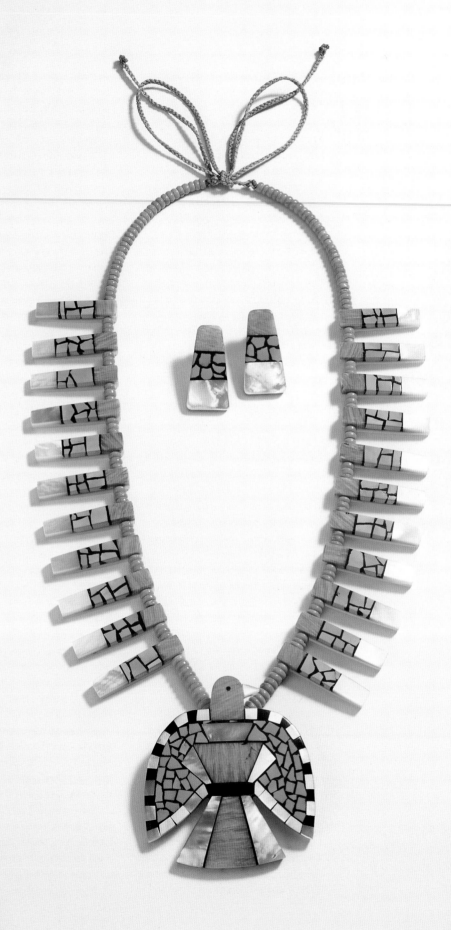

Thunderbird necklace and matching earrings. Martine Lovato (Santo Domingo Pueblo). In an artful and dramatic expansion of the Thunderbird necklace, Martine Lovato replaces the low-cost materials used in historic Thunderbird necklaces with fine materials including turquoise, mother-of-pearl, spiny oyster shell, and jet. 2001. Total length (without string tie), 25". Collection Museum of Native American Jewelry, Albuquerque, New Mexico

Opposite page:
Martine Lovato wears jewelry of his design and making and holds his "Star" bracelet created in 2003.

200

MYRON PANTEAH

Navajo (Diné) and Zuni
Bear Clan (Zuni) and Water Edge Clan (Navajo)
Zuni Pueblo, New Mexico

My family used to live in California, but they would send me back to my father's family at Zuni for the summers. I would stick with my grandmother all the time. My cousins picked on me because, even though I was darker than my cousins, I was the "white boy." So I would sit with my grandmother and watch her work on her jewelry. She let me heat the wax she used to put the stones on the ends of matchsticks so she could grind them really small for the petitpoint jewelry. In California, I'd watch my dad make jewelry, the little bit that he could in-between his jobs.

By the time I got to high school, my parents divorced and I was sent to my Navajo grandparents. Then jewelry became a way for me to make money to buy my own school clothes and support myself. I learned the traditional Navajo style of jewelry, but I would go to my dad's books and magazines and see Richard Chavez, Jesse Monongya, and Charles Loloma, and their contemporary styles of work. So I tried to copy that work because it was different and I liked it. It was a good learning process. That way I knew I could do that style but still learn different things from it and develop my own style. I always say: "I don't want to be a master jeweler; I just want to be a better jeweler."

I was taught by my grandfather that you've got to do things for yourself. If you can't afford something, you can always make it, so that's how I learned to make my own tools and develop my own style of working. For a while I worked for a defense contractor, working 18-hour days, but still I'd come home and work for a couple hours on my jewelry.

Since I grew up in California and then later lived on the Navajo Reservation, I'd never really lived in Zuni. My dad did a lot for the family and after he passed away, there was nobody else to pick up where he left off. I wanted to find my Zuni heritage, so I've lived there for almost five years now. At Zuni, in their eyes, I'm still a kid even though now I'm almost forty. I've got a little brother who's eighteen and he's considered a Zuni "man," so it's kind of funny. There's a lot I'm learning around Zuni, and I'm seeing petroglyphs different than I've seen anywhere else. I'm putting these things back into my work. There are certain religious things that you can and cannot do. When I'm not really sure, I talk to the religious leaders and ask if it's okay.

In my style of jewelry, I insert a blade through the sheet silver and saw the designs out. People think I use a laser to cut out the designs, but it's all done by hand. I use a lot of texturing, and I'm getting back into lapidary work again. The stones I use come from all over the world. I don't work in turquoise or coral or lapis, like most Southwest jewelers. I like agates and jaspers because of the busy-ness and colors in them . . . greens and peaches and oranges, which are hard to find in other stones. The way I was taught, you don't value one thing more than another in something that's natural.

I use a lot of symbols in my work, like the migration spiral symbol. Everybody has a migration symbol in their fingerprints, and, on the tops of their heads, they have that little spiral that's like the solar system. At home we pray for rain, so most of the symbols I use pertain to water, like lightning and clouds and frogs and dragonflies. People ask me what the petroglyphs and other traditional symbols mean, and I explain to them what they're seeing. So the knowledge goes to them, and they spread it along. Sometimes kids have a Boy Scout troop, and they're the Zuni group or the Navajos or the Hopis, and they have all these little tribes going. They see that I'm an Indian and they ask what tribe I am. Parents will bring their kids so I can explain things to them. So through my art, it spreads my culture out there to other cultures.

And I do other symbols too. I go to galleries and shows. I get ideas from everywhere—light fixtures, pottery, driving through the mountains in Vermont, seeing things that are different than what you see at home. I think it was like that a long time ago, too, when they traveled to the oceans to bring back shells. They would see something different and come back and put it on the rocks in petroglyphs and pictographs. That's what my work shows, connections to new things.

I keep the contemporary and traditional art separate, mainly for the older people. If you add something contemporary to the traditional, they get after you for it. And I understand, because the older people feel like they're losing a lot right now. So if I do something like *manta* pins for a lady's traditional dress, then I'll make those real traditional, with the big turquoise and the silver. When I do my contemporary, far-out things, I'll show that to the older people, and that's okay . . . they like to see a bit of tradition in the contemporary, but they don't want to see any of the contemporary in the traditional. They do like to see new things and know that we're out there being educated and seeing different things because they've never been out to see that. But they still want what's traditional to be traditional.

Belt. Myron Panteah (Navajo-Zuni). Silver, 14-karat gold, Montana agate, fire agate, psilomelane, red moss agate, Boulder opal, green moss agate, ocean jasper, velvet obsidian. 2003. Total length, 48". Collection Sally and Ron Clonts

RICHARD CHAVEZ

San Felipe Pueblo
Algodones, New Mexico

When I got into the jewelry-making business, I had no idea it was going to be a part of my life for twenty-eight years. I had been working as an architectural draftsman in Albuquerque, and going to the University of New Mexico, planning to get a degree in architecture. I was married and I had a child, and it was difficult to make ends meet on a minimum wage. I had to supplement the income so I bought a book on how to silversmith, Navajo-style, and sat down one day to make a bracelet. I had no idea what I was doing. I turned the torch on, and nothing happened. I sat there for half the day trying to make the solder flow but it wouldn't do anything. In frustration, I took off the small torch and put on a larger torch which threw out a bigger flame . . . all I wanted to do was melt the bracelet down. Well, then the solder flowed, and I said, "Okay—the bigger the piece, the larger the flame you have to use!"

Early on I didn't know how I was going to market my work or where to get advice. I'd seen people sell work at the portal at the Palace of the Governors in Santa Fe. So I went and set up one morning, but I just couldn't sell my work that way. It wasn't my way so I packed up. I decided to try Santa Fe Indian Market, and I met Martha Hopkins Struever from Chicago who was looking for a new artist for her gallery. So that fall I went to Chicago for a show. It was a new experience for me, a person from the pueblo who had never been outside of New Mexico . . . it was my first plane trip. I had to just sink or swim and learn everything as it came along.

At the beginning, I made one traditional piece, a silver ring with turquoise, but I couldn't see myself in it. There was no identity in it as mine, as a "Richard Chavez." I kept exploring; pretty soon the different colors of stone came together, and I could see my style. I use a lot of semi-precious and precious stones in different colors. I've never done all turquoise jewelry because I feel there's enough out there already. I use turquoise only for accents.

After a year of doing jewelry part-time, I needed to make a decision. There was a demand for my work . . . should I go into it full-time? But school was an important part of my life; my grandfather had always stressed education; he believed you needed it to succeed, especially if you were a minority. So I really had to think about it. I never went back to architecture, and I don't regret it because the jewelry business has been great for me and my family.

I'm married to a woman who's Hopi-Tewa and Navajo. She grew up in a boarding school, which was difficult for her because she lost a lot of her culture. I came from a traditional background. When we had our first child we had to decide if we wanted to live in the city. We decided to move back to San Felipe and have our children grow up feeling good about who they are. And it has been good for them. The oldest daughter has pushed herself in education, and now she's in a position to make a difference as a Native American. She works as an associate curator with the Smithsonian's National Museum of the American Indian in Washington, D.C. We're proud of her accomplishments.

My designs are influenced by whatever I see . . . buildings, paintings, sculpture, etc. But I don't use symbolism in my jewelry because it contradicts my culture. I feel good about the jewelry I'm doing today because it's pure art that I make. I put my whole self into the work from start to finish. When someone purchases a work of mine I feel honored that it's appreciated. When I first got into jewelry-making, my grandfather said, "Your talent doesn't just come from you, it comes from some higher source, so don't ever take it for granted. Make sure you give your thanks and that you share that gift that you have." And that's what I try to do.

I feel I've made a difference as a Native American going out into the dominant society because there are so many people who are still unaware of Native Americans —that we still exist. We're out there. We're doing what everybody else is doing, trying to make a living, taking care of our families. I think people appreciate knowing that we're just like any other people.

Bolo tie. Richard Chavez (San Felipe Pueblo). Black jade, dolomite, coral, turquoise. 2003. Length, 3". Courtesy Garland's Trading Post

204

RIC CHARLIE

Navajo (Diné)
Flagstaff, Arizona

I base a lot of my designs on growing up on the reservation. My family uses modern amenities but is traditional; we go to traditional ceremonies. At the same time, my elders have always spoken to me in English. They were preparing me for the modern world, too. Back then I admired the artists that started in the early seventies, like Charles Loloma, Kenneth Begay, Preston Monongye. I saw that they did a lot of lapidary work and fabrication and casting. I really admire the lifestyle these artists were living and the freedom and the joy that they had in creating their work. So, I decided early in my life that I wanted to be an artist.

I lived in Phoenix for twenty years, but it's not necessarily a beneficial thing for me. The city lights and the lifestyle were exciting as a younger person. But now those kinds of materialistic things don't mean a whole lot to me. I feel more in need of peace of mind and something more spiritual in life. So I've come closer to home.

I'm known for my tufa-casting work. Tufa is a volcanic ash that has been compressed into a soft stone. I take it out of the ground myself and cut it into blocks. Then I carve my design into the stone. I have to create a passageway for air to escape as well as a sprue hole where molten metal flows into the mold. Once the main mold is created, I use another piece of tufa as a backing, and sometimes I carve it too so that there's a design on the backside. I have to match the two blocks up exactly perfect—there's no room for error. Before I pour in the molten metal, I put on a coating of soot to lubricate the stone and help the metal flow. Once the piece cools, you separate the mold, and you've got your cast piece in silver or gold. When you pull out the piece and relieve it from the mold, it somtimes rips out the whole design with it. Usually I can get only one creation out of a mold. If it's a simple design with no undercuts, you might get multiple pieces from one mold. But a lot of the work I do has undercuts, so it's all one-of-a-kind castings with my work.

When I carve both sides of the mold—in other words, both sides of the piece—it means there will be a design on the back, maybe against your wrist if it's a bracelet. I think every part of the jewelry should be created with beauty. The backside should be just as beautiful as the front.

On my dad's side, we're from a place near Monument Valley, Arizona. I feel close to that part of the reservation. I have a strong, rooted feeling in that valley. I actually had an out-of-body experience one time. I was talking to a friend of mine —nowhere near Monument Valley—and all of a sudden, I was *in* Monument Valley. I was on top of the buttes. But the mesas and buttes were actually *yé'ii* [Navajo holy beings], and they were slowly looking over the valley. I couldn't understand why I was there and why I was eye-to-eye with them. And I could I see myself in the valley, where all of these *yé'ii* were slowly looking around, guarding the valley, protecting it.

I went over to Monument Valley the next day, and drove into the valley in a jeep. Since I felt like this was my home, I drove off the main road, and I went deep into the valley. The strong force of the rock told me to stop, and it drew me like a magnetic force over to this mesa. I put my hands on it, and, like a computer relaying messages to me, it told me: This is who I am; this is what I'm all about; I'm here to stay—I cannot be budged. Ever since then I've had a strong sense of being a part of Monument Valley. So a lot of my work has the Monument Valley scenery. Every time I feel down, I always think about my place in life. And I feel that I have something to give into this world. I continue to try as hard as I can to be who I am, and I try to express that in my work.

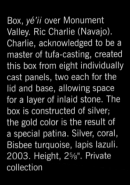

Box, *yé'ii* over Monument Valley. Ric Charlie (Navajo). Charlie, acknowledged to be a master of tufa-casting, created this box from eight individually cast panels, two each for the lid and base, allowing space for a layer of inlaid stone. The box is constructed of silver; the gold color is the result of a special patina. Silver, coral, Bisbee turquoise, lapis lazuli. 2003. Height, 2⅝". Private collection

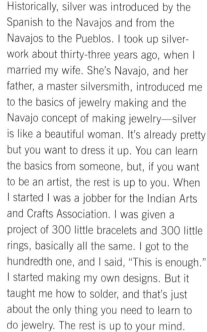

206

PHIL LORETTO

Jemez and Cochiti Pueblos
Cerrillos, New Mexico

Historically, silver was introduced by the Spanish to the Navajos and from the Navajos to the Pueblos. I took up silverwork about thirty-three years ago, when I married my wife. She's Navajo, and her father, a master silversmith, introduced me to the basics of jewelry making and the Navajo concept of making jewelry—silver is like a beautiful woman. It's already pretty but you want to dress it up. You can learn the basics from someone, but, if you want to be an artist, the rest is up to you. When I started I was a jobber for the Indian Arts and Crafts Association. I was given a project of 300 little bracelets and 300 little rings, basically all the same. I got to the hundredth one, and I said, "This is enough." I started making my own designs. But it taught me how to solder, and that's just about the only thing you need to learn to do jewelry. The rest is up to your mind.

I was nationally known as a painter for a while, but my paintings got too political. It was a political time—the late sixties and early seventies. I was part of a group of young activists who wanted to make a change in Native American politics, trying to get better benefits for Indians in any field, whether it was engineering or plumbers. So when you're in that life, you don't have much time for yourself. You exhaust yourself, and it's not healthy for the family. Artwork was what saved us. In the art world, I kept my mind intact, and I started focusing my mind toward creativities.

And I realized you can't sell your ideas of aggression to people; it's not a good way to make a living, making explosive artwork that rubs people the wrong way. You can make a statement, but after a while it's only for your own relief. So I decided to drop out of painting because I knew that jewelry would be more economically sound for me, especially when I was going to college.

One time I was at my lowest, thinking I was not going to make it in the art world. I was sitting on the porch on the Navajo reservation, and I was worried, "Gosh, can anything get any worse?" And here comes a spider, crawling along the ground, really moving along. And there was a little rock, but it looked like a big boulder next to him.

Next thing you know one of his legs hits that rock. Bam! That spider flipped all over the place, and I cracked up. I thought, "Well, that guy has eight legs, and he's still having problems." So I got up and went into the workshop. I always use that memory of the spider as my mentor.

Historically the Southwest has been difficult for jobs because it's so rural. Especially after the wars, World War II and the Korean conflict, the soldiers came back, and they didn't have jobs. A lot of them resorted to doing artwork because that was one of the few means they had of making money. That's mostly how people trained to be an artist. Because it was that or construction. The construction trades took a lot of men away from their families, because they had to move to cities. So a lot of times, the men who could, chose art.

In Santa Fe, New Mexico, artists sell their work under the portal, the front porch of the Palace of the Governors on the plaza. It's a marketplace that's been there since the Spanish came in. I basically grew up under the portal, selling jewelry from the time I was about four or five years old. It's a good place to sell to the tourists and for them to see your work. And it's a good way to make money. But you ask yourself, What are my feelings about this? What can I do that sets me apart? What's my objective? What's the jewelry saying to me about myself? Is this going to be my destiny, to always produce pieces that I know will sell but that don't necessarily challenge me creatively—something that's so nice that it floats? We all have to think about making money for our families, but the difference is the time and effort that you put into a particular piece. That's what sets you apart as an artist.

Making the art, the jewelry, takes a lot of endurance. It takes a lot of faith. Sometimes when you're doing a particular piece, it takes knowledge, a background check on your history. In the contemporary work you have to use a bit of the old look and a bit of the future, to create the pieces.

In reality, one stone is not better than another. But you like to pick out the best stone that you can. Sometimes you're cutting a stone so small, the size of your eyelash, and you want to put a curl in it. That one stone might take twenty hours to cut and fit into one particular slot. So you don't want flaws in your stones. You want it to be just as clean as it can be.

When I first start on a piece, I don't know what I'm going to make. I peer into a piece of metal, and the peering comes back, and I start from there. Sometimes I do drawings right on my beads and bracelets and buckles. I guess I've recorded history in my jewelry, because I draw what goes on in Pueblo life or in Navajo life— the traditional dances and people working in their fields. It used to be a tradition with the Pueblos and the Navajos that the Pueblos would do the vegetables, and the weaving, and make traditional garb, and then they would go to the Navajos to trade for silver adornment, and sheep, and goats. We would trade them pumpkins, apples, pears, chilis, melons—whatever we grew.

I read a lot; it's one of my passions. Growing up in Santa Fe, I got my first library card when I was five. I would read five books a week on Native American culture. Later I majored in Southwest studies and in art. I incorporate a lot of myths and legends from South American, Mexican, and Canadian Indians in my jewelry.

I like to work with just about everybody. I'll sit down with a client and find out where they're from, their background, their heritage, favorite colors, their ideas, faith, convictions. I look at their builds, and then I design pieces around the particular person. Jewelry is like a healing process sometimes, because I consider my pieces to be very dear to the people who wear them. They purchase jewelry because they want to remember something, or they have a special occasion. My personal feelings go into the piece so that when the buyer gets it, that becomes part of their enjoyment. I like to say that a jeweler or an artist is much like a doctor—somebody who brings the healing process to the person who's receiving the art.

"Butterfly Songs" necklace. Phil Loretto (Jemez and Cochiti). Red coral, fossilized ivory, turquoise, jet, abalone, mother-of-pearl, Royal Web turquoise, silver. Ca. late 1970s. Pendant length, 3⅛". Collection Jim and Val Reeks

208 ANTHONY LOVATO

Santo Domingo Pueblo
Corn Clan
Santo Domingo Pueblo, New Mexico

Our ancestors always had personal adornment. At places like Chaco Canyon and Mesa Verde [home to ancestral Pueblo Indians through the 1200s AD], they found different shells and necklaces, bracelets, and feather ornaments. That's proof that we've always made jewelry. Today, jewelry is a source of income, but it's also used in the tradition, especially the shell work. I hardly make any traditional-use jewelry because only the different religious societies can create pieces for their own use. I create pieces to sell to people and different galleries.

My grandfather, Santiago Leo Coriz, was born in 1913. His family had a ranch, so he made horseshoes and other metalwork that was needed. He also learned to do silver jewelry, so I'm a third-generation jeweler. My father did silverwork, but nobody ever told me, "Come here and learn this." I just started watching; that's how I picked up jewelry. When I was in high school I took jewelry classes, and then I majored in metals in college, just to go further. And once I finished that, I moved back home to Santo Domingo, and I've been a full-time jeweler since 1984.

But I've been selling jewelry since I was about thirteen. I sold at the portal in Santa Fe for my parents, so I know what tourists are looking for. A lot of the different peoples that have come to the United States have lost their own culture and are looking for their own spirit or their heritage. So I do spirit pendants. The spirit, I believe, is the other side of the life that we live . . . like day and night, male and female, positive and negative. The balance is in-between the two.

I pursued the metalwork instead of *heishi* or pottery because I wanted to be different. Metal to me is more magical and more forever than pottery and turquoise. And I wanted to become well known. So I created my own style. I do concho belts, bracelets, watchbands, bolo ties, necklaces, squash blossoms, rings, earrings, and also bigger pieces like canteens and wedding vases in metal. The bigger pieces take more time—at least two months— because of my technique. I do the tufa-

casting. With tufa-casting, normally you have to buff it down, remove all the metal scales. But nature has its own designs, so I leave it up to nature when I do my cast work. That's why I leave a lot of texture on my work. In fact, one of my accidents one time was an overflow effect that I hammered back onto the piece. And now that's kind of a signature mark of my own.

I use silver and 18-karat gold, which is my favorite because of the color. It works better for me than the 14- or the 24-karat gold. And I use all kinds of stones from all over the world—Russia, Africa, Madagascar, Brazil, Peru. A lot of the jaspers that I use are from Montana and other states, and I use tourmaline topaz from the San Diego area.

I moved back home to the pueblo after college. Santo Domingo has two religions— the Catholic religion and our own Indian religion, which is off limits for us to talk about because of the Spanish influence. It's not right for a Pueblo person to talk to a non-Pueblo person about his Indian religion in depth, and by this I think we're both better off. It has nothing to do with hate. When the Pueblo people do their prayers, it's for the whole world's harmony and not just in the one place. It's important to me to be at the pueblo, because the creative spirit is easier to capture if you live and work within the village, neighbor to neighbor, house to house. I think if I lived in a city my jewelry would be more contemporary than what it is now. We are a tool for the creative spirit as artists. When we do our prayers, we ask for help and guidance.

Spirit pendants. Anthony Lovato (Santo Domingo Pueblo). Tufa-cast silver set with stones: (left to right) Corn Spirit, malachite azurite; White Buffalo Spirit, jasper drusy; Rain Spirit, blue topaz; Mother Earth with stars, Carico Lake turquoise; Night Spirit, Pilot Mountain turquoise; Rain Spirit, blue chalcedony. Average height, 4½". Private collection

JAMES LITTLE

Navajo (Diné)
Scottsdale, Arizona

I remember the ceremonies from when I was a boy . . . how they sang the songs, how it smelled, the fire dancing. I remember how it was, how I breathed it. It's something that gives me ideas for making my designs. I get ideas from lots of places, like when I have a trip, like a scene, or a landscape, or something from my mom or my dad . . . it all makes a history. I saw a glass elevator in California. I had never seen that before, the people going up and down . . . that was something. I made that elevator as a pendant. Or when my mom is weaving a rug, weaving some traditional design, she tells me the history, and I might come up with an idea to turn it contemporary. So it's like that—something happens to me, and makes the designs come out.

I had a hard time hearing when I was growing up, and that's why I didn't go to school. I was born with a problem in my ears. I still have problems these days . . . sometimes, I can't hear people that well. So I lived about twenty years with my mother and my father. I learned from my mom how to make beadwork for the ceremonial things. My mom was a rug weaver too, and I watched her. She used a lot of traditional designs, and I put those designs in my beadwork. Later on, people got to know that I made good things. So different people, like the son of the medicine man, asked me to make special orders. From the time I was ten to about eighteen, I made a living making things. My father is a medicine man. I would go help with the ceremonies as a drummer, to be a part of it and so I know what the ceremonies are.

When I was over twenty years old, I started to learn arts in a classroom. My brother was studying drawing and said I should come take classes for the summertime. I'd never done anything like that. I learned from Stanley Mitchell, a traditional Navajo-style jeweler. He taught me how to bend the silver and solder. I went back home, and I stayed the whole year with my mom. But I wanted to learn some more. So I went to Navajo Community College in Many Farms, Arizona. I met Kenneth Begay;

he was the teacher there, and I studied another couple years with him.

Then I got offered a job in Flagstaff, Arizona. At that time I didn't know hardly any English. On the reservation, I didn't learn it because everybody spoke Navajo. So that summer, it was hard, but I went to work in a jewelry store in Flagstaff. At first, I didn't know what to do with that curly wire and sheet silver, but I learned. Designs just came out, and ideas of different ways I could work that wire; I called it "twist the wires" design. People started to like that kind of design. So that's how I started, I learned from school, and then learned more from the shop. Because at the shop, it was silver everywhere; I made jewelry eight hours a day for two years.

Some people named Mr. and Mrs. Kirkhuff had bought my jewelry in Flagstaff and really liked it. They invited me to dinner and the first time was tough, because I didn't speak English very well. I went to the restaurant, and I didn't know how to order. I used to just point to a picture as best I could. We got to be friends, and they asked me to go to California to work. I think it was about October of 1976 that I went down to live in their home. They didn't have any family, any kids. They were just so nice, like family, and I got very comfortable. All the time they talked to me in English so I began to learn. I spent almost three years with the Kirkhuffs. Sometimes I wanted to go back home; I missed my dad and my mom. I grew up there, I understand my own language better, but I wanted to learn English too.

I moved back to Sedona, Arizona in 1978. My jewelry and my picture were in the magazine *Arizona Highways*. Through that, a lady named Lovena Ohl said she wanted to have my jewelry in her gallery in Scottsdale. Lovena was a very nice lady. The jewelry and all of the Indian art in her gallery was top of the line, so I was nervous. I didn't think my jewelry was even close; it embarrassed me a little bit. So the first time I met her, I lied and told her I didn't have any jewelry with me, maybe next week.

Having my jewelry in her gallery with all those top artists gave me ideas and made me more creative. It was a lot of education. And it was so nice . . . I don't know how to explain it . . . it was like a family. When I moved to Scottsdale, Lovena got me a special teacher to learn to read and speak English well. I studied a couple hours every night, for five years, summer and winter. I thought I heard the right way, but I would say words a little bit wrong, because that's the way I heard them. Once I knew about that, I learned a lot for myself. So then, finally, I could read a menu.

There's two different ways to think about making jewelry. Sometimes when people work, they look at the time and the hours going by, and they think about how many hours a piece takes. This is the principle people live in—the dollars. And sometimes I have to live in that principle too; I need the dollars. But sometimes, I just enjoy making that thing, touching it with my fingers, what I'm feeling, especially with the stones. Those times I don't think about the dollars. Time keeps going.

Mother and Child ring. James Little (Navajo). 18-karat gold, diamonds, turquoise. 1999–2000. Height, 1½". Collection Dolores Schapiro

BIBLIOGRAPHY

Adair, John. *The Navajo and Pueblo Silversmiths*. Norman: University of Oklahoma Press, 1944.

Benedict, Ruth. *Patterns of Culture*. Boston: Houghton Mifflin Company, 1989.

Brody, J.J. *Anasazi and Pueblo Painting*. Santa Fe: School of American Research, 1991.

Brown, Steven C., ed. *Spirits of the Water: Native Art Collected on Expeditions to Alaska and British Columbia, 1774–1910*. Seattle: University of Washington Press, 2000.

Cordell, Linda S. *Ancient Pueblo Peoples*. Washington, D.C.: Smithsonian Books, 1994.

Dubin, Lois S. *North American Indian Jewelry and Adornment*. New York: Harry N. Abrams, Inc., Publishers, 1999.

————. *Jesse Monongya: Opal Bears and Lapis Skies*. New York and Manchester: Hudson Hills Press, 2002.

Duffek, Karen. *Bill Reid: Beyond the Essential Form*. Museum Note No. 19. Vancouver: The University of British Columbia Press, 1986.

Dutton, Bertha P. *American Indians of the Southwest*. Albuquerque: University of New Mexico Press, 1983.

Drucker, Philip. *Indians of the Northwest Coast*. New York: The American Museum of Natural History, 1955.

Frank, Larry. *Indian Silver Jewelry of the Southwest: 1868–1930*. West Chester, PN: Schiffer Publishing, 1990.

Furst, Peter T. and Jill L. Furst. *North American Indian Art*. New York: Rizzoli, 1982.

Holm, Bill. *Northwest Coast Indian Art: An Analysis of Form*. Vancouver/Toronto: Douglas and McIntyre Ltd., 1965.

Holm, Bill and William Reid: *Form and Freedom: A Dialogue on Northwest Coast Indian Art*. Houston: Institute for the Arts, Rice University, 1975.

Jernigan, E. Wesley. *Jewelry of the Prehistoric Southwest*. Santa Fe: School of American Research, 1978.

Jonaitis, Aldona. *From the Land of the Totem Poles: The Northwest Coast Indian Art Collection at the American Museum of Natural History*. New York: The American Museum of Natural History, 1988.

Jonaitis, Aldona. *Chiefly Feasts: The Enduring Kwakiutl Potlatch*. New York: The American Museum of Natural History, 1991.

Kabotie, Fred and Bill Belknap. *Fred Kabotie: Hopi Indian Artist*. Flagstaff: Museum of Northern Arizona, 1977.

Kessell, John L. *Kiva, Cross, and Crown: The Pecos Indians and New Mexico, 1540–1840*. Washington, D.C.: National Park Service, U.S. Department of the Interior, 1979.

Kirk, Ruth. *Wisdom of the Elders: Native Traditions on the Northwest Coast*. Vancouver/Toronto: Douglas and McIntyre Ltd., 1986.

Lévi-Strauss, Claude. *The Way of the Masks*. Seattle: University of Washington Press, 1982.

MacNair, Peter, Robert Joseph, and Bruce Grenville. *Down from the Shimmering Sky: Masks of the Northwest Coast*. Seattle: University of Washington Press, 1998.

McLennan, Bill, and Karen Duffek. *The Transforming Image: Painted Arts of Northwest Coast First Nations*. Seattle: University of Washington Press, 2000.

McMillan, Alan D. *Native Peoples and Cultures of Canada: An Anthropological Overview*. Vancouver/Toronto: Douglas and McIntyre Ltd., 1995.

Ostler, James, Marian Rodee, and Milford Nahohai. *Zuni: A Village of Silversmiths*. Zuni Pueblo: A:Shiwi Publishing, 1996.

Sando, Joe S. *The Pueblo Indians*. San Francisco: The Indian Historian Press, 1976.

Shadbolt, Doris. *Bill Reid*. Seattle: University of Washington Press, 1986.

Sheridan, Thomas E. and Nancy J. Parezo, eds. *Paths of Life: American Indians of the Southwest and Northern Mexico*. Tucson: University of Arizona Press, 1996.

Simmons, Marc and Frank Turley. *Southwestern Colonial Ironwork: The Spanish Blacksmithing Tradition from Texas to California*. Santa Fe: Museum of New Mexico Press, 1980.

Stewart, Hilary. *The Adventures and Sufferings of John R. Jewitt, Captive of Maquinna*. Vancouver/Toronto: Douglas and McIntyre Ltd., 1987.

Tanner, Clara Lee. *Prehistoric Southwestern Craft Arts*. Tucson: The University of Arizona Press, 1976.

Whiteford, Andrew Hunter, et al. *I Am Here: Two Thousand Years of Southwest Indian Arts and Culture*. Santa Fe: Museum of New Mexico Press, 1989.

Wright, Margaret Nickelson. *Hopi Silver: The History and Hallmarks of Hopi Silversmithing*. Flagstaff: Northland Publishing, 1982.

Wyatt, Gary. *Spirit Faces: Contemporary Masks of the Northwest Coast*. Vancouver/Toronto: Douglas and McIntyre Ltd., 1994.

————. *Mythic Beings: Spirit Art of the Northwest Coast*. Seattle: University of Washington Press, 1999.

Zolbrod, Paul G. *Diné bahane: The Navajo Creation Story*. Albuquerque: University of New Mexico Press, 1984.

INDEX

Note: Numbers in *italics* refer to illustrations.

abalone, 58
    adornments using, *19, 58, 91*
    in bentwood boxes, *37*
    as sacred stone of Navajo, 192
    used in masks, 58, *103*
    see also specific jewelry
Adams, Art, 111
Ahul, see katsinas
Albrecht, Martha L., 28
Anasazi (ancestral Pueblo), 114
    pendants, *7*
    petroglyphs of, *119,* 200
ancestral Pueblo, *see* Anasazi
animal imagery, 6, 18, 21, 22, 61
    see also specific animals
Apache, 116, 133, 138
apprentices, *37,* 100, 104, 160
art:
    clothing as, 22, 98, *98*
    Haida economy and, 111
    jewelry as, 158
    as political tool, 206
    tradition and evolution of, 102, 106, 110
    as visual language, 16, 18, 21, 22, 27, 102, 110
art, Native American, 16–18, 27, 32, 38, 52, 79
    animal imagery in, 6, 82, 155; *see also* specific animals and jewelry
    collecting of, 28
    formline, 22, 49, 86, 138
    rules of, 89, 96, 100, 200
    supernatural in, 16, 47, 84, 153, 155
    technology and, 6, 22, *124*
    tourism's influence on, 138, 144, 147, 178, 179
    see also specific artists

beads, shell, *see* shells, shell beads
Bear bracelet, *23*
bear imagery, 6, *17,* 21, *23, 79,* 106, *154,* 155
Bear mother and cubs bracelet, *79*
Beaver-Eagle bracelet, *83*

Beaver pendant, *93*
Beck, Victor, Sr., 192–93, *192, 193*
Begay, Harvey, 178–79, *178, 179,* 196
Begay, Kenneth, *135, 158, 158, 159,* 169, 178, 179, 204
Bella Bella, *see* Heiltsuk
Bella Coola, *see* Nuxalk
Benedict, Ruth, 148
bentwood boxes, *37,* 38, 88, 106
Beyuka, Edward, *149,* 186
Beyuka, Madeline, 186
"Big Thunder, Little Thunder" bracelet, *111*
Bill Reid (Shadbolt), 74
Bill Reid Respect Pole, *37*
Bird fetish necklace, *143*
Bird-Romero, Mike, 147, 190, *190, 191*
blankets, 38, *43,* 49
    button, *9, 34, 79,* 98
    Chilkat, 16, 34, *53,* 64, 78, 104
"Blessings" bracelet, *189*
Blessingway, 133, 192–93, 196
Blue corn bolo tie, *20*
Boas, Franz, 13, *45,* 61, 148
Bob, Dempsey, 49, 52, 96, *96*
body adornments, 16, 18, 21–22, 27, 38, 47, 58, 63, 64–65
    ancient forms of, 22
    beliefs expressed through, 32
    body-painting as, 22, 54, *105,* 150, 153
    of Nuu-chah-nulth, 48
    piercings as, 54, 58–60, 150
    social status and, 56, 58, 60–61
    see also jewelry; tattoos, tattooing
bolo ties, 16
    animal imagery on, *17*
    Haida, *19*
    katsina imagery on, *149*
    Navajo, *17,* 29
    Pueblo, *17, 20, 124, 195, 203*
    sky imagery on, *17*
    see also specific bolo ties
Bondell, John, 158
bowguards, *131, 141, 159*

bowls, *51,* 84
bracelets, 47, 49, 56, 65, 81, 84
    animal imagery on, 6, *17, 23, 27, 51, 57, 73, 79, 81, 83, 107, 167, 168*
    Gitxsan, *46*
    Haida, *23, 51, 57, 73, 79, 111*
    Haisla, *83*
    Heiltsuk, *107*
    Hohokam shell, *122*
    horn, *41,* 56, 96, *96*
    human imagery on, *27*
    katsina imagery on, *126, 168*
    Kwakiutl, *see* Kwakwaka'wakw
    Kwakwaka'wakw, *27*
    Navajo, 16, *119, 126, 137, 161, 189, 193*
    Nisga'a, *81*
    Nuu-chah-nulth, *48*
    Nuxalk, *107*
    Pueblo, *117, 143, 151, 161, 162, 163, 167, 171,* 194
    Sun face imagery on, *168*
    supernatural imagery on, 16
    Tlingit, *41, 43, 44*
    Tsimshian, *95*
    see also specific bracelets
bridles, *132*
Brillon, Jesse, *23*
Bringhurst, Robert, 74, 75
Brody, J.J., 151
buckles, *173*
Burkhart, Will, 100, *100,* 102
butterfly imagery, 6, *141,* 155
Butterfly pin, *141*
Butterfly Songs necklace, *207*
butterfly whorl-style hair, *2*
button blankets, *9, 34, 79,* 98

canoes, 32, 33, 34, 38, 74–75, 78, 100, 111
Carpenter, Edmund, 61, 64, 66*n*
carving, 38
    of canoes, 100
    as Haida artistic style, 110, 148
    Hohokam traditional, *122*

ILLUSTRATION CREDITS

Note: Numbers given represent page numbers.

Al Abrams: 119 (top); Tom Alexander, courtesy Ric Charlie: 205; Dale W. Anderson © 1996: 182; © MCC-CMC 1941. Photo by Charles Marius Barbeau. © Canadian Museum of Civilization, negative 88 926: 72; Craig Chesek: 120; Edward Curtis: 9, 45 (bottom); Jackie Beckett: 19 (both), 79; Rolf Bettner: 105; Hillel Burger: 40; Larry Carver; 33, 115 (top); Kari Chalker: 194; Sally and Ron Clonts: 201; Edward Dossetter: 35 (bottom), 45 (top), 59; Courtesy Lois Sherr Dubin: 17, 21 (top), 154, 161, 162 (bottom), 163, 167, 168, 183, 211; Dennis Finnin: 23; O.C. Hastings: 35 (top), 41 (bottom); Jerry Jacka: 162 (left); Karen Hayes: 118; Paul Jones: 122 (bottom); Gregory R. Lucier/WindSong Studio: 189; Tony Marinella: 203; Eliza Massey: 74 (left); Jerry McCollum: 87; Bill McLennan: 21 (bottom), 26, 36, 42, 50 (bottom), 75, 81; E.W. Merrill: 41 (top); Rod Mickens: 11, 37 (top), 44, 51 (bottom), 121, 130; Trevor Mills: 111; Sam Minkler: 204; N. Orchard: 52; Jim Phillips: 135 (bottom), 136, 137 (all), 139 (all), 141 (bottom); Kay Begay Rogers: 158; Fred Schock: 55; Ulli Steltzer: 110; Arch Thiessen: 25, 141 (top), 142; Kiyoshi Togashi: 7, 16, 17, 20, 24, 29, 39, 46, 57, 73, 78, 80, 82, 83, 84, 85, 86, 88, 89, 90, 91, 92, 93, 94, 96, 97, 98, 100, 101, 102, 103, 106, 107, 108, 109, 117, 119, 124, 125, 126, 128 (both), 129, 131, 132, 140, 143, 145, 146, 149, 151, 154, 159, 161, 163, 166, 167, 168, 170, 171, 172, 173, 174, 175, 176, 177, 178, 178, 180, 181, 183, 184, 185, 186, 187, 188, 190, 191, 192, 193, 196, 197, 198, 199, 200, 201, 202, 206, 207, 208, 209, 210, 211; Barb Wilson: 104; Gary and Elsie Yoyokie: 195.

Maps on pp. 14–15 by Adrian Kitzinger

Editor: Elaine M. Stainton
Designer: Binocular, New York
Production Manager: Maria Pia Gramaglia

Library of Congress Cataloging-in-Publication Data
Totems to turquoise : Native North American
jewelry arts of the Northwest and Southwest /
Kari Chalker, general editor ; Lois S. Dubin and
Peter M. Whiteley, contributing editors ; with
essays by Kari Chalker . . . [et al.] ; photography
by Kiyoshi Togashi.
          p. cm.
     Includes bibliographical references and index.
     ISBN 0–8109–5593–8 (hardcover).
ISBN 0–8109–9186–1 (paperback)
     1. Indians of North America—Jewelry—
Southwest, New—Themes, motives. 2. Indians
of North America—Jewelry—Northwest, Pacific—
Themes, motives. I. Chalker, Kari. II. Dubin, Lois
Sherr. III. Whiteley, Peter M. IV. American
Museum of Natural History.

     E78.S7T68 2004
     739.27′089′97078—dc22
2004007284

Printed and bound in China

10 9 8 7 6 5 4 3 2 1

Harry N. Abrams, Inc.
100 Fifth Avenue
New York, N.Y. 10011
www.abramsbooks.com

Abrams is a subsidiary of